a.d. mcmxciv

aroldus iiiin er gulland moritur

a.d. mcmxcv

uaedam puella advenit

a.d. mcmxcix

iii februarius Emma Wel by et Pandora sewell crius tulum partuintur

v October gmis in cubi culo calceorum pueroru m incipit: igitur apody teria puerorum · iam du pla magnitudo apodyterii

SCHOOL STORY

A Portrait of Cumnor House

SCHOOL STORY

A Portrait of Cumnor House

NICK MILNER-GULLAND

THIRD MILLENNIUM
PUBLISHING, LONDON

To Anna

Ode to Apollo and Cumnor House

dive Parnassi nemorisque rector
Delphici, de quo teneros poetas
Castalis pura nive fons soluta
    nutrit et arte,

advoles campos ubi Cumnor aequa
corda doctrina puerilia implet,
semper apricus superisque sedes
    haud minus apta.

hic ubique errat rhododendron, errat
aura per quercus levis, et reportat
dulce ludorum modo murmur, illinc
    iam calamorum;

scaena silvestris feritur cothurno
parvulo, cunctumque lyrae soporant.
cara dispersis domus haec alumnis,
    carus et ille

qui libro nunc tot memoranda certat
contulisse uno. monumenta laetae
si iuventutis petis, hoc volumen
    perlege mirans.

(Apollo, ruler of Parnassus and the Delphic glade, from which flows the Castalian spring, nourishing tender poets with its art and with its waters of pure melted snow, fly down to the fields where Cumnor fills children's hearts with equally good learning, an ever sunny place and an abode no less fit for the gods. Here rhododendrons spread everywhere and light breezes are wafted through the oaks, bringing sweet murmurs, now of play, now of work; young actors' boots tread the sylvan stage, and all is lulled by music. Dear is this place to its dispersed alumni, dear too is he who now strives to gather so many memories together in one book. If you are looking for memorials of happy youth, read this volume in admiration.)

BY MIKE ATKINSON

father of Katie, Jonathan and Christopher (1987–97)

Copyright © Cumnor House School and
Third Millennium Publishing Limited

First published in 2007 by Third Millennium
Publishing Limited, a subsidiary of Third Millennium Information Limited.

2–5 Benjamin Street
London
United Kingdom
ECIM 5QL
www.tmiltd.com

ISBN: 978 1 903942 60 4

British Library Cataloguing in Publication Data
A CIP catalogue record for this book is available from the British Library.

Edited by Val Horsler
Designed by Helen Swansbourne
Production by Bonnie Murray

Printed by MKT, Slovenia

CONTENTS

PREFACE

I can remember everything absolutely

clearly, whether it happened or not.

MARK TWAIN

Those with long memories will remember that Hal Milner-Gulland, my father, published *School Story* in 1976 (at £2 a copy): I have shamelessly purloined the title for my own book. But the two books are different in scope and purpose, not just in price: the first told the story of Cumnor House through articles from CHS magazines over the years, while this book attempts a continuous narrative of the first 75 years of the school's existence, aided by contributions from many people who have close links with Cumnor. Other sources have been CHS magazines, which provide a remarkably complete archive; 'Wartime Memories', published as a supplement to the 1997 magazine; the book *Me* published in 1967 by the 13-year-old Stephen White; published tributes to my parents; private letters; speeches; a long document from which I quote extensively, written in about 1963 by my father, which appears to be the first draft of an unpublished autobiography and came to light only this year; and much material from the CHS archives.

I have avoided the word 'history' to describe this account. The text largely depends on the arbitrary and unrelated contributions which happen to have been sent in, and which I have tried to incorporate into the narrative. Fun though it has been to adopt this approach, the book is inevitably a collection of anecdotes rather than balanced history, and I hope it will be enjoyed as such.

I should like to thank those who have given me much help. First, and most importantly, those who contributed memorabilia – reminiscences, photographs, letters etc. There was such a huge response (over 100,000 words, for a book which was supposedly limited to 50,000) that I had the difficult job of cutting most contributions mercilessly, and sometimes not using them at all. I apologise profusely; but if it is any consolation, every single contribution influenced my perception of how people saw the school, even if I did not quote them all in full. I fear that I shall disappoint some people by failing to mention well-remembered pupils or staff: this is not because they are less important, but because of lack of space or documentation. Although I have tried to verify all facts there will inevitably be mistakes, for which I apologise and bear the responsibility.

I am grateful to those who helped in the planning stages: my successor Christian Heinrich, whose original idea it was; Peter Wigan and Justin Cheadle, who look after the CHS archives; David Burt from Third Millennium; Sir Peter Hall, Simon Williams, Joanna Dodd and Dominic Lawson, who sent material for the brochure; Mike Atkinson, author of the Horatian ode; Bill and Virginia Nicholson and Angela Holdsworth, who gave useful early advice; Ian Edwards and Michel Polacco, who helped with computers; Dick Wheeler, who filled in the gaps in my knowledge of the pre-war years; Peter Gamble of MBA and Toby Milner-Gulland, who produced diagrams; Jean Baldwin, Keith Bennett and La Vigar, who read the proofs and made valuable suggestions; Helen Swansbourne, who is responsible for the beautiful artwork; my excellent editor, Val Horsler, whose advice on all matters from the Oxford comma to the arrangement of chapters has been invaluable; and finally my wife Anna, without whose constant support and interest this book could not have been written, and to whom it is affectionately dedicated.

NICK MILNER-GULLAND   *Valojoulx, 2006*

A brief history of CHS in Latin, produced in 2003 by Julia Nicholson (12), who composed, designed, illuminated, inscribed and illustrated it on parchment which she herself had prepared. It includes such items as the first cricket match, the move to Danehill, coeducation, Peter Wigan, the Barn, the Old Oak, a flu epidemic, Julia's arrival and departure, fire in the bootroom, Kate Jelly losing her voice, sports tours and Natasha Brice's car accident.

THE CROYDON YEARS

1931–39

A spirit of faith and adventure

To found a school or college has always seemed to me one of the noblest and most selfless acts that mankind can aspire to: not only are you providing for the transmission of knowledge and wisdom to generations yet unborn, but you are able to embody in the new foundation your loftiest and most deeply felt ideals. Indeed in the first Inspection of Cumnor House in 1933 HMI refer to its having been being started 'in a spirit of faith and adventure'. But in fact this was not quite the spirit in which Martin Wheeler embarked on his new venture in January 1931: as he later admitted, he founded the school on the advice of his accountant, who thought that schools represented a good way of making money respectably. This was at a time, just after the slump, when earning a living did not come easily. Despite this, 53 prep schools opened in the 1930s, though many soon succumbed to economic pressures and competition from LEA schools.

Martin and Dolly Wheeler's son Dick was one of the first six pupils: the others were Richard Berrill, John Christie, Kenneth Lazenby, Roy Miller and Gordon Wood. Dick Wheeler recalls the early days: 'My father A Martin Wheeler (AM) was the son of a south London GP. Educated at Dulwich and Sidney Sussex College, Cambridge, he taught for a time at Dulwich Prep. As I think was usual in those days he had done what his father expected and started premedical training at the Middlesex, which he didn't take to. It then so happened that his father died and AM pulled out before the clinical course. After war service in the Artillery he tried his hand at various small business ventures and then joined Atkinson (ex-army) and Ibbotson (a classicist) as a partner at The Limes Prep School, South Croydon, which I attended till Cumnor started.

'AM then decided to set up his own school. He bought Cumnor, a substantial house in the rooftop flightpath of the airliners coming in to Croydon aerodrome. He was a good judge of men. He found a crucial recruit in Perry, a man with a grammar school background, as senior master. (I went at 12 with Perry to my first play at the Streatham Theatre where we saw a promising young actor called Gielgud as Hamlet.) He then kicked off with six boys. The numbers steadily increased and AM acquired the two houses on either side and extended the main house for

Dick Wheeler (left) and Harley Sherlock, October 1990

a hall, classrooms, accommodation for a few boarders and an outside swimming pool. He had the use of the sports field over the road. AM had no pretensions to academic prowess. He was more an entrepreneur and a practical man. He was perhaps most at home working on drains with Mr Bacon the builder and with Nobby, his herculean labourer. But he could do a solid stint at maths and Latin. School concerts and

plays owed less to Handel and Molière than to Mabel Konstanduros and music hall: I can still remember much of 'Knocked 'em in the Old Kent Road'. He wasn't so much a pianist as being able to strum out tunes by ear.

'My mother looked after the domestic side. The first prospectus read: "Mrs Wheeler fully understands the importance of a good midday meal for the growing boy." Suet puddings glistened sluglike but there was a competitive response to "hands up for ends". It was very much a family affair. I had two older sisters, Betty (+5) and Janet (+2). Betty wasn't so much involved, being a student, but Jan simply gave up Croham Hurst at 14 (I suppose then that was the legal leaving age) and enthusiastically got down to teaching the small boys. She had had some previous success as she used to hold my head down over Peary's voyage to the North Pole till I got it right.

'More appropriately AM recruited Miss Pring, an experienced teacher, to take charge of the small boys to complement Perry at the top. Some other teachers were more transient, filling in gaps while waiting, for example, for ordination or other courses or just trying things out. One older man, Molony, ex-RAF, practical and handy, taught carpentry and looked after the three cars which did pick-up rounds. He taught me to drive. AM was pleased to be relieved of some social chores as Molony was in demand as a bridge player. An ex-soldier did gym and boxing.'

Perhaps Dick is a little dismissive of his father's academic pretensions. Harley Sherlock (1934–40) has rather different memories: 'Martin Wheeler was, in fact, not only well-qualified academically, he was also a great organiser, and – with the help of a very painful slipper – a good disciplinarian: aided and abetted by his wife, Dorothy, whose words were actually more painful than her husband's slipper.

'One cannot, of course, mention the Wheelers without referring to their beautiful daughters, one of whom was particularly well remembered by some of us for the time when her screams woke up the whole school in what seemed to us the middle of the night. Mr Hutchinson (known to us as 'Hutch'), one of the school's new young masters, was rather fond of practical jokes. Apparently, he had put a stuffed crocodile in Jan Wheeler's bed! Where the offending animal came from – or where it finally went – we children never discovered; but we relished the incident, and teased the victim about it as only schoolboys can.

'The school in Pampisford Road was close to Croydon Airport, which was at the time the airport (I beg its pardon, "aerodrome") for London. There was, in theory, a disadvantage about sleeping so close to it, even in peacetime, because of the nightly, 3 am, arrival of the Junkers passenger plane from Berlin, which flew low and very noisily over the school, to make its landing into the prevailing wind. However, we soon got used to this, and it was only the noise-that-didn't-happen which woke us up, whenever the flight was cancelled.'

Jim Earle (1937–44) recalls Martin's appearance: 'Mr Wheeler, the headmaster, was the dominant figure. He had ginger hair but what this little boy remembers is that some of it grew out of his ears. Can it have been so memorable? His presence at

Cumnor House, Summer 1934. Staff (left to right) Jan Wheeler, not identified, Miss Day, Mr Perry, Martin and Dolly Wheeler, not identified, Miss Pring, Miss Garrard, Betty Wheeler

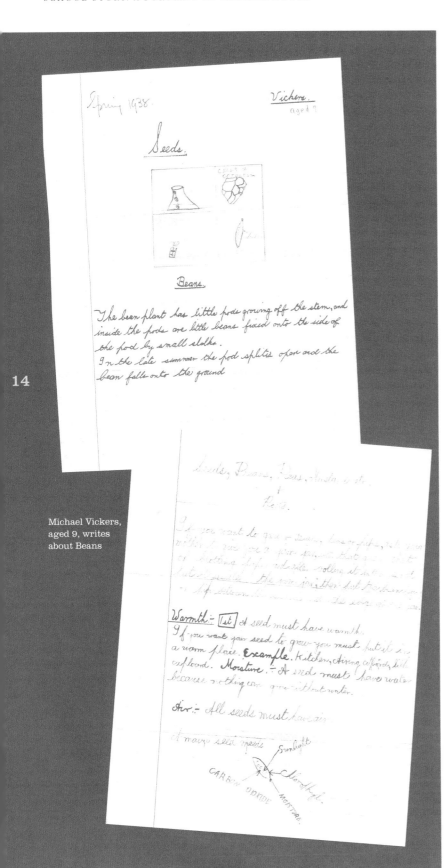

Spring 1938.

Vickers. aged 9

Seeds.

Beans.

The bean plant has little pods growing off the stem, and inside the pods are little beans fixed onto the side of the pod by small stalks.
In the late summer the pod splits open and the bean falls onto the ground

Michael Vickers, aged 9, writes about Beans

14

Michael Vickers as a boy at Cumnor and as Bishop of Colchester

Prayers was serious: I should not have been thinking about a little gadget I had seen advertised in the *National Geographic Magazine* for removing nasal and ear hair, but I know I did.'

Michael Vickers (1936–42) remembers: 'In the light of today's world, one of the memories that I find most remarkable is that of seven-year-old children being allowed to walk by ourselves, as some of us did, a mile or more through an urban area, crossing such major thoroughfares as the London to Brighton road, navigating railway station bridges or "underpasses" such as those at Sanderstead and Purley Oaks, all of it long before the era of lollipop ladies, organised school crossings or sophisticated control of traffic. The best part of the walk to school, and also by today's standards one where young children might be thought to be at their most vulnerable, was the climb up across the Downland between the Brighton Road and Pampisford Road, up and of course down again after school.

'It was during the walk home from school that I first had a helpful lesson in the application of justice. It was my custom to stop off, morning and evening, at the hospitable home of Patrick and Barry Lyndon. Their parents were Irish Roman Catholics; Patrick was a close friend of mine and a Cumnor contemporary, while Barry joined the school later, I think. Mrs Lyndon was an outstanding cook, which may have had something to do with my regular stop-offs. Unfortunately another day boy, who also walked to school from Sanderstead and shall remain anonymous, was the only bully I remember from my Cumnor days. One afternoon, in the yard at the back of Purley Oaks Station, he set upon Patrick who was considerably smaller than he was. I went to my friend's help and, in fending off this other boy, landed a punch on his nose, which began to bleed profusely. The outcome was that the other boy's father lodged a complaint with the headmaster and, when we were all summoned next day to Mr Wheeler's study, I reckoned I was really in for it. The outcome was somewhat otherwise. The bully was severely admonished and, although Mr Wheeler gave me a good ticking off for my vicarious retaliation, he did it with a twinkle in his eyes. I have never forgotten that: he was clearly a headmaster with his finger on the pulse of what really went on in the school.'

A story, doubtless apocryphal, relates how in the early days Marcus Molony was detailed to walk round the centre of Purley with an armful of prospectuses, dropping one in every pram. Certainly the reputation of the new school grew, and numbers rose rapidly: 20 in September 1931, 50 the following year and 99 by the outbreak of war. Academic successes followed: Dick Wheeler, with a scholarship to Canford, was Cumnor's first public school scholar, followed by Roy Miller in 1934. Martin Wheeler wrote in the first school magazine (*The Cumnor Chronicle*, 1934) with quaint nonchalance: 'We must congratulate Miller on bagging a Bursary of £20 at St Lawrence', and the following year 'We've pulled off four scholarships'; until 1947 all scholarships were recorded on the Honours Board

with their monetary value (between £20 and £100 a year). An innovation which was started in 1935 and has continued till today was that boys would sit termly trial CE papers, the results of which would be sent to parents with the reports. School functioned on Saturday mornings, and the 1935 magazine records that 60 out of 80 parents were in favour of introducing a half-term holiday (from 4 pm Friday till Monday morning!) – but only in the summer and

The first Honours Board

The swimming pool

Christmas terms. The magazine was a strangely discursive document, with the first issue containing articles on Lord's, brake linings, Stonehenge and 'Bugs and All That'. It was intended to appear half yearly, but it never did.

The first eight years were a time of constant building, adapting and buying more property. Martin designed and oversaw much of this work himself. Michael Vickers: 'The New Swimming Bath of 1934 had been installed the year before I went to Cumnor House and I have vivid memories of it. There was a slope up to it from the playground, it had a proper diving-board, it was unheated and often icy cold. I shall never forget the incredibly skimpy red cotton "triangles" we all wore for swimming. I am so grateful that, young as many of us were, we were so well taught not only to swim but to dive – by which I mean entering the water perpendicularly rather than at an angle. I also remember the competitiveness of the Swimming Sports, certainly equalling what took place on our Playing Fields on the other side of Pampisford Road (I write as the winner in 1936 of the Egg and Spoon Race for those under eight!).'

Food seems to have been pretty good. Robin Kennard (1934–39) was a satisfied customer: 'The lunches at Cumnor were so appetising with the exception of cold meat and beetroot on Wednesdays! I have never knowingly eaten beetroot since, and that was 67 years ago. I remember the competition between the boys to see who could down the most helpings at one meal: John Ashford, I recall, claimed three shepherds pies followed by 12, yes 12, helpings of jam tart. In the summer term, a Walls tricycle called conveniently at break every day at the front gate and most of us had a 1d Snowfruit, but the wealthier ones chose 2d bricks or 3d choc ices. One boy even went for a 4d tub – his name was Freeman and it was his father who donated the Freeman Challenge Cups.'

Jim Earle recalls: 'Being a small boy, I remember school meals better than the lessons. There was a welcome regular weekly appearance (Thursdays?) of a minced beef pie. My memory of the filling is not very clear but the pastry is perfectly vivid. By modern standards it was only school caterers' pastry but it was different from the kind my mother made and it still has a specific feel in my mouth. The only other dish I remember was a sort of chocolate custard. I am afraid we unreformed little bigots in those far-off days called it "black man's sick".'

Waffles meant much to Harley Sherlock: 'I was one of the dozen or so weekly boarders at what was primarily a day school. But what privileges we boarders had! And the most prized of these privileges was our access to Cook's secret waffles "which I'll do yer later". By this she meant, when the day boys had gone home and the masters were occupied with their supper. When it was decided that my younger brother, Andrew, should have just one term as a boarder instead of me, I was seriously put out; and I very much disliked cycling home in the rain, with thoughts of those lucky boarders back at school enjoying their waffles.'

Robin Kennard too has happy memories of boarding life: 'In 1938 our parents went on a cruise and Colin and I boarded for a fortnight; we enjoyed it so much that, despite living only 800 yards down the road, we then became weekly boarders under the tender care of the matron "Swetty" – Miss Swettenham.'

Far left: Donald
Campbell, 1935

Left: Early winners
of the Freeman
Challenge Cups

Below: CHS 1st XI soccer,
1938–9. From the back,
left to right: R Kennard,
S J Williams, D W Allen,
J Crump, D Chapman,
B L Nimmo, J M G
Berkley, Mr Carrigan,
R Lazenby, J B Lumsden,
N R Burt, R D Fox,
H Sherlock, B Price,
M Kennard

During these years the school was developing a personality. Martin encouraged the 'firm growth of the corporate spirit among all the boys, not just among those who seem to get all the plums'; he also wanted good cooperation between parents and school – 'not mere negative acquiescence but helpful and constructive criticism'. Pupils were known as 'Cumnorites', and their uniform consisted of a grey flannel jacket and shorts, grey shirt, school socks, scarlet school cap and tie and black shoes. 'Though an incipient giant may be given special permission to wear "longs", they are not part of the school uniform … shorts are more healthy and have to be worn by *all* at many of our best public schools.'

In 1934 the first school cricket and soccer teams played (often twice or more in a season) against the limited number of local schools, and in 1936 boxing was introduced; informal rugby followed in 1939. In 1938 our first century was scored by Robert Lazenby (115* v The Grange); it was to be 20 years till the next. Archery and bowls were also offered. By 1934

A nature study walk with Mr Hutchinson. Boys (left to right) John Thompson, Patrick Lyndon, Michael Vickers, Hodder, John Barr

Right: Robert Crump, Robert Lazenby, F J Carrigan, Bruce Nimmo, Colin Kennard

six sporting cups had been presented, all of which are still presented today: the two Freeman Challenge Cups, given by Captain and Mrs Freeman for outstanding sporting ability allied with good sportsmanship; Bowling (Rowe-Williamson), Batting (Campbell), Fielding (Harold Williams) and Swimming (Morgan). A tradition grew up that the winner of the Mothers' Race on Sports Day had to present the prizes.

Harley Sherlock: 'On the sporting side, I loved team games, especially cricket, which I enjoyed as someone who applied himself, rather than as one with any natural talent. My enthusiasm was encouraged by our mad Irish games master, Mr Carrigan, who was reputedly a bit of a bully, but an excellent coach. His occasional quick temper was well demonstrated when, having kindly agreed to start Matron's rather temperamental old car (and having failed), he threw the starting-handle into the air, and could only watch in horror as it returned to earth via a shattered windscreen. Despite all that, it is largely due to him, and to another good coach at Canford, that I was able to enjoy playing regular cricket until the age of 60.'

Out of school

An impressive array of extra-curricular activities sprang up: carpentry with Mr Molony and natural history with Mr Hutchinson were popular, and a stamp club was started. 'The Truncheon Club' was a pupils' literary club, with lectures by members, which also arranged visits to the Tate Gallery and the Oval, for instance; visiting lecturers included Mr F Handley-Page on 'Aeroplanes', and Jim Earle remembers 'a visit by a distinguished lepidopterist who Mr Gulland stressed was a very important person. The visitor's name I distinctly recall. He was L Hugh Newman and he had written a book. I became an avid butterfly collector.' Music didn't really flourish until the arrival of Ainger Negus in

1938; before that the annual concert consisted of one-act plays and a few songs. Weekly gramophone concerts took place at which 'sometimes more unusual composers such as Sibelius' were represented – which gave my parents, when they arrived in 1938, a lifelong distaste for his works. Mr Baker and Miss Pring 'have been working indefatigably at the singing. We ourselves distinctly recognised several songs last term.'

Epidemics

Throughout the 1930s and 1940s great distress and disruption were caused by epidemics: all cricket matches were cancelled in summer 1935 because the school was in quarantine for mumps, and in the following summer the school closed early because of scarlet fever. In 1937 a much more terrible epidemic broke out, vividly recalled by Harley Sherlock: 'In the autumn of 1937 a dreadful disaster struck Cumnor House School. Mr Perry, Martin Wheeler's very capable and much liked second master, fell ill with what, for three whole weeks, was treated as 'flu, but which turned out to be one of the first cases of Croydon's notorious typhoid epidemic. And, because of the lack of early treatment, poor Mr Perry became one of the first of the epidemic's 47 fatalities. The school was badly hit generally, with more than 20 catching the disease out of about 100 pupils, including me. One rather pleasing result of my typhoid was my father's decision that I should not be burdened with the thought of having to sit for a scholarship at the end of my time at Cumnor. This had an added bonus, in that when I reached my next school (Canford, in Dorset), I was not put into one of the forms which scholarship boys joined straightaway, but into a form which was a whole year junior. I walked off with three end-of-term form prizes before I was rumbled and moved up a year – where, of course, I had to work much harder.'

Dick Wheeler believes that his parents never really got over the loss of Perry. Martin later wrote: 'I lost the man to whom much of the credit for the work and the games of the school was due.' Both Martin and Dolly were also troubled by rheumatism, and by 1938 were keen to find a junior partner, and then retire.

Cumnor House School, South Croydon.

CHAPTER 2

HAL AND NAN
MILNER-GULLAND

Hillcrest,
64 Partickhill Rd
Dear Aunt Lizzie,
    Thank you very much
for your nice bulls eyes; I like them
very much and am eating
them up like lightning. The
last Latin I wrote was
"Incolae insulae reginam
terrent." I wonder what
kind of inhabitants they were
Mother says was it Mary 2. of Scots?
            Love to both Harry.

Hal aged 8, with
one of his letters

domus et placens uxor

HORACE, *ODES* II.14

The idealistic 30-year-old who joined Martin as partner in 1938, my father Hal Milner-Gulland, bought his partnership with a legacy of £17,000. Earlier Hal had been particularly inspired by two remarkable teachers: the first was Gilbert Evans, his prep school headmaster, 'a loveable unworldly Etonian', who had been a family friend in Bushey where Hal grew up, a polymath and keen writer and producer of his own witty plays; it was he who bequeathed Hal much of his library as well as his duck-billed platypodes, having no children of his own to pass things on to. (The platypodes, remembered by many Cumnorians, are now in the Booth Museum in Brighton.) The other was Rooker Roberts, the headmaster of Belmont, junior school of Mill Hill, where Hal had taught for eight happy years before Cumnor:

Rooker was 'a big, dark man 20 years older than the rest of us, with a kind face. In his younger days he had played rugger for Devon, and he claimed to be the first man in this century to bowl Ranjitsinghi (at Fenners in the spring of 1900). He was wonderfully versatile; he spoke perfect French, he was an expert ornithologist and bird photographer and he painted delicate, beautiful water-colours.' He encouraged many of Hal's interests, including astronomy, handwriting, art, architecture and drama.

A further strong influence was Haileybury, where he had been unhappy and had developed a lifelong antipathy to authoritarian and hierarchical attitudes. Later, when as headmaster he was asked on a report form what he thought of a candidate's leadership qualities, he would write 'None, thank goodness'. Later still (April 1962), in a revealing correspondence with Tim Cobb, headmaster of Dover College, he wrote: 'A great deal is written about public schools nowadays, and whatever else is said, one thing is generally agreed, that the public school gives a unique training in leadership. I wonder …? It could be argued that the public school encourages acquiescence, herd opinion, the suppression of individuality and the following of false gods. I can't forget my own experience in coming from an atmosphere of trust and affection at my prep school (inefficient by today's standards, but goodness, how we enjoyed life there) to the bleak discipline of a bad house at Haileybury. After sizing it up for a fortnight, I realised that this was going to be a fight for survival, with no holds barred, and acted accordingly.'

But he had had a happy childhood in Bushey, where he was the much-loved only child of elderly parents. Both the Milners and the Gullands had moved to Bushey so that Aunt Lizzie (Gulland) and Aunt Nell (Eleanor Milner) could study mezzotint engraving at the Herkomer Art School. He was christened Laurence Harry Milner Gulland, with no hyphen; when the unmarried Aunt Nell realised that the name 'Milner' would disappear from the family on her death, she persuaded Hal to insert a hyphen between his last two names, in return for which she would leave him her pictures and all the family silver and furniture. He considered this a fair bargain, even though he later regretted the nuisance caused by such a cumbrous name; but when he was tempted to revert to plain 'Gulland', Nan would quite properly remind him of his undertaking. The family has always enjoyed chuckling over various misspellings.

At Peterhouse, Cambridge, he read Classics, and was runner-up for the Porson Prize for Greek verse. He loved Horace, and kept a copy of his works at his bedside till the day he died; he also loved English poetry, particularly Keats and Shelley. He was a keen rower, and enjoyed student plays: next to him as a

Bacchic maiden in the university production of *The Bacchae* was his fellow Petreian and oarsman James Mason.

Hal and Nan

In April 1934 Hal took his recently widowed father on a Mediterranean cruise, during which he met the vivacious and attractive Australian Nan Bavin, who with her sister was making her first visit to Europe. Within three weeks they were engaged and on August 1st that year they were married; during the remaining 71 years of her life she returned to her much-loved family in Sydney only three times. Even by flying boat the journey lasted 10 days; by ship it was up to six weeks. Her parents had severe misgivings, and were unable to come to the wedding; but they knew her well enough to realise that once she made up her mind she would not be deflected. She resolutely made a new life for herself in England, happily unaware in 1934 of Cumnor House School

Left to right: Hal, Nan's sister Shirley, Nan, Hal's father, 1934

Hal's diary entry for April 30th 1934 . . . and for May 1st 1934

or the immense part that she would play in its development. Robin was born, and it was a family of three who arrived in Purley in May 1938; I was born in 1940. It was a long and happy marriage, lasting over 60 years until Hal's death in 1994.

Opposites attract; and it was certainly so with Hal and Nan. He was reserved, donnish, thoughtful, slow, quiet, precise, meticulous; she was impetuous, gregarious, chatty, generous, impatient, spontaneous, outgoing, always laughing. Rosalie Challis remembers her 'antipodean *force de la nature*, wonderfully extrovert, physically energetic partner to Hal's understated, quiet, modest presence.'

Hal reckoned that human beings, particularly school matrons, were by nature either panickers or non-panickers. I remember one evening when I was

---

Up 9.20 Bed 3.40 big 25
(clocks on 1hr)

Up 7.30 Bed 12 big 18

120   MONDAY, APRIL **30**, 1934.   18th Week.   18th Week.   TUESDAY, MAY **1**, 1934.   **121**

(121-244) SS. Philip and James.   LESSONS.
Matins—Isaiah lxi.; John i. v. 43.
Evensong—Zechariah iv.; Colossians iii. to v. 18.

(120-245)

£ 28   2   11½

Wine bill £5 000
tips etc. . . c £5

Ring 127 - -

It was true after all.

At about a quarter to three tonight as we sat on a coil of rope on the top deck I asked Nan to marry me and she said she would.

N.B. The particulars given below have been compiled by us with the greatest care from information supplied to us by our client: but we cannot hold ourselves personally responsible for their accuracy.

No. 6,617   No. 6,617

Private and confidential Notice of Transfer of, or Partnership in, a successful Boarding and Day Preparatory School on the outskirts of London.

———————— o ————————

Dear Sir,

We have been asked by a client of our Firm, a Cambridge Graduate, to put him into touch with candidates who would either purchaser his School outright or take it over in Partnership with the present Senior Master. In the latter case the purchaser would probably be offered a half-share. The School, which prepares boys for the Public Schools and Royal Navy, was established in 1931 with only 5 boys, and has gone ahead steadily until for the September term 1937 there are 110 boys, of whom 14 are boarders, and the School is quite full. Our client only wishes to give up for reasons of health, as he and his wife have been working exceedingly hard for the past 7 years and are in need of a rest. The premises, which consist of a main building and two other houses, all of which are our client's freehold, are valued by him at £11,000. From the photographs they seem quite adequate for the purpose. The School premises comprise the original house, which has been considerably added to, a house on the north which was purchased for £1,950, and another on the south purchased for £1,750. These two houses are used entirely for accommodating teaching and domestic staff, but their large gardens, added to that of the main building, give grounds of nearly 1½ acres. Two playing fields, one of 14 acres belonging to the local Council, and another of 9 acres, are rented, and both these fields are directly opposite the School.

The School provides comfortable accommodation for 14 boarders, 84 day boarders, and 12 day boys, leaving ample room for the Headmaster and his family, together with 6 resident masters, 2 resident mistresses, matron and sufficient domestic staff to run the School. The prospectus fees for boarders are from 40 to 45 guineas a term, according to age; weekly boarders, from 35 to 40 guineas. Day Boys pay from 10 to 12 guineas a term, according to age, with extras for dinner and tea, with the result that the average day boarder pays from £60 to £65 per annum. Our client tells us that during the whole history of the School there have been only 2 boys who have not paid full fees.

The Gross Receipts for the last three years, ending in May, were -

Year	Receipts.	Profit.
1934/1935	£4,768.	£1,042
1935/36	£5,743.	£1,742
1936/37	£6,672	£2,059.

and based on the numbers for the September term, 1937, the turnover should be over £7,000 a year, and the Profit should reach £2,500. In estimating the Profit no allowance has been made for rent. Our client has kept books of accounts which are open to inspection by or on behalf of a bona fide purchaser.

Our client is asking £6,000 (six-thousand) for the Goodwill and £12,000 (twelve-thousand) for the premises, furniture and equipment. Our client is quite prepared to consider any reasonable proposition with a purchaser who is in a position to put down about £9,000 in cash. This might be either a sale outright or a partnership with the Senior Master, or possibly the formation of a Company in which the incomer would purchase a block of shares.

We may say that the opening seems to us an extremely proa pupil at the school and he was reading to us: one of the former burst into the room shouting that the cellar was on fire. Like Drake summoned to repel the Armada, Hal finished the paragraph at his normal deliberate pace, put down his cigarette in the scallop shell ashtray under a half-crown (to be resurrected later) and walked sedately out of the room. Luckily the fire turned out to be insignificant.

Nan favoured a broad brush approach. When they bought their Périgordin farmhouse in 1963 it was she who charmed the neighbours with her noisy, fluent and inaccurate French, helped by extravagant gestures, while he would speak in stately and measured phrases, with every gender correct and every subjunctive in place. He was a born actor, with an actor's sense of timing, as he showed in speeches, whether on Sports Day or at a memorable series of CHS Dinners in the Barn. He had a disconcerting habit of referring to Nan as 'my present wife'; if anyone queried this, he would explain that 'it keeps her on her toes.' He had a nice touch in mock-humility: if he sensed criticism in the air he would heave a great sigh and say, 'I'm doing my pathetic best.' He had learnt early on that this was an effective way to deflect criticism.

William Maslen (1969–74): 'I remember meeting Hal Milner-Gulland – or, in one of those mysterious splits that separate the child's world from the adult's, "X", as he was always known to us – for the first time: a tall, forbidding presence with, from a child's viewpoint, an exceptionally impressive beaked nose (just the sort of thing a headmaster should have, as the Molesworth books we all read so avidly in the library confirmed). But also his exquisite courtesy and the way he would focus on conversations with children – no hint of condescension, even when, in retrospect, I blush at the inanities I was undoubtedly spouting – courtesy only marred by the fact that he couldn't always hear what you were saying. Not that this deafness was regarded by us kids as any kind of handicap – it was part of

him, adding to his mystique and formidable persona.

'I remember the Pink House where Mrs G ruled supreme, dominating even X (astonishing to us children, but indubitably true). She would have been even more formidable, except that she wasn't deeply involved in day-to-day school affairs and had a twinkle in her eye that reassured – except, of course, when she was being angry. She cared so much about the school – that was clear even to childish perceptions – but she could also be very kind to individual children. I remember, as an A-former, being invited along with other "big boys" (and girls) to sessions with the headmaster in the sitting room of the Pink House, a hallowed place that, surrounded by its walled garden, always seemed special and pristine, filled with fascinating little knick-knacks that, if asked, X would demonstrate or explain. When I eventually visited Valojoulx, it was the Pink House that served as the base of operations as we prepared to leave. It was a high command, a tranquil but significant seat for Higher Things.'

Purley

Hal has left a detailed account of his time at Purley, written in about 1963: 'Fresh paint first attracted us to Cumnor House. It was 1937. Nan and I had then been married for three years, spent in much happiness at Mill Hill. But we lived beyond our means, our elder son Robin had just been born and we had to try and make some more money. A public school seemed the obvious answer, but Gabbitas had told me at 23 that I was really a little bit young for such a job, and at 27 that I was a little bit old. Perhaps the crucial moment had flashed by without my noticing it?

'But Gabbitas and Thring welcomed our proposition of buying a prep school. Years later we were to discover that assistant masters with a few thousands of capital were less common than we had imagined; those with an open-handed Aunt Nell behind them less common still. Now the field was open; we were given 20 confidential handouts, each one furtively setting out the attractions of a high-class establishment in a supposedly healthy district. We visited one or two and did not greatly like what we saw. Halfway down the list came the name of Cumnor House, less pretentious than most, but a good deal better, so it seemed, as a business proposition.

'So here we were at South Croydon. The street was suburban, the house itself four-square, Edwardian and finished with a dark grey pebbledash. The distant view of Croydon gasworks was softened by a dozen intervening acres of plain flat grass. We pressed a bell and immediately a maid in uniform opened the door. We walked along a short corridor, neatly brown-painted to shoulder height, into a spick span and hideous study. A teddy bear man with a shrewd, freckled and pleasant face rose to greet us; his wife, knitting an enormous dishcloth, couldn't quite make it, but gave us a piercing critical look. "Mr *Wheel*er!" cried Nan, as though to a long-lost friend. "Gosh, how you must hate us!" The tension was broken. It wasn't the last time my wife, a politician's daughter, was to set the tone of a meeting, and we started off on the right foot.

'Martin Wheeler was a man of wide experience, both in schools and business, an unusual combination which we had never before met and in fact could hardly believe. Finance was his subject and money was his goal. He ran rings round us as he explained the minutiae of school accounts and the present advantages of turning the place into a limited company. We sat aghast, to hear some of the details; how in the evenings the family ate pork sausages, the junior staff beef sausages, in different rooms and at the same time. Little mention seemed to be made of the boys, and I ventured to ask about them during a pause. "Well," said Martin, "we're getting quite a few nowadays from the Rose Walk and Silver Way area, and they're just the sort who take all the extra subjects without turning a hair." As

for parents, "I often have them round for a chat, but I make a rule never to offer them a drink. It all saves up, you know." Saves what, we thought, but didn't say it; later that day we were both full of *esprit de l'escalier*. And compared with my lofty affectations there was something engaging about this man's single-mindedness.

'We walked round the school. We met a friendly little man called Perry, the senior master – it was the only time we were ever to see him – and there was a longish pause while we listened to an excellent lesson on nature study taken by a part-time master, a clergyman called Hutchinson. Used as I was to the lavish untidiness of Mill Hill Junior School, I was perplexed to see such minute classrooms and tiny blackboards, and only moder-

ately impressed to hear that forms were limited to 12 in number. But what we both liked was the scrupulous cleanliness of everything, the floors, the walls, the desks. This was no showpiece laid on for a visitor's benefit; it was due in design to Martin and Dolly Wheeler, and more immediately to the daily care of one Overbury, a little rabbit-faced man, ex-RN, to whom we were in due course introduced. "He paints," explained Martin, in an aside. "He does graining. I get him to do one or two rooms every holidays." Sure enough, in the dormitories upstairs (for at that time there were already a dozen or so boarders) the walls were freshly decorated in a two-tone ordure colour, which bore a faint resemblance to wood. There was an indefinable something lacking in this school, and yet, it was all so efficient....

'Dolly Wheeler's remarks were few, and mostly designed, where we might have missed the point, to underline her husband's smartness. It was strange how she and I were somehow akin, despite an immediate mutual antipathy, while Nan and Martin spoke the same language. When her husband left us for a moment, she came into her own. There were other aspects to Cumnor House, it seemed, besides finance. "I am in charge," she said without the flicker of an eyelid, "of the spiritual side of the school." Searching for words, and summarising, she said, "What I try to do here is to give these boys a Sound Working Knowledge of their Heavenly Father."

'Our link with Cumnor House was fated and forged from the moment that we reached the front door. There was something exciting about this school which we had not met in any other; moreover, the very things had already been done, the traditions established, which we ourselves could never have created at the outset. Its newness was an asset and an invitation to further development. All this we discussed on our way home. If we could maintain this glittering facade of non-essentials, and at the same time inject into its core certain features which to us

seemed lacking, what possibilities were opened up.

'The deficiencies, as they appeared at that time, were first a regard for learning (less highly thought of then than now), secondly a warmth and affection which had perhaps cooled in seven years of hard struggle to survive, and thirdly the sheer spirit of success. This last quality had always meant much to me, perhaps too much, since going to a 'bad' house at Haileybury, one which at that time was notoriously inept and bottom of almost every competitive exercise. But by myself I could never have maintained the frontal efficiency. In fact since we have been on our own, the cleanliness, the paint and the polish have been Nan's doing. And avoiding the pitfalls of obsessive house-pride, she has kept them up with a light-hearted disregard for her own achievement. To an over-earnest visitor who dilated on the "atmosphere" of the school, "Oh, that's the floor polish" she replied.

'Meanwhile the shortcomings of the place were obvious, but all of them were explicable in their context, of a new school built up from scratch. Martin Wheeler had built, expanded and reorganised, never running quite the same sort of school from term to term. Both he and his wife were worrying types, and their health had suffered. Dolly Wheeler in particular was no longer full of fun and vivacity, as from all accounts she had been in 1931. There were months of negotiations, and periods of hesitation on both sides to close the deal, but by the early days of 1938 the thing was done and we entered upon a partnership which was to last just one year. Martin Wheeler, with characteristic candour, had said, "We can get hold of any number of young schoolmasters like you. The wife was the real worry, but we knew Nan was all right from the first remark she ever made to us." He kept me in my place, but it had better be said at once that during that year he also taught me a great deal, his most valuable lesson being that goodwill and high ideals are no substitute at all for efficiency.'

CHAPTER 3

WAR CLOUDS GATHER
1939

Cry 'Havoc!' and let slip the dogs of war

SHAKESPEARE, *JULIUS CAESAR*

The partnership lasted one year, and it was not an easy one. Hal later recalled that year: 'Nan and I in our inexperience knew nothing of the pitfalls inherent in partnership. Looking back on it now, I think we and the Wheelers probably jogged along fairly well together, but at the time it seemed that we lived in an atmosphere of continual dissension. To us they seemed fussy; they were accustomed to treat staff in a cavalier fashion. Heaven knows how we seemed to them, heartless I should think. Brash and uncompromising, we were inclined to pooh-pooh their alarms, their illnesses and their meticulous anxiety about seeming irrelevancies. "Good God," said Wheeler, a day before the term began, "I haven't made out the list of dining room places." "Never mind," I said. "Just for tomorrow, let the boys sit down as they come in." But this was unthinkable. All lists had to be made out a week before the term began. Now, after 20 years on my own, I do, or try to do, exactly as he did then.

'Martin must have found me insufferable with my daily suggestions, hopefully put forward for immediate and welcome adoption. But Nan at that time had most to bear. Dolly Wheeler, recognising her social gifts, was sedulous in preventing her from exercising them in school affairs. "There's a rock garden," she said, "down there beyond the lawn. The best thing you can do is to give some help with that." Against all her inclinations she set to. She made a good job of that rock garden – but neither of us has done any gardening of any sort since then.

'Punishment was a question on which we were at loggerheads from the start. I mean the expiation of major offences, not the petty deprivations used to minimise negligence. To me, the model relationship between pupil and teacher was that of Lady Jane Grey and her Mr Aylmer – "One of the greatest benefits that ever God gave me is that He sent me so gentle a schoolmaster." Martin's attitude was different, but perfectly open and four-square. The smallest boys had their classroom next to his study. "I open the door," he said, "and when I tan the little blighter, they can jolly well hear him yell." His wording, accompanied by a bright smile, was meant

to shock me, and succeeded. Solemnly I suggested that punishment was a confession of weakness, and that a good schoolmaster could obtain his ends by kindness, cooperation, enthusiasm, the positive approach. He smiled.

'Towards the end of that term I collected a number of exercise books which clearly showed that one of the elder boys had been cribbing. With my assistant master's mentality, I took the matter to Martin for solution. He brushed it off – "I suppose you'd better give him a tanning." So there we sat in my room, I sure of nothing save that I had a slipper within easy reach, Philippe, a friendly and mondain 13-year-old, suavely denying the whole business. Obviously it was a situation that had to be resolved quickly. "I'm very sorry, Philippe," I said, "but this exercise shows without any doubt that you've been copying from your neighbour. I'm going to give you four on the behind. You can jolly well bend over." Obligingly he did so. It's hard to know what would have happened if he hadn't, but then perhaps I was lucky to have had an understanding accomplice. It really did hurt me more than it hurt him.'

The Wheelers retired in March 1939, and a great farewell presentation was arranged for which parents subscribed £135.0s.3d. With some of the money a canteen of 18th-century silver was purchased; the rest was to be spent on carpets. Bruce Nimmo, the head boy, gave a speech and a presentation from the boys and staff, adding that he 'hoped Mr Gulland would not take over Mr Wheeler's accurate aim with a slipper.' Martin Wheeler wrote to express his thanks for the send-off: 'The building up of Cumnor is the big thing we have done in our lives. We are sad of leaving but there is a feeling of satisfaction that we are passing it on to you and Nan, who have already gained so thoroughly the confidence of the parents and the affection of the boys …'. After a period in which Martin worked part-time at Sherborne prep school, the Wheelers

retired to the Isle of Wight, where he died in 1971, and Dolly the following year.

Evacuation

In summer 1939, his first term as sole headmaster, Hal brought in several important innovations. The first was the house point system, which was started with the three houses, Whites, Reds and Blacks (Blues were added in 1943); points were to be awarded for scholarships, cricket, PT, swimming, hobbies, digging, general behaviour – and work. An important feature of the system, unusual then as today, was that there were to be no minus points: a good deed does not become less good if there is a subsequent failing. Secondly, the school was divided into four forms – A (the eldest), B, C and D (the youngest, apart from the few young E formers under eight). Thirdly scouting, which for 24 years was to be such an important element in the school, was introduced.

Hal wrote an optimistic editorial in the school magazine of June 1939: 'The new term has been under way for some weeks and shows every sign of being a happy and successful one. A promising selection of potential scholars, a strong cricket side and a lessening of the political tension have combined to give us a good start.' Within weeks war broke out, Croydon aerodrome became an RAF base and hasty meetings were held with parents to discuss the future of the school. Nic Bellatti remembers that there was even talk of evacuating to Canada. There were 99 boys in the school; 50 of them disappeared without trace, 29 of them came as boarders to the country with Hal and Nan and 20 stayed in Croydon, using as their schoolroom a large room in the Sherlocks' house, The Old Saw Mill in Sanderstead. Longley, who had replaced Molony when the latter joined the RAF in February 1939, was to be the headmaster of the Sanderstead branch. Hal later wondered whether Nan would have seen through Longley,

CHS 1st XI, 1939. From the back, left to right: R Kennard, R Walker, D Allen, J Crump, H Sherlock, R Fox, B Nimmo, F J Carrigan, J Berkley, J Lumsden, R Lazenby, N Burt, B M Jones, M Kennard

but she was in Australia with Robin, making a final visit to her sick father. One by one financial irregularities surfaced, and it slowly became clear that Longley had a serious drink problem. The Wheelers gallantly offered to stand in, but in fact the blitz solved the problem. When machine gun bullets began spraying the classroom walls, it was time for The Old Saw Mill to close down as a school. And meanwhile where were the 29 to go? In Hal's words: 'Nobody remembers when or how we first entered into negotiations with FitzOrchard. He ran a school near East Grinstead called Charters Towers – a seedy place by Wheeler's spotless standards – but there were large grounds and plenty of room. Moreover, another large house was available just over the road, and FitzOrchard kindly suggested that his school should move there while we occupied his present school buildings. He was to house and feed us, at a weekly charge per head. It seemed a satisfactory arrangement, at least to tide us over a term or two; a draft agreement was drawn up, leaving many loose ends.

'When war did come, near the end of the summer holidays, what had seemed an academic exercise became an immediate and urgent actuality. In any case the school was compulsorily turned out, for nobody doubted that Croydon airport would be a primary target. We circularised parents, called a meeting to explain our plans and for three successive evenings went to meet FitzOrchard at a hotel in Godstone. He had changed, we found, from a keen young cricketer into a lynx-eyed businessman. No question now of our moving into his school buildings: we were to go to the house across the road. A row of wooden huts was to provide our form rooms and general headquarters. Moreover, any future new boy was to be enrolled as a member of his school. Those were his terms – take them or leave them.

'We had little option now. There was one saving clause that we managed to insert in the final agreement which FitzOrchard and his lawyer had

ready for us. We could give a fortnight's notice to terminate at the end of any month. Under these unpromising auspices we arrived, 29 boys and a staff of four, the day before war broke out. The outlook was uncertain, near three-quarters of the school had disappeared for ever, but these boys were now our family and we wanted to do our best for them. Also, if it were humanly possible, to reach at least a *modus vivendi* with our hosts. This was responsibility different in kind from anything we had known before.

'Our first memory is of hustling the boys into the basement after the first air-raid siren of the war. Our second is of emerging to find FitzOrchard in the first of many blazing tempers at the top. It seemed that he and his wife had been helping to prepare a meal upstairs, exposed to bombs, while we had been loafing around and enjoying ourselves below. The boys, milling around and keyed up for excitement, mostly found this adult rage an adequate substitute for a real air-raid.

'Some of the more thoughtful ones, indeed, as the days went by and Poland was overrun, showed signs of distress. But the greater part, finding that they were not going to come into immediate physical contact with Germans, quickly became preoccupied with their novel and countrified surroundings. And school work of course went on as usual – simultaneous equations, rules for the agreement of past participles …'.

FitzOrchard regarded the war as a heaven-sent opportunity for restocking his school with fresh boys. At weekends he sat in a window and waylaid our visiting parents with suggestions that they should transfer their sons to him. It is pleasant to record that no-one did so, but the fact only inflamed the violent temper of our host. It soon became clear to Nan and me that these arrangements could not continue; within a very brief time, and with no alternative then in view, we invoked our escape clause and gave notice to leave at the end of the month.'

CHAPTER 4

LITTLEWORTH CROSS
1939–45

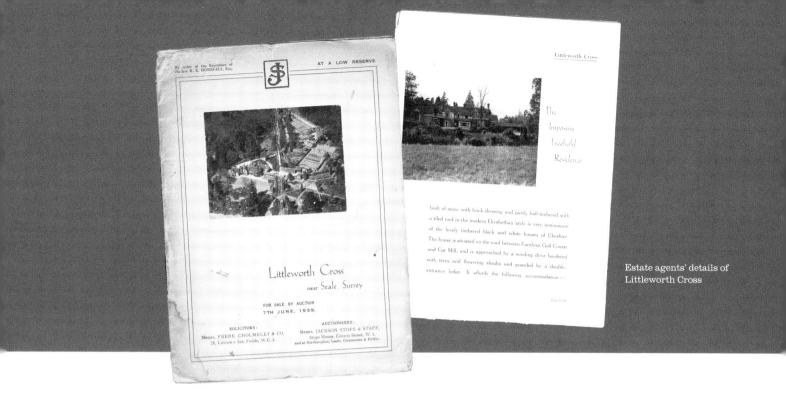

Estate agents' details of
Littleworth Cross

Sweet are the uses of adversity

SHAKESPEARE, *AS YOU LIKE IT*

The fortunes of the school were at their lowest ebb. The move to East Grinstead had been a disaster, and there was no prospect of a new home; several members of staff had been called up, and only two of the pre-war teachers remained, albeit the excellent pair of Rosie Field who was in charge of the D form (the youngest boys) and 'Garry' (Peggy Garrard) who was in charge of the C form (nine-year-olds) and the cubs. Back at Sanderstead Longley's problems were soon to become apparent. Hal had written in the 1939 *Cumnor Chronicle*, only five months earlier, about 'a future to which we look forward with great pleasure and high confidence.' They can have had little cause for confidence now: indeed they must have felt that the school in which they had invested so much hope and money was close to collapse. Yet from the

despair emerged an extraordinary rebirth: despite the war and the problems it brought, the next six years turned out to be, for Jim Earle as for many others, 'one of the happiest, least troubled, golden times of my life.' That the school survived at all was due to an extraordinarily supportive group of parents, the helpfulness and adaptability of the boys, particularly the vintage 1929 class, and the enthusiasm and hard work of my parents and the staff; that it survived so happily was largely due to the discovery of Littleworth Cross, Seale, near Farnham. The house was designed by Norman Shaw, with pigsties and stables by the young Edwin Lutyens, no less.

Twenty years later Hal recalled this time: 'We had a fortnight in which to find ourselves a new home. It was not easy, for we had limited funds and no standing, and many competitors were in the field.

Day after day Nan and I set off and after many false trails we landed at Littleworth Cross, a moderate-sized country house, set in a garden of rare rhododendrons, two miles south of the Hog's Back. Our first impression, for we did not then realise the illusory emptiness of an unfurnished house, was that it was far too big; six years later we were to leave because it was too small for us. At the moment, anyway, it was the only possibility. There was a three-acre paddock which would do for playing fields; we took it, and moved the school for the second time. We relied on old Woodger, the first of a wonderful series of gardeners that fate has sent us. He must by then have been well over 60, but offered immediate willing help in heavy jobs like moving desks and furniture which were right outside his terms of reference. He also scored 34 not out in our first staff cricket match, standing up straight and driving the ball before the wicket in the manner of the previous century.

'We were lucky in our friends during the brief time we had for moving in. Mr Price, who made "Sleepeeze" mattresses, presented us with 16 divan beds and delivered them on the spot. Mr Pruden, a bank manager, came to help with typing and duplicating the circulars with which at that time we had to bombard the parents with every change of plan. And a circular, from beginning to end, can be the best part of a whole day's work. Mr Gooding, an oil magnate, took a week's holiday and helped in his shirtsleeves with every sort of menial job. The Vickers had also taken a house nearby and Mrs Vickers (in those days we did not like or dare to call parents by their Christian names), with her incomparable maid Charlotte, used to come day by day to help with the cooking. This may not sound much but in fact the big cooker on which we had pinned such faith was out of action when we arrived. Not even Mr Gooding could put it right and for the first week every meal had to be cooked on a camp fire in the back yard. Luckily the weather was fine.

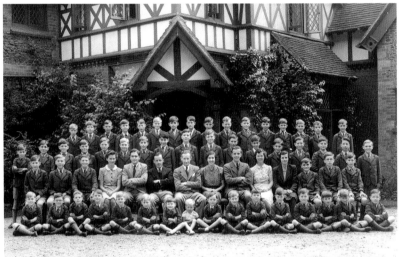

'We came to Littleworth Cross with 40 boys; things had looked up a little since our abortive essay with FitzOrchard a month earlier. We had made a tentative start with forming a boarding community, and it was a wonderful thing to be on our own. The new life was a complicated one. We laid on a bus for visiting parents every fortnight and provided a pleasant tea. It was not quite so pleasant when illness struck us, and we were haphazard and unorganised. Looking through my notebook for those months I find innumerable scribbled lists, though it is interesting to see that, despite the illnesses, 37 out of 40 boys put on weight during that term.

'On foot and by bicycle we went to the local

Cumnor House, 1941.
Adults (left to right):
Rosie Field, Mr
Bullivant, James
Usborne, Hal and Nan,
Mr Robinson, Peggy
Garrard, Miss Dell
(matron)

...you look so long.
My darling son was
laid to rest last

church on Sunday mornings. Not only was the church itself old and beautiful, but the rector, a kind-hearted and elderly scholar, became a close friend. He began to address his sermons almost exclusively in the direction of the school; he interested the boys of all ages. He presented the school with a set of the *Encyclopaedia Britannica* which now bears signs of over 20 years of constant use. To the boys he taught singing and came to give an occasional lecture, rousing historical stuff.'

The war

At Seale the war had little direct impact on the boys. Philip Gaze, who had taught at Cumnor before the war and was now studying for ordination, received a letter from Hal quoting *The Acts of the Apostles*: 'Come over into Macedonia, and help us.' Much later, in a 'Wartime Memories' supplement to the 1997 magazine, Philip wrote: 'On the whole the war's nastier effects passed us by. It was possible to see London burning from the Hog's Back road and one night a German plane discarded a load of fire bombs over us. None hit the house; some landed in the garden. I can remember foolishly extinguishing one by stamping on it in bedroom slippers; the bracken on the common land beyond the boundary was well ablaze and we tried beating it out with whatever came handy, but made little impression till the AFS arrived with heavy shovels to beat it down.'

Jim Earle recalls an air-raid and 'the unexploded bomb': 'The one great excitement with an air-raid was when the Germans bombed the railway marshalling-yards at Ash, just the other side of the Hog's Back, some three miles away. They hit an ammunition train and it went on blowing up all night long. All of us knew far more about air-raids than we ever learned at school. In fact, it underlines the wonderful cocoon that Cumnor managed to weave round us that I have so little to tell about the physical realities of war at school. There was one very exciting time when it was reported that a

strange unidentified object had been found in the stable yard near the pigsties. It had been covered with a cardboard box and the authorities summoned. A long and suspenseful wait ensued until the Bomb Disposal people came, removed the cardboard box and pronounced the tiny thing to be the inside of a golf ball.'

Sports Day 1941 was named 'War Weapons Day' and raised £405 for the war effort. However, the reality of war was brought sharply into focus when there was a death close to the school community. Fl Lt Jack Firth, who had taught at Cumnor from 1937 to 1941, was killed in action in August 1942. His mother wrote to Hal, 'Jack was so very happy with you all at school. I am

Thursday, Sept. 3rd, at
Streatham Park Cemetery.
I know you would
have been there had
you known.
Jack was so very
happy with you all
at school. I am most
grateful for all your
kindness to him.
What a waste of dear,
brave, young lives.
Yours very sincerely,
Ruby Firth

Letter to Hal from Jack Firth's mother, 7th September 1942, and below, Jack Firth

most grateful for all your kindness to him. What a waste of dear, brave young lives.' The rugby cup was given in his honour. P/O Leonard Cox, who had been a member of staff before the war, was killed in an aeroplane accident over the sea in September 1942. Lt Alec Williams was killed on active service in December 1943; he was the son of Mr and Mrs Harold Williams, who had presented the Fielding Cup, and his two scholarships are recorded on our first Honours Board. And finally Peggy Garrard's brother John, who had been one of the first boys at Cumnor and a frequent visitor to the school, was killed while serving as a pilot in Italy in January 1944. Another event which must have brought home the enormity of war was a visit in summer 1945 from a Miss Ashbery with her first-hand description and photographs of the recently liberated Belsen.

Activities

Were there compensations? To an A former who complained that 'Wartime has no pleasures,' Hal wrote: 'To take a few innovations at random, the war has brought to him here scouting, cubs, the "long break", bicycling expeditions, eightsome reels, week-end reading, knitting, pigs, goat, ducks, rhododendrons, the "parents' coach", news periods, National Savings, nature walks, cinemas and conjuring!' Scouts were run by the young James Usborne who arrived in 1940, and they continued to be a large part of Cumnor life for the next 20 years. The 12-year-old Terry Reardon wrote: 'Since I have been down at Cumnor in Seale I have had several enjoyable afternoons scouting. I remember one afternoon in particular with Mr Usborne, when we went on the common and made fires, on which we made toast. Afterwards we had a short sing-song and went home to a very enjoyable high tea. On shorter afternoons we play games rather nearer home. One of these games I like especially is "Getting to Cutmill without being seen". This is not as easy as it sounds, because there are all three patrol leaders and sometimes Mr Usborne looking out for you. But scouting is not all games. It involves hut-building, test-passing and patrol work.'

Hugh Campbell (1936–43) remembers a scout camp at the Vlasto family's farm near the River Wey: 'The finale of the camp was a game of French and English on a grand scale. In groups of five or so, two-

Scouts, 1941

36

thirds set out to make their way back from the camp after dark to Cumnor House. The remaining third were dispersed to catch them. The way ran through woods inhabited by fallow deer and then across Crooksbury Common covered in heather and bracken, to the south gate of the school grounds. Although we started in a group, we split up or were captured. I was on my own halfway across the common when I became aware of someone moving rather fast in my direction. I thought I had found a ditch with good heather cover, but found Nic Bellatti waiting at the end of it – so we went back to CHS looking forward to hot soup. There was no shame in being caught by Nic because he was quite a "Captain Scarlet" in those days.'

John Berkley (1933–39) recalled: 'I must mention the heart of all scout camps, the camp fire, when, in the heat and smell of the wood fire and light of the dying sun, we gathered round in blankets to drink cocoa and sing the old songs, such as "Rule, Britannia", "Little Brown Jug" and "Ten Green Bottles".'

John's brother David (1940–45) remembers the cubs: 'This was an essential part of the week's activities. We graduated from dancing around in a circle demanding to know "Who killed Shere Khan" to lighting a fire with no more than two matches. I am still eternally grateful for learning the difference between a granny and a reef knot, a clove hitch and a round-turn-and-two-half-hitches, a sheet bend and a sheepshank. Then came the proud moment when one sewed a second star beside the wolf head on one's green and yellow cap – Two eyes open!'

Each summer holiday an expedition would be arranged, not only scout camps but a week's sailing on the Broads in 1944 and an amazing bicycling trip to Stratford in 1945. Hal was the one person for whom the Broads trip was not a success: 'Everybody enjoyed the voyage except for the one member of the party who within the space of 24 hours dismasted his boat, slept the night in the lee of a haystack and

Cubs, 1941

crippled himself for several weeks with a gallon of boiling water.'

David Berkley remembers the Stratford expedition: 'The Stratford Shakespeare Memorial Theatre had just been reopened. LHM-G's passion for Shakespeare was such that the occasion should not go unnoticed. He led a party who *cycled* from Littleworth Cross to Stratford, camping *en route* and while there. Did we carry all our camping gear? I can't believe that we did, but I clearly remember Howard Aplin, who had a drop handlebar bike (wow!) toiling over the Cotswolds with a huge communal billy-can hanging precariously on the back. We camped at Stratford for five days, going to a different performance each evening. (But I still haven't caught the Shakespeare bug!)' All got there and back safely (despite no gears on cycles then), even the 11-year-old John Hignett, and saw *Antony and Cleopatra*, *The Merry Wives of Windsor*, *Othello* and *Romeo and Juliet*. (In later life John was closely involved with Sam Wanamaker in the building of the Globe Theatre on the South Bank.)

Left: James Usborne with Maud, and Amelia, above

Animals

James Usborne was a memorable character, who was later to become a successful farmer at Newick. At Seale, where he lived in a 'Gazebo type of room 7ft by 8ft built on stilts in the kitchen garden', he was responsible among other things for the animals, which formed an important part of school life: indeed Michael Kennard observed quaintly that 'until Mr Usborne came to this school there were no animals'. The 12-year-old Tim Moss explained: 'There are many different kinds of animals at Cumnor House School, they are very interesting. There are pigs, dogs, cats and a goat. The sow has had 10 babies which are very pink and fat. The goat Maud by name is very sweet. She once had a baby, but it was sent to market as it was a billy. The dogs run all over the countryside catching rabbits. Peter is the fastest runner of them all and has caught a great many rabbits. The cats have now gone almost wild, but they rid the school of mice. Maud gives a lot of milk and she is milked by Vickers and D Campbell. There are some ducks and two bantams which are laying well. The masters and boys love the animals and so they are well looked after.'

James Usborne later recalled: 'Amelia was the queen of the piggery and regularly every six months gave birth to the required 12 little piglets. We didn't have a boar, Nan didn't think it was quite nice. The result being I and a few boys, of not too tender an age, used to lead Amelia, an awful lot of pushing and pulling, down to Seale village where they had a stud boar. If she wasn't happy about the union we had to go through it all again a day or two later. We also bought two goats to supplement our milk quota. Everything was rationed – food, petrol, clothes etc – and many things such as imported fruits were not obtainable, so the little extra goats' milk was welcome. It was my job to look after the animals. The goats were staked out with collar and chain on grass every morning and even Amelia had her own collar and chain. She ate the grass but unfortunately rooted up the turf which upset Hal and of course the goats Maud and Mabel, so we had to put a ring in her nose. She didn't like it. Again we had no billy goat so we had to take our usual road down to a billy in Seale village.

'Another reason for a pig is of course she ate up all the waste food from the dining room and kitchen and I again being a junior member of staff had to boil it all up in a large 20-gallon drum. I enjoyed the work. There were of course little and sometimes not so little piglets to feed. Later on in the war when we had Canadian troops arrive we had a lot of their waste swill.'

Michael Vickers enjoyed looking after Maud: 'Although I remained a close friend of Donald Campbell, I was jealous of his appointment to milk the goat while I was relegated to be Holder of the Rear Leg. However I was later promoted and GBH was averted.' Nan too remembered Maud 'whose milk nourished our young son' – me – 'until she took to eating ivy which brought him out in fearsome spots; one of her kids couldn't resist the open dining room window and ran up and down the tables with us in pursuit; the pigs used to be scrubbed up to look clean for parents' days – usually with my best carpet brush.'

The 1942 magazine relates another memorable Usborne adventure, part of the folklore which grew up around this extraordinary man: 'To be driving a car at 10 o'clock on a dark winter's night, to see a deer 50 yards away, to draw up, load, and shoot it dead, is no mean feat. Congratulations, Mr Usborne. Venison makes a nice change.' Incidentally the illegality of this exploit consisted not of killing or eating the deer but of shooting from the King's Highway.

James also taught Scripture to the D form: 'We used to make it very informal sitting around on the floor and generally enjoying the Bible stories. However after a time I ran out of exciting stories such as David and Goliath, Pillars of Salt and Ruth, never did quite understand that one myself. So I made up what I thought would be enlightening religious stories having gone through the Lions' Den excitement. The children really enjoyed it, especially about pirates and so on. However it all came to an end when one of the parents, a vicar, wrote to Hal asking where young Usborne found his stories in the Bible. My teaching the Holy Scriptures came to an abrupt end. I took carpentry lessons instead.'

Food

Of course the purpose of the farm was to provide food: fun was a by-product. Mr Woodger the gardener, who had already been at Littleworth Cross for 25 years before the school arrived, supervised the excellent vegetable garden, helped by boys and staff.

Peggy Garrard (staff, 1936–45): 'Food of course was rationed, but we didn't starve. Dried egg was only edible scrambled. Meat was short but plenty of cheese, macaroni and milk puddings…. There were fresh vegetables from the garden, amongst them artichokes which I'd never tasted before and liked.'

Hugh Campbell: 'Quite often we had herrings for breakfast and it was generally possible to have "seconds". This started a competition to see who could eat the most whole herrings – head, tail and backbone as well – possible if they were well fried. Richard Drake was the champion and I was the runner-up. I'm glad to say it didn't put me off herrings and the training stood me in good stead for later boarding school and army food.' Michael Feaver used to look forward to 'Spam fritters, sausages in gravy and, of course, eggy bread made with reconstituted egg.'

Others, like Peter Branscombe (1941–43), had reservations: 'I hated fat and recall plenty of it on the meat at meals. We had to eat it up ("there's a war on"), and I couldn't always drop it into my handkerchief to dispose of later. So I curried favour with Mr Bird, and he made me sit next to him at meals. It was easy to distract his attention and slip the fat on to his plate – where he could leave it, or eat it. I was caught, and rightly "tanned" by LHM-G.'

Nan, according to James Usborne, 'had the brilliant idea that we should hide dustbins full of tinned food, in case of a complete stop of food supplies. We chose a spot in the woods to dig the holes, not the easiest place to dig a hole to take dustbins. However we filled six bins and dug six holes. The tins were mostly of Spam and sardines, the former a horrid American mix of ham etc. We covered them up, only to discover when we got back to the school we'd left the can openers out! So we had to go back, find our hidden bins and put in the openers. We'd hidden them so well we only found five. They're probably still there.'

Boys did their bit for the war effort by picking potatoes and apples. Hugh Campbell remembers 'apple picking on a fruit farm near Chertsey under canvas in a very well organised camp, and hot summer weather. We didn't just climb ladders to pick apples but climbed the trees as well – much better than potato picking in Mr Poulsom's fields near Seale.'

Peter Branscombe: 'Michael Kennard and I formed a disconsolate pair of potato-pickers during the one expedition I can recall in which we boys took a role in war work; we bent over the trenches and picked what we could, grumbling that our parents' ill-afforded school fees were meant to prepare us for Common Entrance rather than digging for victory.'

Surroundings

The large grounds and miles of sandy common land all around afforded marvellous opportunities for nature study, a novel experience for the boys, most of whom came from Croydon. Hugh Campbell, aged 13, wrote: 'It is interesting to note the different birds that come to nest here, in the grounds. We have been lucky enough to have some rare birds. For instance, a little time ago two redstarts nested near Mr Usborne's house by the front drive. As well as the redstarts the pied wagtail is often to be seen strutting up and down the front lawn. Tree creepers and woodpeckers have also been seen creeping up the acacia trees pecking as they go. Then of course there are the tits; tits of all sorts, bluetits, great tits, coal tits and long tailed tits, all of these have been seen swinging on the silver birch trees in the grounds.'

The seven-year-old Bill Sutherland was an expert on robins: 'The robin dus not mac his nest tide. He dus lik the snoe. He dus perch on a holy tree

The gardens at Littleworth Cross

ore a fair tree. He dus sing a luvle soing. His egs are creemy with red spots. His culers are red brest and his back is braon.'

Looking back 65 years on, Peter Branscombe writes: 'The school grounds were very special, rich in trees, birds, beasts and butterflies. I became an expert catcher of grass snakes and lizards (I was nicknamed 'Liggie'), and once for a while even kept an injured adder. My snakes and lizards became quite tame, and locally renowned; one fairly small snake learnt to emerge from my sleeve when I held my hand out to someone as if offering a hand-shake. And a particularly handsome female common lizard obtained a measure of immortality by – unknown to me – emerging from my blazer breast pocket and figuring in a school cricket XI photograph.

'One was dared to jump out of the (ground floor) dormitory windows at night and climb a tall tree, and collect a cone from its crown; or run round the games field in the moonlight; or indeed at first-floor level climb out of one bow window and creep cautiously round the protruding windows and climb back in at the far side. There were turtle doves building their flimsy nests in the rhododendron bushes, a pair of goldcrests hanging their tiny nest from a low branch of a Weymouth pine and nightingales in the under-growth (I don't think I learnt to know and love their song until later). A wheatear's nest in a letter-box near

Cutmill Pond, where great-crested grebes courted. And once I saw a truly immense grass snake slowly cross the raised path in front of me – I knew that it was harmless, but it was awe-inspiring, and far too big to risk trying to catch.'

Problems

Not all was unalloyed joy. Peter Branscombe again: 'There was some bullying – I suffered at the hands and tongue of John Reaveley, whose younger brother James ('James and John the sons of Reaveley', in impious substitution for the name of Zebedee) was a friend; he sang folksongs beautifully. Most of my contemporaries whom I recall at all were delightful people – Michael Vickers (whom I was to remeet at Worcester, our Oxford college, and years later still when two daughters of his studied German at St Andrews), Jim Stanley-Smith, Nick Burt, Howard Aplin, Peter Hines, Christopher Barnes (whose sister was the first girl I fell for), the Berkley, Kennedy and Campbell brothers, Brian Jenks, Mark Fielden, Peter Willan, Michael Feaver ('Beever, beever, where is Feaver? Sitting at the bottom of Crooksbury Hill').

Illness was a much more constant and serious threat than now, and not just the epidemics such as chickenpox which decimated the cast of *The Tempest* in 1942, or measles which led to the cancellation of all matches in spring 1945 and the reduction of the C form to two boys; Nan remembered 'terrifying times, too, in those pre-penicillin days; well I remember taking a temperature with a thermometer registering only up to 105 degrees and finding the mercury trying to run through the end of it as the boy's earache developed into mastoid. Equally memorable was the collapse of an asthmatic boy with measles (then in one of its very severe phases) and the hospital's sending out oxygen equipment minus a vital valve, which had to be fetched by car with our last cupful of petrol. Mercifully both of these, and others equally severely ill, recovered; but, having

lived through those years, I find it hard to speak scornfully, as so many younger people do, of "wonder drugs". Of course they are too often used just as an easy way out, but I have sent up a silent paean of thanksgiving ever since, when I've seen a small white face and prostrate form transformed overnight into a sitting-up convalescent, and the word "pneumonia" no longer fills me with a helpless feeling of panic and dread.'

Peter Branscombe has a bizarre memory 'of lying in a first-floor sick room somewhere at the back of the main building, with window looking out over the cobbled yard. I had fallen from a tree, and was suffering from what might have been glandular fever. The one memory is of a humming, buzzing sound that got louder and louder. It was a swarm of bees. They swirled in through the open window, I dived under the bedclothes, and only recall that I was not stung, though very frightened in my already feverish state. I think my shouts were at last heard, and that Peter Willan and JU contrived to collect the swarm and remove them to a more proper place.'

Out of school

For entertainment the school had to rely on its own resources. Scottish dancing was introduced (as a substitute for soccer when the pitches were frozen!). Wood was hard to obtain for carpentry, but Hal got some offcuts of Perspex from an aircraft factory where it was used for bomb sights, and started Perspex modelling; Garry managed to find some Malayan basket-cane for basketwork; some kind neighbours lent their squash court; there were frequent lectures, films and conjuring shows, and trips were often made to the River Wey with books, lunch and bathing things.

Canon Arrowsmith, Rector of Seale, visited the school each week to practise the music for the following Sunday's church service. He wrote in the magazine: 'In the 18th and 19th centuries music was looked upon in schools as effeminate, a musician being generally represented as a weedy specimen of humanity, with long curly hair and feeble limbs, and an inane expression. All this has passed and good music is regarded as a valuable means of education – in training the ear to beauty in sound, in teaching a sense of rhythm, in cultivating an appreciation of the aesthetic values of life and in providing occupation and solace in days of boredom or difficulty. Few greater gifts can be given to anyone than a love of good music.' Hymns were introduced into morning prayers, and the first carol service was held in 1943; in the same year six boys passed their piano exams.

David Berkley remembers the weekly visit to church: 'Each Sunday morning we would cycle to Seale parish church for the morning service (the younger children were taken in the sedate Armstrong Siddeley). We sat on chairs in the transept in front of the congregation. One Sunday we were to sing, as we often did in wartime, "O God, our help in ages past". "We will leave out verse five (Time, like an everlasting stream, Bears all its sons away. They fly forgotten, as a dream Dies at the opening day): that is not true," said the vicar. Why was he so emphatic, I wondered – and still wonder. Was it because he had his own personal memories, or was it because it was directly contrary to the armistice declaration: "We will remember them"?'

Chris Dalgarno (1943–46) remembers 'cycling en masse to Seale church on a Sunday. We used the opportunity to see who could make butter in a bottle of milk tied to the spokes.' Peter Branscombe: 'Brother Ron and I developed a certain notoriety for fainting during Mattins at Seale Parish Church. I usually began to feel queasy soon after Canon Arrowsmith had intoned "We shall now sing the first seven verses of the Venite", and retired to the churchyard (it was always sunny outside in my memory), where, after Ron had joined me, we could roll marbles on a flat tombstone. One memorable Sunday I survived beyond the usual moment of near collapse, and was there to hear the Canon's querulous chant, "Let us pray", and the immediate loud response, in a fine imitation of the ancient vicar's tone and inflection, "OK". A moment's stunned silence was broken by suppressed laughter, then pandemonium broke loose. The culprit was Bryan Salm. Although I may be wrong, I think there was, in official recognition of his brilliant achievement, no enquiry as to the identity of the sinner.'

Sport

Sport was no less important 65 years ago than it is today, and in 1940 the school enjoyed making many new friends in the neighbouring schools – Aldro, Amesbury, Barfield, Boxgrove, Edgeborough, Fernden, Lanesborough and others. Michael Vickers: 'Despite what I remember as a really competitive spirit in all sport during those years, we were encouraged to be good losers when it came to that and not to get results out of proportion.' In 1940 the 1st cricket XI was very young, and 'when they lost a match they did so with thoroughness.' Next year the remarkable Freddie Fox took all 10 wickets for five runs against Barfield. Harley Sherlock enjoyed the three-acre paddock: 'The football pitch was on such a steep slope that, as goalkeeper, I was easily able to clear the halfway line with a good punt. Needless to say, my rather selective memory does not allow me to recall what happened when we were playing uphill!'

The 1941 and 1942 soccer teams were unbeaten (goals for 70, against 1). Hal sounded a note of caution: 'Personally I don't much like "unbeaten records". They are uncomfortable things to live up to, and tend to drive the joy out of the game and engender the swollen head.' The first school rugby matches were played in 1943, with Hal's old friend from Belmont days, Wilf Sobey, ex-England scrum half, coaching the team. Meanwhile Sports Day had become more serious: gone were such old favourites as the Egg and Spoon race, Sack race, and races for Masters, Little Brothers, Little Sisters, Big Sisters, Mothers, Fathers.

Staff

The stalwarts of the staff, besides my father, were Philip Gaze (part-time), James Usborne, Peggy Garrard and Rosie Field. Philip Gaze stayed till 1950, when he left to become Vicar of Puttenham (then to emigrate to New Zealand in 1962); James Usborne left to go to Agricultural College in 1944; Peggy Garrard became an Essex farmer's wife when she married Francis Seabrook in Seale Church in 1944 (after which there was a reception at the school and the boys ate four gallons of pink ice cream); and Rosie Field left in 1942 to marry John Hutton.

There was also Cyril Robinson, with his blue pinstripe suits; Michael Feaver (1940–45): 'My most vivid memory of him was when, playing Wei the Dragon General in *Lady Precious Stream*, he had to be fiercely beaten. All were willing the protective pillow to slip!' Mr Robinson was said to be 'the only person who dares to stand up to our Nicholas James, just turned three; the latter retaliates by calling him a Big Bully.'

Peter Branscombe: 'Of the other masters, the most unforgettable (for all the wrong reasons) was Mr C W Robinson, "Robie", who even then struck me as ignorant, bullying and unfair. I remember his giving us a spelling test, and mispronouncing the words burglar ("burgular") and orange ("ornge"), thus upsetting my normally reliable sense of spelling (something that 40 years of marking university essays has done nothing to improve). I don't know whether he had a drink problem, though there may have been some reason for the ditty we used to sing: "Oh, it's my delight on a Saturday night/to visit the Barley Mow". One night when we were all chatting in the dormitory, Robie burst in and asked who had been talking. Nic Bellatti said he had, and I too confessed. We were taken down to LHM-G's study and "tanned" pretty viciously with a gym shoe; I recall Nic's stoicism (he was led in first), and I managed to do no more than whimper (and fart hugely).'

David Berkley recalls another Cyril, the Rev

Left: Philip Gaze

Below: Rosie Hutton (Field), Peggy Seabrook (Garrard) and Nan, June 1997

Cyril Maurice Jones, taking him for English composition: 'He took the line often taken by teachers in that situation – "Write a composition on anything you like, but its title must begin with a C." I doubt whether my composition deserved many marks, but I did get a B+ for the title "Cricket Calamity Caused by a Cow".' Hugh Campbell remembers Latin lessons with Mr Bird 'who was tall, thin, dark and solemn. At the first lesson we noticed his large gold ring with the two-headed eagle engraved on it. Lessons passed but by this time a certainty had formed. It was our opinion that Mr Bird was a German spy. Whispers circulated and altogether we didn't give him a very nice time. I don't think Mr Bird stayed much longer. I hope he wasn't really aware of our unpleasantness because he was a kind and peaceful person.'

Hal's teaching was remembered more warmly. Jim Earle recalls being taught the Marion Richardson style of handwriting: 'I still doodle those patterns where a group of letters is written continuously over and over and then repeated upside down touching the first row.' Michael Vickers remembers Hal's 'highly memorable and quietly dramatic French lessons. He would "transport" us in imagination into a Parisian

Philip Gaze

Philip Gaze, who was on the staff from 1939 to 1950, liked to celebrate his colleagues in verse. Here is his tribute to the substantial figure of the friendly and popular Marcus Molony, who was much missed when he left to join the Balloon Barrage.

As the Lilliputians chattered
　　Underneath the Giant's eye,
So of old did Cumnor infants
　　When the Irishman went by.

He was lofty as the mountains
　　And his head was in the clouds,
And the motorists fled before him
　　When they met him on the roads.

But his smile was like the sunrise
　　When it warms the dew-wet earth,
And the heart that beat within him
　　Was the equal of his girth.

He is lost among the cloud-drifts,
　　Wandering far beyond the moon,
Clinging, clinging yet more firmly
　　To an RAF balloon.

James Usborne was the subject of this poem:

There was a wildness in his hair,
　　There was a wildness in his eye,
There was a wildness in his voice,
　　And it struck the passer-by.

He was ruthless in the form-room,
　　He was kindly in the sty,
He was raucous in the garden,
　　And he shocked the passer-by.

He was deadly with a shot-gun,
　　Where the rainbow-pheasants fly,
He was deadly with a Bren-gun,
　　And the Hun shall not pass by.

He also immortalised Jim Earle and his brother Bob in verse:

Jimmy and Bobby Earle I next behold,
Delightful boys, who looked as good as gold.
Bobby, endowed with large and serious eyes,
Would gaze at you in innocent surprise
Should you the slightest accusation bring
That he had been remiss in anything:
It was an excellent accomplishment,
And often saved young Bob from punishment.
That Jimmy can be serious I know,
(And when he is, beware, for tears may flow),
Yet seriousness was not his constant mood,
He most was merry, sometimes even good!
Ent'ring with joy on all that came his way,
Soccer or scouts, plain knitting or a play.
With equal zeal displayed in his intent
Whether on schoolwork or on mischief bent.

A PAGE OF WRITING PATTERNS 5

café where he came round as the waiter, taking our orders and bringing them to us with explanations and recommendations.

'A difficult and potentially dull subject such as algebra was presented as a challenge in problem-solving. I am sure this is why, in a scholarship mathematics paper in May 1942, when I was surprised to find such questions (apparently out of context) as "What is wrong with the following proof? All fishes can swim; Mr Winston Churchill can swim; THEREFORE Mr Winston Churchill is a fish", I was not totally fazed.

'I also remember the day, just before I left Cumnor after a year as head boy, when he called me into his study and told me to choose as a gift any book from his collection. When I started to go for something "less", he steered me in the direction of an exquisite little volume, a 1636 small red edition of *Virgilii Opera Cura D Heinsii* with a map and some unusual red printing in the middle. It was so typical of his generosity and kindness. Although I think I was always going to go the way of history and theology rather than the Classics, I treasure this in memory of him along with his equally generous final headmaster's report.'

Slightly more critical is Peter Branscombe's summary: 'LHM-G was a powerful, feared, but admired figure with his strong, hairy nose; he could be distant, and he could be very kind and understanding. He read books to us in his study of a Sunday

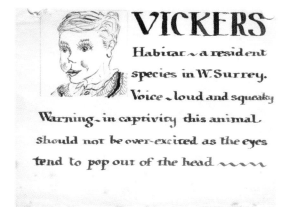

Michael Vickers as seen by Hal

evening – I particularly recall Dorothy Sayers' *The Nine Taylors* (she and Conan Doyle remain the only writers of crime fiction whom I've ever read). And he was very good at games, not always patient with those whose ability was impeded by nervousness. Favouritism was sensed (as, surely, in most schools).'

David Berkley too remembers story time: 'It was obvious that LHM-G enjoyed reading to us in his study on a Sunday evening as much as we enjoyed listening. We were treated to several chapters each week of some gripping stories. I don't remember anything of the exploits of the one who, at moments of high drama, would declare: "It is I, Colonel Etienne Gerard". That was repeated with much relish whenever any one of us wanted to make a dramatic impression! We sat spellbound through episodes of Captain Hornblower, and on tenterhooks

to know what would finally happen to Brown On Resolution.'

Two features of the school were unusual at the time: one was the increasing use of Christian names rather than the surnames which were customary before the war. The second was the introduction in 1942 of Saturday tests instead of end-of-term exams. This system, still in place today, was to gain much wider acceptance later as 'continuous assessment', but at that time it was a novel idea. Years later Tom Tickell was to write to Hal from Westminster: 'We are now in the middle of exams – how I wish we had them at weekends, as we did at CHS, so that one's sins caught one up in manageable proportions and not in one great rush.' Details of boys' work are revealed in the school magazines with breathtaking, today almost libellous, candour: 'Barry Murch wriggled his way into Bradfield', and 'There are still too many old men in this class: Tony Hines is only spasmodically hard-working, and Ian Knill-Jones somewhat apathetic.'

John Alexander (1942–50) recalls: 'In my last year I became head of Blue House, a responsibility I took very seriously. The chief task was to collect the house points, made out on little squares of paper by the

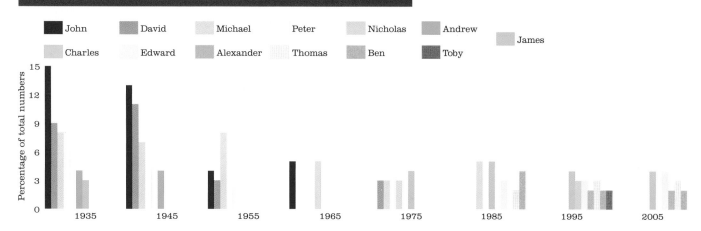

Changing fashions in boys' names 1935–2005

teachers. I badgered my house members so successfully that in my last term Blue House won the cup, much to my satisfaction. I was also patrol leader of the Kingfisher Patrol in scouts. I enjoyed this very much. We were allowed to take our patrols camping in the grounds. This involved making up blanket beds and taking them down to a tent set up in the woods. We would cook cocoa over an open fire in the evening. I was expert in finding the brittle twigs underneath the holly trees to start the fire. In the morning the dawn chorus awoke us with a deafening noise.'

The play

I have left till last in this chapter Hal's most important and lasting innovation: the Shakespeare play. Peter Branscombe: 'Perhaps the most powerful influence on me that I take from my Cumnor years is the discovery of Shakespeare ("discovery" simply because he was to become a quintessentially personal, private force, whom I prefer to read than to experience in the theatre). But *A Midsummer Night's Dream* and *The Tempest* (the first in Seale Parish Hall, the second in the school grounds) made a profound impression on me. Michael Vickers as Bottom and, especially, as Prospero, are still the personae that come to mind in these roles (I was prompter for *MND*, learnt the play almost by heart and cannot forget the enthusiastic comment of a visiting headmaster to LHM-G, "You have a magnificent Bottom"). John Alexander, Mustardseed in that production, remembers: 'We wore specially made trunks, and carried a bamboo wand, ingeniously made with a battery in it and a little bulb at one end.' Michael Vickers, the magnificent Bottom, valued 'the coaching we received from LHM-G in matters of voice production, the subtle use of vocal "light and shade" and the superlative value of managing pauses. This was not exactly a hindrance when I was a sergeant-major during National Service and, even more critically so, after I was ordained. Sitting, often unrecognised, in the congregation when I have been preaching, one criticism my wife has not often overheard is that I was inaudible! The plays at Cumnor House, both in the Jubilee Hall in Seale and in the garden at Littleworth Cross itself, have in themselves an almost disproportionate place in my happy memories of those days, but I never foresaw at the time the positive impact that they were to have later. Of the Jubilee Hall productions, I often wonder how we managed successfully to squeeze even LHM-G's abbreviated version of *A Midsummer Night's Dream* (December 1941), in which I was Bottom the Weaver, into those particular premises, but it was with open air productions in the rose garden at Littleworth Cross that I felt a new dimension of

Romeo and Juliet, 1943. Jim Earle (Benvolio, left), Hugh Campbell (Mercutio)

"magic" appeared. *The Tempest* (Summer 1942) was, for me, almost a life-changing experience.' It was in this performance that Barry Murch, playing Alonso, had been doped by Dr Hobbs against his asthma. So he really did fall asleep on the stage in Act II Scene I. But luckily he awoke at Ariel's call.

That much-remembered *MND* – the play about which Nan said, 'There is only one drawback to *A Midsummer Night's Dream* – it spoils you for any other play' – was the first Shakespeare play produced at CHS. Jim Earle remembers it well: 'There had been earlier plays – I remember *Nix-Nought-Nothing* by Naomi Mitchinson – but the performance I recall was the first Shakespeare. It has been followed by 60+ years of open-air Shakespeare productions but this first adventure was indoors in the very typical wooden country village hall in Seale, and by great good fortune I had the part of Puck. Three defining moments stand out. The first was LHM-G saying to me "Music ho!" (in his unforgettable, husky voice) whilst we were getting things ready on the day. By this time, LHM-G was immersed in the schedule by which he did all the make-up, and he wanted background music. The record that we were using in the play was already on the turntable of his gramophone in the wings, and the command meant I was to put it on. It was a suite of Purcell dances put together as "Ayres for the Theatre" and performed by a string group conducted, I clearly remember, by Anthony Bernard. It was and remains sheer magic; I cannot ever hear Purcell dances now without being back in that moment.

'Mr Usborne had rigged up some lights and had a hand in hanging the large red velvet curtains taken from the big B form room at Littleworth Cross, which were big enough to form a backdrop and wings and looked splendid. They looked even better later in an open-air *Romeo and Juliet* in the rose garden. The thought of that later production still takes my breath away.

'During our rehearsal period I was taken, as a treat, by LHM-G into Guildford to buy the material to make the ass's head. He was constructing this on a wire frame with strings to make the ears wag and now needed a length of shaggy grey velvet to cover it. This was acquired and we went into a restaurant for a wartime lunch. My second unforgettable moment came when we ordered our meal and I passed over the attractive jam tart in favour of prunes and custard. LHM-G was amazed that a small boy would make such a choice but I was always fond of prunes and had not had them for ages. I cannot encounter a prune to this day without remembering the moment.

'Puck was played as a skinny brown elf with not many clothes on. The brown was applied in a bath of body make-up at school. I was barefoot and I still can

feel the dusty floorboards of Seale village hall underfoot. The performance passed in a sort of high-octane dream and was over all too soon. Puck parted the curtains and delivered the Epilogue from the fore-stage, and as I finished the final couplet, something unexpected happened that we had not rehearsed: the audience started clapping. I was momentarily unsure what to do next, indeed whether to laugh or to cry. That third moment sealed my fate. I went on to become devoted to Shakespeare, to read English at Oxford and to have a lifetime addiction to poetry and the theatre. I, like all Cumnorians of my time and later, have many, many things for which to be deeply grateful to LHM-G. High on my long list would be Purcell, the prunes and Puck's surprised applause.'

Jim Earle was a member of the sailing trip to the Broads, and Hal later recalled the origin of a long tradition: 'Milk was unobtainable and we lived for a week on black coffee. To strain this we used a large red and white spotted handkerchief, and I remember on one occasion Jim's hoisting it to the masthead of our ancient craft as a signal of distress. This handkerchief has a long and unusual history. Bought at Woolworths in Watford before the war, it was used as a dishcloth for our first two scout camps at Elstead. Surviving this, it now began its stage career, first as a headdress for the Master in *The Tempest* (1942).' It continued to appear as a sort of talisman for many years.

Although the school's numbers climbed rapidly to about 60, Cumnor was still a very small school indeed. It really was possible to create something of a family atmosphere for the boys, most of whom had had no previous experience of boarding. It engendered great corporate feeling, and virtually everybody was included in the teams, the plays and the hobbies. It is probable that, as Peter Branscombe hinted, certain star pupils received too much attention, and that is a failing which Hal later recognised in himself; but in general Cumnorians of that era look back on Littleworth Cross as little short of an earthly paradise.

CHAPTER 5

BIRCH GROVE

1946–49

Below: Harold and
Dorothy Macmillan at
Birch Grove

We were, fair Queen,
Two lads that thought there was no more behind,
But such a day tomorrow, as today,
And to be boy eternal

SHAKESPEARE, *THE WINTER'S TALE*

'No-one could leave Littleworth Cross without regrets,' Hal wrote, 'especially with the rhododendron season just ahead, and a generation of boys will remember it with affection. Recollections, happy and sad, crowd the mind; a book could be written of them if there were ever time to do so.' But the school had grown, and the house which six years earlier had seemed so large was no longer suitable. The decision was made to rent Birch Grove House, Chelwood Gate, on the edge of Ashdown Forest, the large and elegant home of Harold and Lady Dorothy Macmillan. It was a fine stone and brick mansion, built in the Palladian style by Harold's parents in the 1930s, almost too grand for a school, with beautiful grounds and views of the Downs. Liz Turner, who joined the school at that time as secretary, cook, babysitter and general factotum, recalls that many of the overmantles, the surroundings and the grates came from Lansdowne House, the London residence of the Duke of Devonshire, Lady Dorothy's father, after substantial rebuilding there in 1931/2. Despite its use by the LCC during the war for evacuee children, Birch Grove House was in a good state.

OPPOSITE PAGE

Top: Birch Grove

Left: In the snoy [*sic*]
(see page 54)

Lady D

The Macmillans, who lived at Gosses, a farmhouse on the estate, became good friends of the school, particularly Lady Dorothy, who was memorably described by the 10-year-old Anthony Brooking (1942–50):

> ### Lady Dorothry
>
> In sussex there is a village called Chelwood gate, and just outside Chelwood there is a house called Birchgrove were our School was moved to. The owner of the house is Lady D. Macmillian, her husband is a member of paliment and a book publisher. I have seen electric bells all over the house with writing above them like so – Lady D.s Bedroom etc. Now that it is fine wheather Lady D asked the boys if they would like to do some gardening and she has got a lot of violentears to do some gardening. She has got 24 daughters according to a boy called Leonard, and one of them has a pet wolf. Lady Ds apperance is as follows:– grey hair, rather old, usually wearing a brown and grey suit, and wrinkles on her face, and very bright. She is nice.

Janet Brown tells a story which is typical of Lady D: 'It was Sports Day, and Tyler who must have been around seven or eight was eagerly waiting to take part in a race. As luck would have it, he missed it. A kind woman who was leaning against a tree saw how upset he was, and asked "What is the problem? Why is he so unhappy?" I explained that he had missed the race, and she turned to him and said, "Never mind, I'll race you from this tree to that one over there," then picked up her skirts and ran with Tyler who flew like the wind, all disappointment forgotten. I discovered afterwards it was Lady Dorothy Macmillan. I often think of how happy she made one little boy.' Tony Poulsom (1946–53) is one of several who have happy memories of tea with the Macmillans after Sunday afternoon walks.

The move

In the final term at Seale it had been possible at last to enjoy the delights of fireworks and a bonfire – the first time that this had been allowed in seven years. Moving a boarding school 60 miles is not a great problem, and almost all of the Littleworth Cross boys transferred to Birch Grove. However, no move is simple, and the 1946 magazine describes the operation: 'The Christmas holidays, protracted to five weeks, were filled with preparations for the move and its execution on January 1st–5th. First there was the clearing-up at Seale, a gigantic task which could hardly have been accomplished but for the efforts of those four stalwart boys, Nic Bellatti, Jimmy Earle and Terry and Martin Reardon, who gave a part of their holiday to this hard and dirty work, at the same time keeping up our spirits with their uproarious merriment and hearty appetites. The final clearance by Jim of the B form rafters brought to light (you will hardly believe it) 51 ping-pong balls, two dozen handkerchiefs and a toffee which he remembered throwing there five years before. All this was only a preparation for sterner tasks at Chelwood Gate. There, Mr Straker's exertions and the help of Christopher Carter, who asked to come back a week earlier, just got the school clean and ready for the general return on January 24th.'

This is the first mention of Jack Straker, who after demobilisation from the Army joined the staff for one term (the school's final term at Seale) and stayed for 34 years. During this time his contribution to the school was immeasurable. Jack and Hal, with their complementary qualities, remained firm friends, with Jack as senior master in charge, among other things, of maths, rugger, chess, printing, lighting for the play and the timetable; he also played the piano for the hymns and for the end-of-term sing-song, and in his spare time wrote a series of excellent detective stories. Described as 'bluff, genial and the best of company', he was voted the

Margaret Straker with Ranald MacDonell (Titania), 1953

Away match, 1948:
Jack Straker and the
(unbeaten) 1st XI

and

Away match, 2006:
Matt Mockridge and the
(unbeaten) 1st XI

happiest member of staff in 1949. As a D form pupil I well remember the anticipation one felt before one of his 'Mystery' lessons. Rhoddy Voremberg in the 1960s was impressed by Jack's teaching him, among other things, how to peel even the most difficult orange. John Alexander remembers: 'In those later days at Cumnor, we had a rambling club, run by Major Straker. He taught maths, and had arrived after the war, after service in North Africa. I was the secretary, and I used to write up each ramble carefully, with an illustrated map. I also clearly remember my scout first class hike, with Michael Allen, over Ashdown Forest; we camped under a pine tree, making a fine fire to cook boil-in-the-bag jugged hare.'

Jack's wife Margaret had an extraordinary talent for producing play costumes, which she continued to do for 40 years, until 1986. In 1959 Hal wrote: 'It is hard to know how we would manage without Mrs Straker in the summer term. For a month before our plays she sews and mends, washes, irons and presses, without respite and often long into the night. A few urgent demands with which she has been faced in recent years have been – "four cobblers' leather aprons", "grey plastic warts for Caliban, and fins along his arms", "a new set of servants' costumes, blue for Montague and yellow for Capulet", "a pink bud growing out of green foliage for Peaseblossom", "tall shoes for a giant, and uniforms for an army". All these orders she has executed without turning a hair, declaring indeed that she enjoyed them. The Straker connection continued for two more generations: Jack and Margaret's son Ian was a Cumnor pupil, together with Ian's children Matthew, Clare and Oliver, and Ian's wife Jo taught art at the school (1980–85).

CHS Croydon

On the very day that Cumnor started at Birch Grove, the Croydon branch, which had finally been vacated by the RAF, reopened with Hal's old Belmont colleague Jock Air as headmaster. Hal continued to have a financial stake in the school until 1962. A piece appeared in the 1946 magazine: 'In January this year Mr and Mrs Air and Mrs Smurthwaite set up house again in our old premises, relinquished with great reluctance at last. No words can describe their early struggles, nor the tact and determination needed even to get their furniture in. After six years of bombing and troop damage, there is much to be done in the way of repairs, but the exertions of the staff have got the place into efficient and even attractive order. The first five boys joined the school in January and a dozen are expected next term, but we need more boys, and would be most grateful for recommendations to parents in the district who are looking for a day school.'

Numbers rose to 93 in 1948, and the school started to win some matches. In the Christmas term of 1946 an anonymous correspondent wrote: 'We found a few schools including you at Chelwood Gate who were kind enough to play us at football. As one of our team wrote, "The object of the game is that they (the players) must get the ball up the field and into the opponents' goal, but it is not so simple as that as the other side is trying to do the same." I am afraid it was the other side who continually complicated this simple problem for us.' The school had not yet developed its later formidable sporting reputation, particularly for cricket.

Today CHS Croydon is a thriving day school of 370 boys, with a fine record of academic and sporting achievement.

Moving a school

Liz Turner remembers helping with the move to Birch Grove: 'Although I had been educated at school to a certain extent, my real education began at Cumnor House, because I was between the ages of the oldest of the boys and the youngest of the teaching staff. They were, I think, the three and a half most enjoyable years of my working life, and I had an amusing, interesting, sometimes hair-raising time. We worked hard, from early morning to late at night. I chose not to have days off; I was basically so lazy that working had never really come into my scheme of things. I was a post-war drop-out; I was the difficult teenager of my era, but I'd decided to prove I wasn't as useless as my family thought I was.'

Liz found it hard to communicate with Hal, who was deaf and suffered from an ulcer, for which he had to go into hospital for much of the first term at Birch Grove: 'Hal was so quiet and polite and deaf, that I didn't quite know … I had nothing to say to him. I don't think I understood how deaf he was. He'd got an ulcer, and he wasn't eating very much; all his food had to be sieved, and he had to have milk or a milky drink every so many hours, and it was my job, when Nan wasn't there, to make sure that he ate and drank regularly. He was so uncomplaining, and in pain a lot of the time, isolated in his deafness. I used to creep around taking him hot milk and things; I'd go into the study, where he'd be sitting; do I say hello, what do I do? I'd just go and put his drink beside him, and make the fire up, because he probably hadn't noticed it had gone out. And he always looked up, as if he wasn't expecting to see me, and said "Oh thank you, Elizabeth". And that was it; there was no small talk for Hal. And if I did speak to him, I was never sure whether he heard. At the time he was definitely "Mr Gulland" to me, not "Hal". Nan, of course, you couldn't not talk to her!'

Food

Rationing was still in force, and the sweet allocation was very precious. John Golding (1946–53) remembers: 'Although I am sure the food supplied to us was very nutritious I know I was always hungry and there were times when the only way I could think of getting something into my mouth to eat was to go up to the bathroom and eat toothpaste. Sweets were on ration. We had a sweet cupboard located near the junior dormitory and the top shelf was for A Form, second shelf for B form etc, and parents would give you a tin and send you various sweets which had to be handed in to matron to put in your tin. On Monday, Wednesday and Friday you had

The swimming pool,
Birch Grove

two sweets only and would have to present them in your hand in front of matron before you went away. On Tuesdays, Thursdays, Saturdays and Sundays you were allowed three sweets. Again my hunger always got through to me until I worked out the system and realised that if my tin fell on the floor I could scoop up my sweets but always leave some on a little ledge that lay underneath the sweet cupboard. I didn't push my luck but regularly did this and left sweets for myself, until one day somebody must have worked out what I was doing because when I went to collect my sweets they had pinched them all. I never tried this trick again.'

Life in the kitchen was not easy, particularly when Hal commandeered the Aga for shaping Perspex models. Liz Turner explains: 'I would put down the hotplate lids to be able to generate enough heat to cook the boys' supper. I'd be sitting in the kitchen thinking, now when shall I start boiling the kettle for tea, and in would come Hal with a troop of his boys and open the hotplates. The first time, I didn't know what they were doing; they'd got these transparent strips which curled up when you heated them, and then they moulded them. There was nothing I could do, he was my boss, and Nan was probably doing something else. When they'd finished, I was able to put my hand flat on the hotplates and there wasn't any heat. Once I burst into tears because I couldn't boil a kettle for tea! And staff tea was so important!'

Nigel Stainforth, aged 10, enjoyed his sausages: 'There are many kinds of sausages, for instance

those red kinds. At school we have them every Saturday. I am very fond of the small brown ones (the ones we have at school) especially the fried sausage-meat that comes out of the ends. Sometimes in shops, they are made into strings. I also very much like sausages and mash. I am always wanting seconds of sausages on saturday.'

Liz Turner again: 'It was incredibly difficult working out menus; we were still relying on home products, as there was nothing yet coming in from Europe. It was a worrying position to be in, not to be able to fill up 50 or 60 small boys with bread or potatoes. We systematically set out to find farms where they were prepared to let us have supplies. Not daily, but certainly two or three times a week, with our very limited petrol ration, Nan and I used to go round the farms, and I remember it was sometimes dark by the time we got to the last one. We were knocking on the door and saying, is there a chance …? On the whole people were very good to us. One particular lord of the manor somewhere managed to keep us going until supplies came. It was quite a challenge to find enough for us all, but I don't think anybody starved.'

The big freeze

The winter of 1947 with its great frost posed enormous problems: Hal later recalled that 'we were rapidly running out of fuel; the road was impassable to lorries; and the whole school might have to be sent home within the week. In the face of this threat several fathers approached me with clandestine offers, and by Monday evening six tons had been delivered at the back door.' All rugby matches had to be cancelled, and there was an outbreak of chickenpox; however there were compensations for Barry Thorne, then aged seven:

In the Snoy
We cood not play footboll be cos ther wos to much snoy on the cround so we had snoy ball fits and we had Fortris wich we cood go be hind and froy snoy balls at eech uthr we cood not go be hind the uthr Fortris and froy the snoy balls.

At Birch Grove almost every member of staff was new. Among them were those twin pillars of the Cumnor community, Joan May and Peggy Chard, who were to serve the school for 18 and 17 years respectively.

Joan May

Joan May presided over the C form from a huge and imposing wooden desk; she had a reputation for strictness, as John Mitchell remembers from pre-war days at another school, but really had a heart of gold, and Elspeth Tissington was one of many who remember her 'with love and respect'. She taught basketwork, ran the stamp club and filled up the ink wells every Sunday evening; each week she gave up her free afternoon to take the bus to Haywards Heath and buy items that boys had asked for on the 'shopping list'. Nine-year-old Terence Storry claimed that 'Maths is my best lesson I think, and Miss May takes the lesson. At the moment we are doing Desimls and Fracshions.' In a report on one of her pupils she wrote 'He does well at maths when grasped.'

John Golding remembers: 'We used to walk all along the roads in crocodile from Birch Grove along the country lanes (there was very little traffic in those days) to the little church in Chelwood Gate across the main East Grinstead to Lewes Road and then walk back. One of the mistresses was Miss May who seemed to us to be extremely old with a large bosom and very sharp tongue and very strict. I always seemed to get on the wrong side of her and one particular time she checked to see if we had been to the toilet before going to church as there was no toilet and we were not allowed to go out during the service. I was so petrified of the thought of wanting to go out and finished up with a Wellington boot full

Above: Basketwork with Joan May

Above right: Peggy Chard

when I was caught short. That never happened again as I was mortified.'

Joan had some endearing quirks: she pronounced 'poetry' as 'poytry', and would produce charming malapropisms such as 'He's so contraceptive: he won't do anything I say,' and, on finding a beetle in the library, 'There's incest in the bookroom.' I'm not sure that she ever quite got the measure of my father, and although he didn't bully her, I do remember one hot summer day when he walked into her form room while she was in mid-lesson and asked 'Anyone for swims?' Stampede! On another occasion he found that boys were not putting their vests on after swimming, and announced that he would appoint Elspeth and Miss May as Vestal Virgins.

Stephen White (1961–66), in his remarkable book *Me*, written between the ages of 12 and 13 and privately published in 1967, describes Joan as follows: 'She would blow out her cheeks and a

"shpu" noise would exude from her. She had short, grey hair and saggy jowls. She would begin her sentences and then leave the listener suspended. "It's nothing to do …" "You've no business …". Clomping one's head, she would say "You know as well as I do, it's nothing to do …". One had to guess what she was talking about, and write what was "something to do". She would suddenly invent a person and ask him a question. "Er, Elliot, explain the metaphor in line two." There would be a silence, and she would be reminded that Elliot never existed. Despite all this, I came to like her and to realise that she was in fact extremely kind, which I had not realised at first.'

Joan retired in 1964 to Croydon, where she died in 1993, having kept in close touch with the school in the meantime.

Peggy Chard

Peggy Chard joined the school as matron in 1946. John Turner (1947–53) remembers 'Miss Chard and Miss Bacon – their names still make me smile – and their liberal stocks of gentian violet, strict inspections every morning of ears, teeth, and hands and nails, "cruel" stripping of beds that had been artfully rolled back and their distribution of sweets (three on Tuesdays, Thursdays and Saturdays – is that correct?).' Jeremy Carlisle (1962–66) had 'great respect if not a little fear for Miss Chard', and remembers morning surgery with 'boys forming an orderly queue to have cuts and bruises brushed with iodine.' David Duvall (1956–61) recalls: 'She was a wonderful combination of brisk efficiency with a very kind heart – not easy to achieve, but she could

LHM-G remembered an occasion when Joan broke her leg. 'I worked out her lessons for the next day but when I walked in to take her Scripture, there she was, her foot propped up and all ready to start as usual.' Adam Ogilvie in a letter home remembered the occasion

do it in a single word: "Miss Chard, I've been sick." "Where?" Meaning, yes, I'll help you but we won't make a drama out of it.'

One's heart bleeds for the seven-year-old John Golding: 'On my very first night away from my parents and a long long way from Halifax you can imagine that I suddenly thought of the enormity of what was happening to me and that I just couldn't turn round and ask for my mother. I remember that evening as though it was yesterday, lying in my bed below the window when matron, Miss Chard, walked in and went round the room asking if everybody had "managed properly". Everybody said either yes or no and when it came to me I just stared at her not knowing what to say and she thought I was being clever. In the end she said "Have you sat on the toilet?" I thought she was being clever and said "How do you mean?" and by this stage all the other boys were laughing and I felt very small, as though they knew each other and were laughing at me. This was the first time I started to feel homesick. I gradually recognised what she was asking and was able to say yes and had no more problems on that score when she asked every night, as she did.'

As with Joan May, Stephen White found that the initial impression of Miss Chard's fierceness was misleading: 'I later found her to be very kind and helpful.' Nan wrote in her obituary in 1970: 'She dispensed a discipline that was firm, impartial and loving; she expected high standards, adhered to them meticulously herself and showed favouritism only to boys in need of special help, and to a long line of fat and lazy cats on whom she doted.'

Arson

One member of the kitchen staff turned out to be not quite what he seemed. Liz Turner: 'We started having little fires in funny places, inside the house, and he was always the one who came, in great excitement, and said "There's a fire!" I went into the sitting room, which was the maids' sitting room in the old days, and found a smouldering armchair; I was a bit worried about it, but he came running in saying "There's a fire! There's a fire!" So I went to tell Nan, and we all came and patted it out. But then we realised that he was starting the fires himself, though he denied it; he was a pyromaniac. We didn't dare tell anybody! I think there were about three fires, but the armchair was the worst because we had to throw it away. I don't think we ever had to get the fire brigade or the police; he was dismissed.' He had some other curious habits. On learning that some of the boys' bicycle tyres had been let down, he offered to stay up all night to catch the culprit – in vain! On another occasion as the cook was working at the Aga, an egg splattered on the wall in front of her; she looked round but the culprit's head was buried in a newspaper. He ended up burning down a rope factory in Bridport, and Hal went to give evidence at his trial.

Boarding

After the war the boarding community began to change. While the school was at Littleworth Cross most of the pupils were evacuees from Croydon, who but for the war would probably have been at a day school. Now boys came from further afield: a number from London and beyond, and a growing number from overseas, often sons of Colonial Service families, including Liz Turner's apparently inexhaustible supply of brilliant nephews from Nyasaland, the Tappers and the Corries, and their friends. A little later came Andrew and Tim Kieft, their cousins Adam and Graeme Ogilvie whose parents were living and working in Calcutta, another pair of cousins, Simon and William Thompson, whose parents were abroad with the Army, and then some family friends, also from Calcutta, Gavin and Alan Turcan.

The eight-year-old Ian Corrie (1956–62) wrote about Africa in 1957: 'I live in Africa: with all the dark brown people, they are very nice except the Mau

Maus who used to kill and eat you, but now they just kill you. Last summer holidays I flew over to Nyasaland with my brother. On that journey I was sick 36 times; and an average of 22 times in two days.'

Many families, in John Golding's opinion, felt that boys of his age, whose fathers had been away in the war and who had been brought up in a female environment, needed the male discipline that a boys' boarding school could provide. In John's case the family made considerable sacrifices to send him to Cumnor: during his time at the school (1946–53) they had no car, no telephone, no television and didn't own their house. He describes the journey from Halifax: 'Obviously I was coming further to Cumnor House than most other boys. I would have to get up at 6 am and catch the train to either Bradford or Leeds from Halifax, then on to London King's Cross and then change tubes twice before arriving at Victoria Station where there used to be a large blackboard with all the names of the various schools travelling back, the time the train was departing, and from which platform. There was always a lot of merriment and excitement as we met up with our friends on the train and by the time the train boys had come via the bus we were integrated back into the ways of school and suddenly what had been for most boys a miserable few days before the end of holidays, became a pleasure when we met all our friends and there was always a new form, a new type of game and just the excitement of being. We were always met at Haywards Heath station by a very old Bedford bus, I think green, which used to transport all the boys off the train via Horsted Keynes through to Birch Grove. The cost for my mother and father to escort me down to Victoria and then go back the next day became prohibitive and at the age of eight and a half I suggested that I was fully confident that I could make the trip by myself and reluctantly my mother agreed, though she gave the head waiter on the restaurant car in Bradford or Leeds 10 shillings to look after me and feed me, which he did.'

Peckham boys

In August 1948, a party of 45 small boys from Peckham came to enjoy a fortnight's holiday at Cumnor House under the Children's Country Holiday Scheme. Hal wrote: 'Analogies with our own boys are a great source of interest; a distant rumble overhead, as of furniture moving at high speed, brings back a nostalgic feeling of term time.' Two of these boys, Denis Cozens and Harry Hooper, returned as boarders in September: it was a bold experiment, and not always easy, as John Golding discovered: 'Harry had been in the worst part of the East End and lived rather like a feral youth leading a band of six- and seven-year-olds roaming through the sewers and gutters and bombed-out buildings drinking, smoking, looting and entering into gang warfare. I remember one early morning at Birch Grove, we were aghast to see Harry Hooper in his pyjamas and dressing gown with the tassel belt hanging untied by his side, walking round the 12-inch ledge that went below the windows on the outside of the third floor. He walked completely round the house by holding onto the window ledges and the wisteria and Virginia creeper that covered the house. How he didn't fall off or trip on his belt, we could not imagine. When he came to

Cumnor House he was certainly out of his depth in the early days and found it extremely difficult to conform and proved a real headache to all the masters and mistresses.'

Later he had an unnerving encounter with Harry Hooper: 'In the summer term, when we wore blazers, he followed me into my dormitory and closed the door behind me and said that since he had been at the school for about a year he recognised I was the leader of my form and he was not used to having anyone above him and therefore wanted to fight me. I said this wasn't the way we did things and I never felt a leader: we were all just boys getting on and having a good time. He said this was not the case, he wanted to fight me and drew out a knife from his back pocket and started to threaten me as you see on films. Aged about nine, I was confronted with a totally unexpected problem. I suddenly thought that if I took off my blazer and moved around in a way which would disconcert him, I would then flick the blazer in his eyes to cover them, which I did, and followed up with the biggest kick in his genitals and as his head came down I thumped my knee into his face and then kicked him in the stomach at which time the knife fell down and I stood with my foot on his neck and immediately when he had caught his

LHM-G and Ron Branscombe OC with a group of scouts, 1949

breath he said "You're the leader and I'll follow you from now on".'

Inspection

Hal describes the inspection of October 1948: 'Cumnor House was first inspected and "recognised as efficient" in 1933. I had applied for reinspection in 1938, being then new to the job and standing in need of advice. Ten years, and a war, were to elapse before the visit came; it was awaited, of course, with great interest, but I am glad to say with a complete and indeed studied absence of window-dressing ...'.

As a result of HMI's recommendations, 'More emphasis is now being put on practical skills and art, partly by encouragement towards display in form rooms, but chiefly by the introduction of a "hobbies" period for the elder boys every evening. It began in a modest way by the formation of groups of boys interested in singing, dancing, acting, stamps, painting and eightsome reels. The singers embarked gallantly on *Trial by Jury*, the painters held an inter-form competition and the Highland dancers, mostly of pure English descent, were able to give quite a polished little display after our Sports.... Other later activities have included lettering, boxing practice and a discussion group, an interesting and popular innovation run by Mrs Gulland. This is not to mention Miss Russell's lessons in pottery with the A forms.'

The introduction of hobbies, or 'evening occupations' as they came to be known, was the most important change to come from the inspection. There had of course been several hobbies before this, both at Seale and at Birch Grove, but now their scope and variety were much increased, and a special time was allotted to them each weekday evening. In other schools this time would normally be devoted to prep; but Hal was not a great believer in the value of prep, viewing it as generally a counter-productive and time-filling exercise, and felt that boys were better occupied getting involved in hobbies which they had opted for.

John Golding enjoys a twist, 1948

Cubs and scouts continued as at Seale, and there was an adventurous camping trip to Newtonmore in the Highlands; 20 scouts went up to Scotland, and it was only sad that they chose the wettest week in the depths of September. The cooks, rising to prepare breakfast, were often confronted with the carefully sited cooking trench swimming in murky water, and a real camp fire was possible only one evening. The following year they had a much happier camping experience at the Essex farm of Mr and Mrs Seabrook.

John Golding remembers making 'twists': 'We had to sharpen a twig and then dip it into a mixture of flour, water and sugar and then roll round as a firm twist and heat it in the open fire till it became crisp and chewy. With my constant need for food I was in seventh heaven on these cub evenings.' On Sunday afternoons children were free to roam around the surrounding countryside. The eight-year-old Matthew Carter (1945–51) explains: 'Down a steep hill there is a stream, and on sundays we go down there. There is a sertain place were it is shallow and posable to build a dam so we built one. The next time we came the water on one side was two or three feet deep. So we construcked a bridge and worked from it. Then when the stream (witch was a lake now) had realy got full we let go of the dam. You can imageine the rush of water pouring out after half an hour or so we were able to wade in it. Further on up stream some boys were building a pretty little waterfall and now it looks quite sivilized instead of a ruff werlpool.'

Rod Meikle (1941–51) has a memory of visiting Viscount Cecil: 'At some time while Cumnor House was at Birch Grove, we being cubs or scouts were asked to collect material for inclusion in a magazine that was to reflect the surrounding area. With another Cumnorian, J M T Ford, I think, we approached the home of the Viscount Cecil of Chelwood. We dithered about by the front gate for a while, trying to summon the courage to knock at the door. I suspect that the maidservant had been watching our antics through the window as the door was opened immediately and we were taken to the drawing room without question. The great man reclined in an armchair in front of a fire and he too must have been aware of our approach. For at his side, on a small table, was a plate of ginger biscuits, which he offered to us before anything else was said. Fortified by ginger biscuits we made our request. The maid brought a note pad and fountain pen and Lord Cecil, with great care and consideration, wrote the note that is illustrated.'

Viscount Cecil's note

Sport

We got to know a new lot of sporting opponents: Ardingly, Ashdown House, Ashfold, Brunswick, Fonthill, Grove Park, Sharrow, Temple Grove. Sport continued to go well: in summer 1946 we had our first ever unbeaten cricket 1st XI, and in 1948 our second. John Golding had a memorable encounter with Ashfold: 'I remember when I first came across my adversary – James Fox, later to become a film star – who was captain of the Ashfold Under 11s when I was captaining the Cumnor House Under 11s. The only difference between us was that he was a very confident young boy with immaculate white shirt, trousers and buckskin white boots with studs whilst I had a white shirt, borrowed white flannels and our standard gym shoes which naturally had no studs. He had a very bad temper and was a fast bowler. I remember he had a cable knit sweater which he used to take off theatrically every time he was going to bowl and it was with the greatest pleasure that I hit him for fours and sixes. We always seemed to win against Ashfold, much to James' displeasure.'

On the day of Princess Elizabeth's wedding in November 1947 lessons were cancelled and five soccer teams took the field against Ashdown House and a sixth against the Staff, male and female. Not bad for a school of 70!

Sgt Markwick came to teach boxing in 1947; one of his very promising pupils was John Hignett, who went on to win a boxing blue at Cambridge. John Golding remembers a boxing match: 'I was always entered for the school boxing and one of our main matches was against Fonthill. In the last match we had against them, we had beaten them at every weight up to me, and as I was the last boxer in the ring it looked at though it would be a whitewash. After three rounds I had liberally belted my opponent, Dufton, to the point where there was no question who the winner was. As two of the judges were from Fonthill and only Mr Tissington from Cumnor, he was aghast to see that they had voted for Dufton. Naturally as a young boy you cannot complain so I shook hands and walked out of the ring. Mr Tissington came up and said, "That is just the most appalling decision I have ever known." Later when he remonstrated with the Fonthill headmaster he was told that Fonthill didn't want a whitewash and that was it.'

There was no gym at Birch Grove, but we were able to borrow the huge Sports Hall at the Isle of Thorns, a mile away, where we used to play lethal games of roller-skating hockey on Sunday afternoons.

Academic

An important change took place in the A form in 1948. Hal explains: 'Last summer Mr Straker and I, concerned about the present high entrance standard to public schools, decided to split the top form into A1, for scholars, and A2, for those whose Common Entrance prospects were at all uncertain. At the same time Mr Straker's deft manipulation of the timetable added some three hours weekly to the elder boys'

lessons.' In A1 the results were startling: new subjects such as Latin verse, Greek and advanced maths could now be undertaken by the form as a whole instead of by individuals, and of the original ten boys in A1 no fewer than eight went on to win academic awards. One of the dangers of such a split, however, is that the second group may conform to what they see as lower expectations; this didn't seem to happen, but Hal was always alert to the possibility.

The most pleasing academic successes of this period were my brother Robin's scholarship to Westminster in June 1949, our last term at Birch Grove, followed by that won by Robert Symmons the following year. The father of John Roberts had discovered that Westminster boys were admitted free to the Lynsky tribunal (a *cause célèbre* at the time), which seemed to all three families as good a reason as any to choose Westminster for their sons. It was the beginning of a long and happy link with a school with which we felt we had much in common, particularly in its unstuffiness, its lack of ostentation, its liberal attitudes and its ability to do well for many different types of pupil.

The play

There were only three open-air plays at Birch Grove, as in 1947 *Richard II* was performed in March in the village hall. *The Tempest* in 1946 was Martin Reardon's farewell to the Cumnor stage: he had come to Prospero via Miranda, Juliet, Valentine and Oberon. He himself was keen to try Macbeth, regarding Prospero as 'a silly old man', but nevertheless his performance was superb; the memory of it leaves a lump in my throat even 60 years on. The following year *Richard II* starred the excellent Barry Warren as the king: Barry was one of several Cumnorians who went on to pursue a successful acting career. Another was Charles Metherell, who was a memorable Puck in 1948 and Mercutio the next year. Hal was always keen to attempt a cut version of *Hamlet*, but each year his courage failed him.

Last move

In 1949 the lease of Birch Grove House expired and Cumnor House moved to its fifth and final home, Woodgate at Danehill, also leased from the Macmillans. It had always been understood that when the Macmillans wanted to move back into Birch Grove House they were free to do so, and the school would move down the road to Woodgate; with the return of a Conservative government, in which Harold was about to become Minister of Housing and Local Government, the time had come. For all its size and elegance, Birch Grove had not been ideal for a school; Woodgate certainly was.

Romeo and Juliet, 1949. Right: Donald Gale (Romeo), Robin Milner-Gulland (Juliet)

CHAPTER 6

COMING OF AGE

1949–60

Woodgate c. 1940 (left) and in 1903 (below)

Come, my friends,
'Tis not too late to seek a newer world

TENNYSON, 'ULYSSES'

OPPOSITE PAGE

Above left: PT, 1951

Left: Cricket, 1953

Martin Reardon (1939–46), ex-pupil, ex-parent and close friend, wrote: 'Hal created an environment in which children wanted to learn, to achieve and to enjoy the fullness of life; at Woodgate he was at last free to transform the environment to his own purposes.' The school had led a nomadic existence for its first 18 years – eight and a half at Croydon, a month in East Grinstead, six years in Seale and three and a half at Birch Grove. No wonder that on reaching Woodgate in summer 1949 Hal wrote: 'very pleasant it is to feel a sense of permanency and to have a school planned almost exactly as we want it.' As with the move to Birch Grove, several senior boys offered their help – Bob Earle (brother of Jim, who had helped in the earlier move), Jim Meikle and Ronnie Branscombe.

Although the school was owned by my parents, the house was leased. But it felt like home in a way that the palatial Birch Grove never had; moreover, it was to prove much easier now to obtain permission to build, to adapt and to develop it as a school. The building was a large but homely Victorian house, much altered and added to over the years; during the war it had been used as a billet for Canadian soldiers, after which many repairs had been necessary. There was an extensive south-facing flagstoned terrace leading to a large grassy area, which 40 years before had been used for croquet and tennis, and after some extension and levelling would be ideal for cricket; by a strange coincidence a cousin of Hal's had been a frequent guest here of the Corbett family for weekend shooting and tennis parties in its Edwardian heyday. Fonthill School, East Grinstead, generously gave us turf to form our cricket square. The 12 surrounding

acres, including a large lake ('the old swimming pool') and a huge and ancient oak tree ('the old oak', see page 139), would be marvellous for games, tree-climbing, nature study, bicycling and camping; there was a beautiful vegetable garden enclosed by a rare 'crinkle-crankle' wall, and an orchard in which Hal and Nan were later to built the Pink House; and in one corner there was a sloping nettle patch which, with much self-help, a bulldozer, stones from a demolished part of the terrace and the imaginative designs of Leslie Gale, architect father of Donald, the 1950 Prospero, became the Open Air Theatre, just in time for the first production.

Alastair Lack (1950–56) recalls: 'It was truly country house living. Walks in the wonderful countryside came in two flavours: "nature walks" taught us about wood anemones and identification of trees; "Sunday walks" were endless through the Macmillan estates that seemed to surround us – pheasant feathers and spent shotgun cartridges. Nature was a large part of life – building dams in the streams on the common, swimming in the lake at the bottom of the grounds and building lairs of wattle and daub. And all those wonderful trees to climb. Could one get from the tennis court all the way round to the front gate without touching the ground – through the rhododendrons? The great yew tree on the way to the boys' gardens, and the theatre. The time that a boy fell and broke his arm – great excitement!'

Aerial view of Woodgate, *c.* 1952

OPPOSITE:

This photograph, taken by John Saunders of his son Robert, appeared on the front page of the *Sunday Times* of 27th September 1953 with the caption 'Keeping a stiff upper lip'.

Above: *The Tempest*, 1950. Graham Hornett as Miranda, in Hal's mother's white muslin dress, *c.* 1890. John Greenway, later a winner of the Queen's Gallantry Medal, as Ferdinand

Centre: Prospero and Miranda, on the opening night of the new theatre

Right and below: Charles Metherell as Henry V, 1951

Much later Ursula Cholmeley (née Bennett, 1978–82) remembers the grounds: 'I won one prize in the whole of my school years: the gardening prize at Cumnor. I also remember, in my final term, mapping all the trees in the school grounds, and I still remember how rare some of them were. How appropriate that I should now be the driving force behind the revival of an enormous garden in Lincolnshire. The Latin has become very useful (hurrah, there is a purpose to learning Latin) as I have no trouble holding onto plant names. As I wrestle with the health and safety implications of allowing people just to visit our garden, I often think of the death slide, the old swimming pool, catwalk and adventure playground at Cumnor and how much fun they were. Camping out in the grounds with a fire with Francesca Faridany and Claire Packman are all part of what fuels my ongoing love for the English countryside. We used to eat the gooseberries raw out of the kitchen garden and look with amazement at the figs growing. I can picture clearly the acorns and sweet chestnuts on the ground under the trees, the squidgy bark of the wellingtonia, the bamboo, the semi-feral cats and the smell of the incinerator.'

The one thing urgently needed was more dormitory accommodation, and a large one-storey L-shaped block was built (the 'Red' and 'Green' dormitories). This block was universally agreed to be hideous, but with the shortage of money and the post-war restrictions on building materials it was the best that could be done at the time to fulfil an urgent need. Despite later carpeting (over the original lino), false ceilings and constant redecoration, it was always cold and austere, and was criticised by HMI in 1966; it was not until 2001, with an imaginative conversion into changing rooms with dormitories above, that it became anything other than an eyesore. Alastair Lack remembers 'the anthracite stoves glowing cherry red at night in the winter – no Health and Safety then! Ice on the washbasins in the morning.' The only boy who seemed to like the dormitories was Christopher Morshead (1971–74), who in 1971 wrote: 'I like the dormeteries. You get a feeling of a family, and because I have the best bed, all the others go thunk whereas mine goes boing. And you bounce off again when you jump on it.'

John Golding remembers the 'downstairs dormitories' where 'we slept in rows of beds with the youngest at one end next to the house captain going up to the bigger boys at the far end,' where the only heating was a solid fuel stove which bubbled and hissed if you spat on it. In summer the dormitories could become very hot and 'tempers were often frayed. We would then hear the door open and silently Hal Milner-Gulland would come in with a wind-up gramophone and play two or three records without uttering a word or looking at anyone. When he had finished he would quietly pack up and go into the next dormitory, and we all settled down and went to sleep.'

Other building work followed. In 1950 the old stable block, on the left as you enter the drive, was converted into a small gym, and the next year a new three-classroom block (now the dining room) was added, with sliding partitions so that the three forms could be supervised by one member of staff if necessary. In 1954, after plans were abandoned to use the lake as a swimming pool, a new pool was built, but so badly that it had to be rebuilt later. Ruth Steketee-Engledow (staff, 1949–51), who had taken over from Liz Turner as 'secretary', remembers that 'times were still austere: ration books, coupons and vouchers were still very actual, and combined with fuel shortages and a temperamental Aga, flexibility was the keyword.' Although Hal bought a pre-war Rolls-Royce in which he transported school teams round the Sussex lanes at a sedate pace, the impression of opulence was illusory: money was always short, and with boarding fees of 60 guineas a term (ie about 15 shillings, or 75p, a day), life was lived on a shoestring. Nick Corrie (1948–55) recalls another car that was useful for team transport, the once luxurious Armstrong Siddeley (c. 1937) which had survived civilian ambulance duty during the war: 'it had been feared that we would be attacked by poison gas, and a fading painted patch was still visible on the Armstrong Siddeley's front wing, having been applied during the war to warn of the presence of gas by changing colour.'

The Red dormitory, 1953. Richard Robinson as Philostrate

In 1952 the school's coming-of-age was marked by a great dinner at the Hyde Park Hotel. Later that year there was a visit from the novelist Angela Thirkell, who 'told several stories about her cousin, Rudyard Kipling, and struck an original note with her caution to prize-winners against self-deprecation.' Two years later prizes were given away by Dame Margery Corbett Ashby, who had spent her childhood at Woodgate: she advised everyone that it is quite untrue that 'a little knowledge is a dangerous thing'. Patrick Moore, who visited in 1959, asked four boys to estimate the magnitude of seven irregularly variable stars. David Duvall writes: 'I joined the Junior Astronomical Society's Variable Star Section and didn't have to do shoe-cleaning at ten past seven the next morning. I remember Hal's inspiring encouragement to those of us who aspired to be astronomers, and his kindly, patient suggestion that what I thought excitedly was the Aurora Borealis might just be the lights of East Grinstead reflected in the sky.'

Hal's first Rolls-Royce

Cars in the drive: 1956 ...

... and 2006

Academic

1953 was a bumper year for scholarships (Bradfield, King's Canterbury, Loretto and Westminster), and two years later Richard Tapper won our first Eton scholarship. In the same year Hal took a group of prospective scholars on a reading party to the Dordogne, which later became an annual event for 17 years. It is interesting to look at the timetable from this period: both A forms had seven Latin lessons a week, each of 40 minutes, and the A1 had four Greek as well. In 1955 the A1 put on *The Bacchae* of Euripides (in Greek) in what was then the gym at the top of the drive. Ranald MacDonell (1949–55) remembers: 'I played Pentheus who had his head torn off in a Bacchic frenzy by his mother (played by Johnnie Roach) and various Bacchic maidens (played by Robert Saunders *et al*). Many local dignitaries were invited, including the then Minister of Defence, one Harold Macmillan.' No

wonder the school produced so many fine classicists. Jack Straker taught 29 lessons a week, and Hal 24, including four games each. No sign yet of science, DT or PSHE. Tom Tickell (1952–56) recalls: 'There were occasional sex talks for boys going on to public schools, but I missed out. Even as nine-year-olds, we all had some idea of where the mechanics of conception started, but not much more.'

Science did not feature on the timetable until the 1960s; but Richard Hunter (1955–59), aged 10, wrote in 1956: 'This term, in one of the school's evening occupations, there is a most interesting occupation called Bioligy. We collect things like Frog's and newts and later on we disect them, and Mr Cashell shows us intresting things like the heart or Gaulbladder. He told us the Frog eats flies and insects and when it sees one of these, the Frog's tongue whips out a catches the insect by some sticky moisture on the end of its tongue. We sometimes are

TIMETABLE   **EASTER 1955**

Time	Form	MONDAY	TUESDAY	WEDNESDAY	THURSDAY	FRIDAY	SATURDAY
9.30 to 10.10	A1	Maths S	French Sp	Latin X	Geog T	French Sp	Maths S
	A2	French Sp	Maths S	Maths S	Latin X	Latin X	Latin X
	B1	French O	French O	Eng. Sp	Maths S	Maths S	Latin O
	B2	Maths T	P.T. T	Latin O	Latin O	Maths T	Maths T
	C	Maths M	Maths M	Writ. T	Maths M	French O	Maths M
	D	Maths Sn	Maths Sn	Maths Sn	Maths Sn	Scrip. M	Maths Sn
10.15 to 10.55	A1	P.T. T	Maths S	Maths S	Latin X	Latin X	Latin X
	A2	Maths S	French Sp	Latin X	French Sp	Maths S	French Sp
	B1	Latin O	Poetry O	Latin O	French O	P.T. T	Maths S
	B2	French Sp	Draw Sn	Maths T	Maths S	Latin O	Latin O
	C	Scrip M	Writ. T	Maths M	Scrip M	E.Gram M	P.T. T
	D	Read. Sn	Scrip M	Read Sn	Read Sn	Redd Sn	Read
11.10 to 11.50	A1	Latin X	Greek X	Greek X	Greek X	Maths S	Eng. X
	A2	Geog T	E.Gram O	P.T. T	Maths S	French Sp	Eng. O
	B1	Maths S	Maths S	Maths S	Scrip M	French O	Scrip M
	B2	Eng. O	Scrip M	French Sp	French O	Scrip M	French Sp
	C	Games Sp	Games T	Read M	Games O	Games T	Draw Sn
	D	Games	Games	Games	Games	Games	P.T. T
12.00 to 12.45	A1	Games X	Games X		Games S	Games X	Test Sp
	A2	Games Sp	Games S	Scrip M	Games O	Games S	Test T
	B1	Games (O)	Games (O)	French Sp	Games (T)	Games (T)	Test T
	B2	Games	Games	French O	Games	Games	Test T
	C	Hdwk Sn	Nature Sn	Hdwk Sn	Eng. M	Read. M	Test M
	D	Geog T	Hist Sp	Games T	Hist Sp	Writ Sn	Test Sn
3.00 to 3.40	A1	Geog T	Latin X	Games X	Maths S	Writ T	
	A2	Scrip M	Eng. O	Games S	Scrip M	Writ T	
	B1	Eng. Sp	Latin L	Games (T)	Hist Sp	Writ X	
	B2	Latin X	Maths S	Games	Hist Sp	Writ X	
	C	French O	Hist Sp	Hist Sp	French O	Sing L	
	D	Writ. Sn	Spell Sn	Poetry Sn	Geog T	Sing L	
4.00 to 4.40	A1	Eng. X	Maths S	Latin M	French O	Greek X	
	A2	Hist Sp	Latin X	Latin M	Hist Sp	Latin L	
	B1	E.Gram M	French O	Latin M	Geog T	Maths S	
	B2	E.Gram M	French Sp	Eng. Sp	Geog T	Poetry T	
	C	Geog T	Poetry X	Geog T	Maths S	Spell M	
	D	Nature Sn	Draw Sn	Hdwk Sn	E.Gram M	Spell Sn	
4.45 to 5.25	A1	French Sp	Hist Sp	French O	Hist Sp	Poetry X	
	A2	Eng. O	Maths S	Geog T	Maths Sp	Poetry T	
	B1	Geog T	Sing L	Hist Sp	Eng. O	Latin L	
	B2	Geog T	Sing L	Hist Sp	Eng. O	Maths S	
	C	Story M	Story O	Story M	Story M	Story M	
	D	Story Sn	Story Sn	Story Sn	Story T	Story Sn	

shown, on the Blackboard, the inside of a frogs belly. It sounds horrible but it is not as bad as you would think. Really Bioligy is very intresting.' In the same year Hal wrote: 'Twelve years ago it was possible to treat the Common Entrance with a proper disregard. Now it demands to be taken seriously; there is considerable competition for a limited number of places in the better public schools, and this state of affairs is likely to continue at least till 1960.'

An interesting survey into boys' reading was carried out in 1958: eight out of 27 A formers had read at least nine of the following 'old favourites': *The Wind in the Willows*; *Black Beauty*; *Treasure Island*; *The Jungle Book*; *Tanglewood Tales*; *Gulliver's Travels*; *Alice in Wonderland*; *The Three Musketeers*; *Lorna Doone*; *The Pickwick Papers*. Alastair Lack remembers 'sitting at LHM-G's feet in a circle listening to Nevile Shute's *An Old Captivity* with the meaningful pauses for us all to turn round to the beautifully drawn maps of the seaplane's flight to Greenland; or Jim Corbett's *Man Eaters of Kumaon*. Again, sitting at his feet to be told of the king's death in 1952.'

Tests continued on Saturday mornings, with all the marks read out after Prayers on Monday morning and then posted on a board in the hall. To some this was an agonising experience: Matt Mockridge (1966–72) and Patrick Sherlock (1968–73), to name but two, remember the bitter shame of having short-comings so painfully exposed. 'In the early days,' Matt recalls, 'I would wait in Prayers for my test marks to be read out to the whole school. The ignominy as I came bottom of the school yet again!' However Matt's younger brother Jeff (1969–75), aged eight, had a different opinion: 'My beast day is Monday because at prars we have the test results read out and I, whel i look forward to see if i come first or not.' Furthermore the annual magazine used to publish CE percentages, real and predicted, until 1967; I find it strange that my father, usually so sensitive to his pupils' feelings, should have paraded

19 CHRISTMAS 53

A1

	English Oct Nov Dec		Maths Oct Nov Dec		Latin Sep Oct Nov		French Oct Oct Nov			
	17 14 12		10 7 5		26 24 21		3 31 28			
M. Elliott	71 67 48	62.0 (=7)	47 - 72	59.3 (3)	77 60 66	67.7 (4)	56 51 42	49.7 (2)	59.7	4
C. Hall	71 54 60	61.7 (9)	31 60 63	51.3 (6)	54 60	57.0 (=5)	74 69 63	68.7 (3)	59.9	3
R. MacDonell	58 62 68	62.7 (6)	27 26 52	35.0 (9)	67 61 77	68.3 (8)	66 79 58	67.7 (5)	58.4	6
P. McMullan	66 56 57	59.7 (10)	53 36 75	54.7 (5)	27 49 53	43.0 (8)	60 59 40	53.0 (7)	52.6	7
A. Marshall	73 74 73	73.3 (1)	63 65 77	68.3 (2)	59 55	57.0 (=5)	34 38 34	35.3 (8)	58.6	5
D. Marshall	52 57 77	62.0 (=7)	48 31 28	35.7 (=7)	33 39	36.0 (10)	30 32 38	33.3 (10)	42.3	9
J. Roach	70 61 75	68.7 (4)	52 75 48	58.3 (4)	30 43	36.5 (9)	30 29 26	28.3 (10)	49.0	8
B. Rowson	62 60 71	64.3 (5)	28 44 13	28.3 (10)	40 47	43.5 (7)	30 39 27	32.0 (9)	41.9	10
R. Tapper	67 72 70	69.7 (3)	72 70 83	75.0 (1)	- 72 81	76.5	44 67 72	61.0 (4)	70.0	1
D. Stewart	67 81 66	71.0	39 36 32	35.7 (=7)	83 85 80	82.7	58 80 74	70.7	65.0	2

A2

	English Oct Nov Dec		Maths Sep Oct Nov		Latin Oct Oct Nov		French Oct Nov Dec			
	17 14 12		26 24 21		3 31 28		10 7 5			
D. Burnett	67 51 61	59.7 (3)	80 79 75	78.0 (1)	82 73 81	78.7 (5)	53 62 49	54.7 (5)	67.8	3
N. Corrie	38 32 26	32.0 (9)	43 39 15	32.3 (9)	54 40 60	51.3 (5)	63 69 73	68.7 (2)	46.0	5
C. Fox	40 31 22	31.0 (11)	33 19 17	23.0 (11)	- 6 7	6.5 (11)	12 5 14	10.3 (11)	18.7	11
P. Hallowes	71 78 70	73.0 (5)	68 76 74	72.7 (2)	84 86 89	86.3 (10)	70 64 54	62.7 (3)	73.7	2
E. Jeffery	60 36 46	47.3 (5)	45 38 8	30.3 (10)	38 29 32	33.0 (2)	17 31 29	25.7 (8)	34.1	8
T. Nichols	74 55 77	68.7 (2)	67 70 71	69.3 (3)	84 78 76	79.3 (6)	77 73 85	78.3 (6)	73.9	1
R. Osborn	37 32 25	31.3 (10)	58 45 39	47.3 (7)	49 32 53	44.7 (6)	40 39 24	34.3 (4)	39.4	7
R. Robinson	53 54 50	52.3 (4)	68 54 64	62.0 (4)	67 53 61	60.3 (9)	51 66 60	59.0 (4)	58.4	4
C. S...h	48 50 24	40.7 (6)	57 36 56	49.7	37 28 37	34.0 (9)	37 33 31	33.7 (7)	39.5	6

Above: Test Marks, read out after Prayers every Monday and displayed in the hall

Right: Printing

their academic performance for public scrutiny.

The 11-year-old Richard Kennard (1978–84), in a moving piece called 'Chain', also remembered the agonies of academic pressure: 'I am chained behind a wall from the devil echeoing around, forcing me to give up. I can't work I am never to be good at work. The evil spirits jab wicked fingers into my head like a concorde or a roller coster winding round my brain. I was paralized. And then a master from school belted "Kennard! Pay attention, whats an adjective?" "Oh er … its a person, place or …" I was interupted by the rest of the class shouting "Er – thick!" "I mean a doing word." I had got it wrong. "No a describing word", I had got it wright. The spirits shouted a never ending cry rewinding inside me. The good crushes it into thin air, destroyed by the bad that spat into the eye of good. I am trapped behind a wall of evil dragged on the ground of hell. My head twizzels around in circles, vibrates viontley like a propeler. At last the devil submits. I am free.'

holidays
am and
chips and
's old
out to
west plane
per Const-
-Comet. I
know I
in India
remem...

...downwards

I have been swimming every day so far this week because it has been fine, but today it looks very gray and dull and I expect that it is going to rain.

You know the boring vicar we have, well he is leaving sometime this term, quite soon I think. All I can say is that I hope the next vicar is less boring. Mr Gulland said a couple of days ago that he knew we were bored...

...couldn't really stop going to church because it would be rude. He even admitted that he was sometimes bored. He also said that Mr Cornish (the vicar) hadn't got the knack of talking to boys. Today is Whit-Sunday so I suppose that the sermon will be extra long. Can't be helped I suppose.

We had a ghastly history and geography test yesterday. I don't think I will get very much for it.

We had tennis-coaching last Friday although we didn't expect Bourne-Newton to come. Mr -Newton to come. The trouble is when he teaches us to serve we got to touch our backs with our... Not very good diagram... Whereas Mr Matthews doesn't he just goes straight with the shot.

...done over 300 miles on my...watch is fine. I am staying...in Half-term. This letter is...writing than usual, I do...see you soon!
Lots and Lots of Love from Adam

We won 11-0. It...match and...

Last Wednesday there...Under Eleven match against the Dane Hill Village school Under Eleven. I bet at least half of them were over Eleven but anyway we won 5-1. It was a football match.

The new vicar is jolly good at giving sermons but the only trouble with him is that gesticulates too much and he repeats.

This time I promise that there is no more news. I will now have to write about dull things. What date are you due to arrive back here?

I am going out with J. Parke today. I hope Graham is better and that he does successfully in his pantomime. Has any of you got the mumps yet?

P.S. I have Lots written to thank Auntie...

Lots of
Lots of
Love from
Adam

THE NEW VICAR SETTING UP A BREEZE.

Adam Ogilvie is bored in church

The new vicar is a better preacher

Hal enjoyed writing pastiche; here are three examples

Poem for Parents ('54)

When I first send my eldest to Cumnor House School
    (Said I to myself, said I)
I'll work to a new and original rule –
    (Said I to myself, said I)
I'll insist on respect for his elders and betters,
But I won't let his grandmamma knit him his sweaters
And I won't smuggle chewing gum into his letters,
    (Said I to myself, said I).

I'll avoid dropping hints that his highly-strung nerves
    (Said I to myself, said I)
Don't get the respect their importance deserves –
    (Said I to myself, said I)
His work is a subject I'll be most discreet on,
I'll never assume he's a scholar of Eton
Because in the D form his marks were unbeaten,
    (Said I to myself, said I).

His masters at school I will try to support
    (Said I to myself, said I),
And thank goodness I don't have to write his report
    (Said I to myself, said I).
I'll encourage his keenness and sit on his grouses,
I won't mind a bit if he has to change houses,
And I'll ask before sending him back in long trousies,
    (Said I to myself, said I).'

Schuleboy's Lament

Sumer is igoen out,
Lhude sing bhu-hu!
Endeth play, and holyday
And starteth schule anu –
Sing bhu-hu!

Olde boy greeteth olde friend,
Yearneth after mum nu;
Master curseth, matron nurseth
Earlie case of flu.
Sing bhu-hu!

Lines written to a young master given to theorising ('59)

Had we but world enough, and time,
This correspondence were no crime.
We would sit down and plan which way
To fill the long scholastic day.
Thou by Lancastrian Ribble's tide
Shouldst theorise: I by the side
Of Ashdown Forest muse. Each day
Would open up some new-found trait
Of character, and every soirée
Adjust th' IQ of Thomas Corrie.
A hundred years we might consume
Conning the works of Locke and Hume;
Three hundred (since we need not hustle)
In re-appraising Bertrand Russell.
But at my back I always hear
The Common Entrance hurrying near;
And every scholarship exacts
Such grasp of mere material facts.
Now as September draws in sight
I have the magazine to write,
And make out, to avoid disaster,
Schedules of work for every master.
September little time affords
To fix the Games and House Point boards,
Carpentry, football, scouts and swims,
The lists of forms and baths and hymns,
Shoe-cleaning, birthdays, new boys, houses,
Dormit'ries, lodgings with the Prowses,
Furniture mended, books replaced,
Rooms decorated, all in haste;
And all the time (for that's not half)
To shops and tradesmen, boys and staff,
Booksellers, parents, duns and debtors,
A never-ending stream of letters.
Then farewell Freud, Adler adieu;
Let's leave the psychiatric crew
And tear our way, tho' undiscerning,
Thorough the jungle paths of learning.
Thus, though we cannot make our sun
Stand still, at least the school we'll run.

Staff

Bill and Elspeth Tissington arrived in 1950, he straight out of the merchant navy and as yet with no teaching qualification or experience. 'As I was about to enter my first classroom ever to see my form Jack Straker paused to give me advice. I guess he knew I could navigate a ship but I had not an O level or A level to my name, let alone a degree. "You'll find it easier if you get rid of Golding and Greenway," he said; "I'll give them some jobs to occupy them until break." I did as Jack suggested and later realised what a sound move it was. When I told the boys, "Golding and Greenway to Mr Straker," John Golding said, "I haven't done anything!" He might have added "yet"!' Alastair Lack remembers Bill 'leading the cub and scout activities – teaching us Morse and semaphore as he had done it in the Navy. Teaching us Orion, Betelgeuse and Bellatrix, and very primitive celestial navigation, along with the difference between a church with a tower or a spire on the OS maps; also LHM-G's mnemonics for Morse code – Beautifully, Continental, Dangerous, Elephants in Straw Hats, Time Marches On – how can one forget them?'

Bill himself writes: 'When I consider the two rocks of CHS as I saw them, I feel sure of my ground. Hal and Jack were outstanding schoolmasters, one in a refined, restrained, aesthetic way, the other dynamic, noisy, hilarious. Both were very well organised and full of understanding of what appealed to boys. The staff set a fine example in showing that laughter was a vital element in life – not least in the classroom. Jack Straker told me that he couldn't teach without laughter in the class. What a treat it was for all boys to go to his noisy, jolly classes with such a brilliant teacher. No wonder he was admired and loved by everyone.'

Christopher Matthew (staff, 1958–60) has vivid memories of the school: 'When I first arrived, the staff comprised Nick's parents; Jack Straker who drove in every day from Horsted Keynes, taught

Elspeth Tissington and basketwork

Below: Lunch, 1951, in the dining room (now the old library). Bill Tissington is on the left

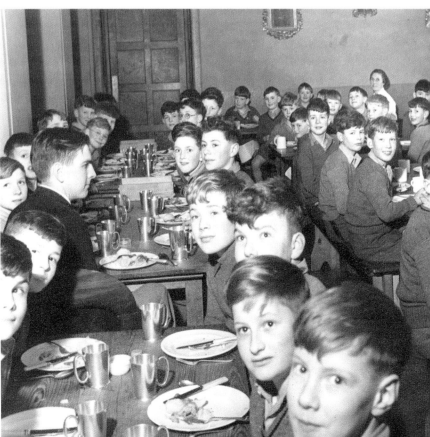

Above: Christopher Matthew, 1960

Right: Bert Chappell (left) and Richard Tapper

Michael Bridge as Edward II, 1959

maths, played the piano at Prayers, and wrote thrillers in the holidays; Patrick Cashell, who was a keen games player and taught French; Ninian Millar, who always wore shorts in the summer, and sometimes a kilt, and took charge of the scouts; Joan May who taught C form; and Hazel Ward who would have made Brian Sewell sound common, had jet black hair which she once dyed platinum blonde, was very funny and later went to work for *The Lady* magazine. She was in charge of the very small ones in D Form. We were later joined in the staff room by the extraordinarily gifted Herbert Chappell, who, while at Oxford, had written musicals for the Edinburgh Festival Fringe, wrote advertising jingles for ITV and would go on to be a senior music producer at the BBC. Tim Sutcliffe returned after a few years' absence in the autumn of 1959. He was exceptionally skilled with his hands and with a group of boys built a tree-house down by the pond. He later left to run a boatyard on the Thames. Another member of staff was Holly Robinson – a jolly and extremely capable young woman from Yorkshire who seemed to be able to turn her hand to anything, from cooking to secretarial work.

'By today's standards, Cumnor was a small school, consisting of no more than 70 boys – all of them boarders, except for one day boy called Tombs who lived just up the road. And because it was small, and because of the intimate atmosphere created by the Milner-Gullands, the place felt less like a school than like a private house in which family members gave lessons, played games with the children, enjoyed delicious dinners and amusing conversation and relaxed in the evenings in front of the telly (black and white, of course) or up at the Coach and Horses.

'The atmosphere of a busy family house in the country was helped in no small way by the beautiful gardens. The cricket nets were set up just next to the ornamental rose garden, the cubs met in the kitchen garden where the Pink House is now (Cashell was Akela, I was his Baloo) and the summer play was performed in one of the most beautiful outdoor theatres in the country. Nick's father always produced the play in those days. In the summer of 1959, it was a double bill of *The Shoemaker's Holiday* and *Edward II*. One of my old photographs is of Michael Bridge standing on the terrace, splendidly costumed and made up as the eponymous king, before heading down to the theatre for the first night. It was in one of these productions that I first saw Simon Williams on the stage. Little did one know where that would lead.

'There were lessons too, of course. My form was B1 – 10- and 11-year-olds, most of whom would sail through Common Entrance and some of whom would move up to A1 and win scholarships to Westminster and Eton and King's Canterbury. All were bright, funny, highly individual and generally excellent company. One boy called Richard Hunter always seemed old beyond his years. I remember sitting down next to him at breakfast on the morning of Sports Day and him saying with utter disdain, "Oh, sir, not suede shoes with a blazer." The scholarship form was the headmaster's and the standard – especially of Latin and Greek – was astonishingly high. I doubt I could have taught them much, or even kept up with some of them.

'The B1 classroom was the middle one of three in the modern wing that ran out beyond the kitchen. They were divided by folding doors, and any sounds from one room could clearly be heard in the next – very clearly when I first arrived and had not quite got my lot under control. Not knowing him at that stage, I fully expected the headmaster to burst in and make his feelings known in no uncertain terms. I couldn't have misjudged him more. During break in the library, he came over, gave a little cough and murmured, "In my experience, the more one raises one's voice in the classroom, the more the children will raise theirs in competition." That was it. Nothing more. And no more noise from B1. He was a great headmaster, and a great man.'

Dominic Lawson (1964–70): 'I self-centredly think of myself as an innocent, largely unaware of subterfuge – except my own, that is. I think this is because at Cumnor we were always treated with kindness and openness. When I went to other prep schools – playing away games for CHS – I often sensed a darker, harsher atmosphere. So, just as I believe that children might have left those schools with a more pessimistic and cynical outlook, I left Cumnor thinking that the world was a friendly place with my interests at heart. I am not sure that thereby Cumnor did me an enormous favour; there are times when one might have gained from a bleaker (more realistic?) view of one's fellow human beings, but on the whole I think it is right that children should be brought up to be capable of being unpleasantly surprised, even shocked, by human nature, rather than little adults constantly on their guard against the malign.'

Tom Tickell recalls his schooldays: 'One great bane of our lives was going down to the church in Danehill in a crocodile on Sundays. The walk there was all right but the service, run by a man called the Rev Pym Cornish, was dreary – and his sermons seemed abysmal. Everyone's morale on walking back up the long road to Cumnor House was much higher, because we did not have to face another sermon for at least another week.

'Hal's handwriting was beautiful, but the horrors of having to learn Italic script come back. At first there were pens with nibs that often went missing and ink in ink wells which invariably got on my fingers. That meant endless rubbing with pumice

79

Hal on handwriting

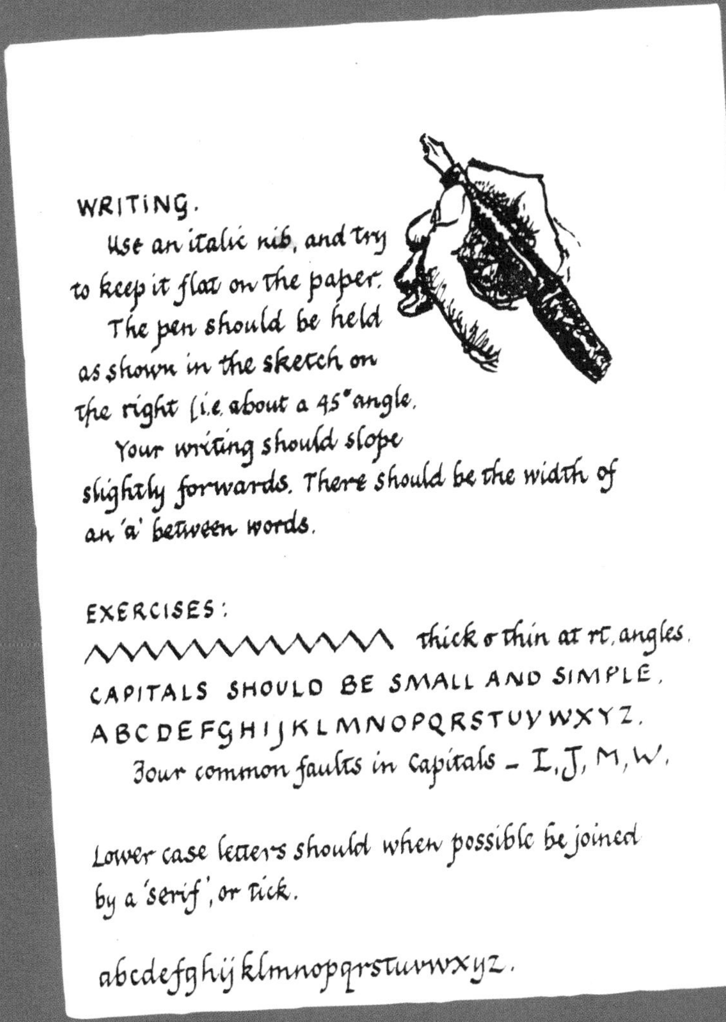

WRITING.
Use an italic nib, and try to keep it flat on the paper. The pen should be held as shown in the sketch on the right (i.e. about a 45° angle. Your writing should slope slightly forwards. There should be the width of an 'a' between words.

EXERCISES:
∧∧∧∧∧∧∧∧ thick & thin at rt. angles.
CAPITALS SHOULD BE SMALL AND SIMPLE.
ABCDEFGHIJKLMNOPQRSTUVWXYZ.
Four common faults in capitals – I, J, M, W.

Lower case letters should when possible be joined by a 'serif', or tick.

abcdefghijklmnopqrstuvwxyz.

Adam Ogilvie writes to his parents in Calcutta about a lecturer

...use Yesterday of evening a Captain
...CC, Lawson-Smith came and gave us
...eath, a lecture on "Deep Sea Diving."
He was dressed in a diving-suit
when he lectured to us and on
a table he had lots of things
a diver uses such as the helmet
...nch and the telephone which goes
...every in the helmet. And that a stone
which was used in quite shallow
...be water. Also another type of flame
...even cutter which was used in very
...on deep water. and many more things
...there such as high explosives. the
...defence, was very funny and this is one of
...being the jokes he told us:-
...than He also told us about
...first the signals which a
...one diver gives. He said that
...is on a diver must give 4
...tugs on the lifeline
...he needs help I.E. WHEN THE SHIP IS SINKING.
"CAPTAIN SAYS, COME UP"

...fast in the grip of a mermaid.
I had a lovely time with J. Parke
last Sunday when he took me out.
His parents were staying at Grave-
tye Manor, a rather nice hotel
near Chelwood Gate. There was
a ping-pong table there and Parke

BY AIR
PAR AV
AIR LE
AEROGRA

Letter home
from Robert
Saunders, 1952

Telephone: Danehill 347

Cumnor House School,
Danehill,
Haywards Heath.
Sussex

Chère mère et père
I hope you are well. Merci Beaucoup
de votre lettre. J'ai scored
des more goals dans football.
Sur le work tableau j'ai got
Dix ispept maison points.
Sur Samedi nous had un
match v Belmont et la score
was vingt - Deux - trois
to out. This test was a une french
Un. Je got about Quatre - vingt -
dix. Yesterday Je played rugg and
the score was dix - huit - dix huit
Love from Robert

stone to get it off again. My handwriting was not good, though it gradually developed traces of Italic.

'Food was normally excellent – and I can still recite the lunch menus for Mondays, Tuesdays and Wednesdays. I was – and am – distinctly greedy but I loathed onions and most forms of fish. There was one occasion on which we were given "Cod Portuguese" which combined both, and I managed to slide most of it into a grubby handkerchief. I then had a sneezing fit – and all the fish and onions fell out onto the floor (I think in a classroom). I can still feel the extraordinary sense of shame.

'My parents seemed deeply embarrassing – but then my children tell us that we are too. The good news was that my father had a 1925 open air Bentley, which attracted a lot of admiration as it throbbed its way down the drive. But I remember his handing over some documents to Nan, and saying genially "Have you anywhere to put them? If not just pop them down your cleavage." She thought it funny but I was mortified.'

Adam Ogilvie (1956–61) remembers food: 'The relentless predictability of the weekly menu – I can still specify the main components of any given meal for any day of the week. Most dreaded, for me, were Sunday tea (hard boiled egg) and Monday lunch (slice of cold Sunday roast, baked potato and beetroot). Lovely treats though (queuing for after-lunch sweets, Tuesday ice-cream van, Wednesday doughnuts, Saturday cakes). As a small boy, I remember the sense of limitless space under a huge sky afforded by the top playing field – with the favourite evening pastime thereon of guarding the terrace against fiercely hit tennis balls.'

In the 1950s not all was sweetness and light. Nick Humphrey (1952–56) has grim memories of one particular teacher: 'I'm sure LHM-G had no idea what was going on under his nose. The chief culprit, as I remember, was a (supply?) teacher, who slept in a room next to Blue Dormitory, and regularly abused boys in the dormitory next door.

1st XI, 1956, "the best prep school side that I have ever seen" (LHM-G). Standing (left to right): Clive Mitchell, Nicholas Narishkin, Neil Annand, Andrew Kieft, Michael Latreille, Michael Eke; sitting: David Monk, Malcolm Gilbert, LHM-G, Jeremy Ray, Robert Saunders; in front Ceri Hankey

But the boys themselves could be pretty awful to each other. We in Blue dormitory were unimaginably mean to one boy, teasing him mercilessly about wetting his bed.'

Sport

The 1950s and 1960s were memorable for a series of brilliant soccer teams, including eight unbeaten 1st XIs. Hal declared the 1956 XI 'the best prep school side that I have ever seen'. In the previous year four consecutive games produced these results – W12-0, W15-2, W11-0, W21-0; 'such embarrassing successes did not endear us to neighbouring schools.'

One remarkable cricketing feat was by Jonathan Krish, who in a house match took six wickets in seven balls, all bowled; another was Ian Cockburn's 102* for the all-victorious 1958 XI, our first century since Robert Lazenby's 20 years before. In 1952 the first Old Boys' cricket match was played: for many years this was organised by John Berkley, the beaming moustachioed wicket-keeper, and regular attenders included Hugh and Thea Campbell, Robin and Yvonne Kennard, and Harley and Folly Sherlock.

Above: Cricket, 1953. The 1st XI watch with understandable concern

Left: Stalwarts at the Old Cumnorians' match: left to right, Martin Reardon, Harley Sherlock, John Berkley, Robin Kennard

Out of school

Many boys developed all-consuming interests, particularly in the natural world, about which they were encouraged to write in the magazine. Here are three examples:

My Hobby

My hobby is keeping and breeding moths; I am especially interested in foreign silk-moths, these are very beautiful and very large. Some of the English hawk-moths are also very beautiful, and have a wing-span of about four inches. I buy my moths, usually as caterpillars or chrysales, then hope that they will develop, mate, and lay eggs.

Sometimes I have to use very large cages for the giant silk-moths, as the caterpillars are about six inches long. I have got the largest insect in the world, which is the Atlas Moth from the Himalayas, although it has not hatched out yet. It is very beautiful indeed and can grow to a wing-span of one foot.

Tom Carter (11)

Snakes

My hobby is rather an unusual one, but it is very interesting it is rearing snakes and lizards. Snakes can often be found on any bank by a lake or stream, but are very well camouflaged. Lizards live in the same haunts and besides being difficult to see are very quick moving. Feeding is the main problem with these reptiles as both pretty well have to eat their 'victims' alive, lizards eat bugs, large flies, and dragonflies, snakes eat frogs, newts, and English common lizards (whole!). If either have eggs they can be hatched by keeping them warm in sand, when they hatch keep the young well away from the parents as they might get eaten!

Andrew Sanders (12)
[one of whose snakes emerged from his luggage on the coach on the way back from the Royal Tournament, causing much alarm]

How I Caught Beetles and Newts

We have a lily pond. It has newts and beetles in it. We catch them in boxes. We sometimes catch things like newts, toads, beetles, pond mussels, dragon-fly lava, leaches, water-boatmen, and water skaters. We put them in jam-jars, pots and tins. I help my friend Michael Wills he is a naturalist. After brekfast we go to the pond. The bell goes for prayers in half an hour. I have given my insects to Wills. I am not taking my things home. Next term I hope to catch more insects each different, big and small, long and short, fat and thin. Good Bye.

Timothy Hyde (8)

Nick Corrie (1948–55) was a plane spotter: 'CHS was a happy hunting ground for those of us who were plane spotters, both due to the variety of types and because the school was evidently situated in a low-flying area. Types of aircraft included those left over from the war (Spitfires, Lancasters, Mosquitoes and Tiger Moths), early jets (Meteors and Vampires), naval aircraft (Wyverns, Gannets and Fireflies), airliners and miscellaneous types, some of them pre-war. The father of one boy (Malcolm Gilbert) even had his own private Auster plane, painted bright yellow, and he sometimes entertained us by circling the school at low level. Most exciting of all were the fast jets, mainly Meteors, flying low and deafeningly over the school.'

The play

John Golding remembers his contribution to *The Tempest* in 1950 and *Henry the Fifth* in 1951: 'In my first year in the plays, I was Second Thunder in *The Tempest*. I only rattled the thunder sheet in extreme moments which in fact was only once during the whole play. The rest was done by First Thunder. I felt I had greater talent than this. In *Henry the Fifth* I had two parts, Mistress Quickly and a soldier called John Bates. I had only about three lines for each part. On the first day I was incredibly nervous and

King Henry the Fifth,
1951. Nick Corrie (Alice) and Barry Thorne (Princess Katharine)

The Tempest

In 1958 Jack Straker wrote a neat Shakespearean pastiche on *The Tempest:*

> There be some tasks are painful, but not mine,
> For my good will is to it. Full many a Tempest
> I have eyed with best regard, and many a time
> I have seen a Prosper and his minions strut
> Here on this grass-plot. The harmony of their tongues
> Speaking the well-known lines (which the Producer
> Took pains to make them speak, taught them each hour,
> Did them such good instruction give that each
> Knew his part well, had time to speak it in,
> And made him no mistaking) hath into bondage
> Brought my too diligent ear. For several virtues
> Have I liked several plays. Here, the king's ship,
> All tight, and yare, and bravely rigged, was virtue;
> The spectacle of the wreck, and its dismantling
> By Prosper's airy sprites, was nimbly done.
> So too the scenery; John Verney, then appointed
> Master of this design, did give us grace
> And dignity. And marvellous sweet music
>
> From singers, flute, and tape-recorder came;
> Sounds, and sweet airs, that gave delight and hurt not,
> Did hum about mine ears. One too there was
> Did train the electricians, and teach them how
> To use the bigger light, and how the less
> That burn by tree and stage …
>
>   One word more.
> Never till this day had rain bemarred our pleasure.
> But at the first performance – oh, the heavens!
> The sky, it seemed, would pour down stinking pitch,
> And so it shortly did. Brave souls there were
> Who did not move before the time was out
> (For this, be sure, that night they did have cramps!)
> And some donation freely did estate
> Out of their bounty. But I prattle wildly;
> I must not too much muse. Praise in departing, sir,
> To thee and to thy company I give.
> For these sweet thoughts that now refresh my labours
> I thank thee, and now rest myself content.

when I walked on as Bates I said the Mistress Quickly lines. When I came off and realised what I had done, I had to decide what I should do when I had to go on as Mistress Quickly after a costume change. I decided that a 9–10 year old was inconsequential to the bigger picture so went on and said exactly the same lines as I had said before, but this time as Mistress Quickly. The audience did not seem to notice or were too gentle to titter.'

I have vivid personal memories of *The Two Gentlemen of Verona* in 1952 when Jonathan Krish (Valentine) was ill and I went on for him at 24 hours' notice, doubling with my original part of Julia. Backstage there was much rapid changing from farthingales to doublet and hose and back. After this production my father and Mr Riseley, whose son John acted Proteus, commissioned Mr Etherton, the Danehill blacksmith, to make a pair of gates to the auditorium, in which the letters G and R are interwoven: they stand there to this day to commemorate Gulland and Riseley, the Two Gentlemen of 1952.

Romeo and Juliet, 1956, a painting by John Verney

CHAPTER 7

WINDS OF CHANGE
1960–74

David Buchanan's portrait of Hal writing reports

Bliss was it in that dawn to be alive,
But to be young was very heaven

WORDSWORTH, 'THE PRELUDE'

During the 1960s there were few signs at Cumnor, or at any other schools, that an era was about to end. Hal was at the height of his powers, the school continued to attract extraordinarily talented boys, the demand for boarding places at eight seemed not to be dwindling, there was not much difficulty in filling the 15 or so places which became vacant every year, a series of very gifted teachers joined the staff and the school had a reputation for distinctiveness and excellence: Pamela Hansford Johnson, wife of C P Snow, declared it to be 'a somewhat eccentric, but kindly and academically distinguished prep school', and Dr John Rae, headmaster of Westminster, told parents that it was 'the best prep school in the country.' Nigel Lawson, it is true, had reservations: 'There was just a hint of a resemblance between Cumnor House and Waugh's Llanabba Castle,' but a pupil, eight-year-old James Healy, was thoroughly satisfied: 'I fike that the school is perfick becasis you have lots of thing to do and D and C form play foot ball nerly ery day I fick that Come the House is the best school I have ben in all my life.'

However there were several straws in the wind. Hal would be 60 in 1968 and was beginning to worry about the succession. HM Inspectors in 1966, although praising the 'humane and gentle direction of the headmaster' and the industry and enthusiasm of the teachers, were critical of the living accommodation, the 'haphazard' system of promotions, the lack of qualifications of the staff and evidence of 'a certain inflexibility of teaching technique and a preoccupation with examination requirements, narrowly interpreted.' Salaries were so woefully low

OPPOSITE PAGE

Above left: The first two girl boarders, 1970: Louise Gibbon, left, and Lucy Artus

Left: Adam and the Goliaths. Adam Ogilvie (centre) with, left to right, Norman Johnson, Simon Williams, Paddy MacDonell, Michael Wills

that few young teachers were attracted to prep school teaching as a career. Hal noted about one applicant for a job in 1963: 'age 39, sounds very good, married; a little too keen on money' (he had asked for £1150 *per annum*). Heads of traditional boys' boarding schools were beginning to consider ideas such as coeducation, pre-prep departments, day pupils, expansion, ideas which in the 1960s struck many as unnecessary or undesirable (though Hal and Nan were both keen to admit girls), but ten years later were to gather irreversible momentum.

A further problem was the precarious nature of the school's finances. In 1970 income was £36,000 and the surplus £235. Some years Cumnor ran at a profit, some years not. Hal was always apologetic when notifying parents of a fee rise. Leo Wynne was later to say with some justification that 'both M-G generations have the same Achilles heel: they abhor asking people to pay for their children's education. They think that education and money should be kept apart. For choice they'd prefer to have run the school without fees; they've been subsidising it for years.' In fact when the school was evacuated in 1939, Hal had reduced the boarding fee to £45 per term in order not to exploit the situation as other schools had done. It was not until 1972, when Leo became bursar and a director of Cumnor House School Ltd, that finances gradually began to be put on a secure footing, with substantial rises in fees and salaries.

No-one could give a better flavour of Cumnor in the 1960s than Robert Gussman (1959–64): 'I joined the school in September 1959, just short of my ninth birthday, and I vividly recall the sense of adventure that dominated my feelings as I arrived. I had bumbled along in a very nondescript way at my previous school, unstretched and undistinguished. Now, I felt like a butterfly emerging from its chrysalis, and delighting in the new opportunities. After a week in D Form, I moved up into C Form and then ever upwards and onwards. It was as if there was something in the air that fired me with

confidence previously unknown. I felt that I was being given permission and encouragement to grow into the person I was meant to be. The school offered me exactly the context I needed, that was both caring and stimulating. In other institutions I have experienced an unwelcome pressure to conform to a particular predetermined model, as though I was being forced into a mould. But at CHS I felt a freedom to discover myself; there seemed to be a deliberate policy to cherish the uniqueness of each person. It gave me some of the happiest days of my life.

'Later on, during my time in the scholarship form, I remember specifically LHM-G urging each of us to identify some field of interest that we could make our own. In one way, the wide range of evening occupations seemed to be an invitation to explore as many different activities as possible, not just to broaden our general understanding of the world, but to try out our innate potential. Life at the school felt wonderfully free. Of course there was discipline and certain elements that could be irksome. But I was conscious that some of the traditional punishments that we knew other schools used were not to be countenanced here. For instance, the practice of writing out umpteen lines was unheard of. Indeed, there seemed to be very few actual rules other than a general encouragement to respect one another and the place we lived in. If there was one rule LHM-G seemed very keen on, it was "Never say 'shut up': saying 'shut up' is the sign of a really nasty boy!" Just very occasionally serious misdemeanours merited a beating with LHM-G's slipper, but it seemed to cause him more pain and grief than it gave the culprit, and he might offer a polo afterwards as a consolation. There were moments of drudgery too – but alongside all of that was the sense of school life gently introducing us to an adult world that was both civilised and privileged. I recall the winter afternoon when LHM-G came in for a Greek lesson bearing a covered silver dish containing small squares of hot

Left: President Kennedy
and Nan, June 30th
1963

Above: Lady Dorothy
Macmillan

buttered toast with a mouth-watering smear of anchovy paste, one for each of us. Or there were the delights of Sunday afternoon walks out into the countryside where we might encounter Mr Macmillan shooting, and we were bidden to call out "Good afternoon, Prime Minister!"

'The great events of the world went on around us, but though we were kept up to date listening to the six o'clock news on the Home Service every evening, the outside world did not normally seem to affect us. Not so on that day that is for many one of the defining moments of the century, Friday November 22nd 1963, when President Kennedy was assassinated. We were in the big red dormitory getting ready for bed, and the master supervising us had brought his portable radio in to share the latest news. I wrote in my diary: "At 7.00 heard that President Kennedy had been shot. Did not believe it until told through [sic] the radio. He died at about 7.30. Felt very shocked and frightened as to what was to happen to the world." We had a particular reason to feel this event, for many of us had only recently met the man himself. At the end of June, the US President had come to England for talks with the Prime Minster, Harold Macmillan, and came down to Sussex for the weekend at his country home, Birch Grove. On the Sunday morning, we were invited by Lady Dorothy Macmillan to go and line their drive to cheer the visiting president on his return from church. When his car reached the bottom of the drive, he stopped, got out and walked all the way to the house, shaking hands with every other boy. I was one of the lucky ones. I found the entry in my small diary for Sunday June 30th 1963: "Breakfast – not bad. Went and saw Pres Kennedy and shook hands with him."

'I remember Nick coming down from university and taking his turn at teaching us Latin and Greek, and also delighting in stimulating other aspects of our education. I recall the time he put up a chart on the board in A1 with Boo and Hurray words: he wanted to encourage us to broaden our vocabulary and avoid lazy speech. We were not to use "aggravating" in its colloquial sense as a synonym for irritating. We should avoid euphemisms like "Please may I be excused, sir" when what we meant was that we needed to go to the loo.

'It must have been as a 10-year-old in my first term in A1 that I remember LHM-G chiding me for not recognising a line from *Macbeth* as I stood at the desk to have some exercises corrected. When I confessed that I had not read the play, he spoke of having worked his way through the whole of Shakespeare before his 14th birthday. I took this as a challenge and set myself the task of doing the same but with the extra requirement to do so before I was 13. That very largely determined my reading for the next three years. And of course it complemented the great feature of the CHS year: the play. It seems astonishing that he produced the whole thing in just the last six weeks of the summer term. I know it was not the only thing we did then, but it seemed to take over our lives and fill us with a complete new experience. We were at that age such malleable material in his hands, and I sensed what a joy it was to feel one's way into becoming the character we were given. And when it was over, with what reluctance I removed my costume and make-up for the last time, and felt a certain diminishment as I reverted to being just me. That whole experience – playing our role, learning our lines, timing our every movement exactly, working together, learning how

to project – was an education in itself.

'It was a measure of the broadmindedness of the school that we were not all required to excel in every sphere. I was hopeless at sport, and the reports I had for soccer spoke of my speed in running away from rather than towards the ball. I entered the annual boxing competition on several occasions, and was matched against my friend Angus Frazer, who managed to beat me every time, despite his acute short-sightedness. In our last summer, a group of us were permitted to withdraw from cricket and we spent our afternoons devising our own game, entitled Finickity; rather more time was spent devising and perfecting the rules than we ever spent in physical exercise. Sports Day I loathed, but I do remember when Bishop Mervyn Stockwood came to give the prizes he spoke of the importance of not expecting everyone to win or feel that they must become the leaders of the future. Success means distinction more than it means winning a competition. That was a huge and welcome relief.'

Jeremy Carlisle too remembers President Kennedy's visit in his stretch-limo complete with TV and a glass roof at the back. 'Do you like my bubble-car?' he asked. And when he asked to hear the school song we had to admit that we didn't have one. Andrew Sinclair (1957–63), then 12, wrote home to say 'Daddy I bet you've never shaken hands with the President of the United States.'

Staff

Patrick Cashell joined the staff in 1956. He was a fine sportsman, and shared Hal's passion for real tennis; he taught French, and was responsible for the introduction of science into the curriculum (though science did not become a compulsory subject in the Common Entrance until 1971), first with the Esso scheme, then in 1967 with the Nuffield Project, for which a new lab was built above the present dining room. When Hal and Nan built the Pink House in 1962, Patrick as housemaster and his wife moved

Holly Robinson,
1970

into their old rooms. It was a relief for my parents to have them living in the school, particularly when in Spring 1963 they took a sabbatical term – Hal's 100th term of teaching – in the Dordogne and left the school (in the term of the big freeze) in the capable joint hands of Patrick and Jack Straker.

Bert Chappell, who arrived in 1959 after studying music at Oxford, gave a tremendous boost to the music, in particular through the evening occupation in which he and a group of enthusiasts set Vachel Lindsay's *The Daniel Jazz* to music. Dedicated to Hal and Nan, it was published by Novello and was said to have sold better than any publication since the *St Matthew Passion*.

Simon Templer had two stints teaching French and history in the 1960s. In 1966 he produced a remarkable film called *The Five-Foot Ruler*, a story of pupils taking over a school, with echoes of *Animal Farm, Lord of the Flies* and *If*. The boys much enjoyed filming the scenes of staff being beaten up or shoved into cellars and bodies thrown off roofs. Rhoddy Voremberg (1963–67) remembers 'at least two

summers spent filming *The Five-Foot Ruler* with SGT and his team of aspiring cinematographers – first in 8mm and the second version in 16mm, with editing sessions up in the attic alongside the theatrical wardrobe. SGT also introduced me to the lighting and sound for the play, and all the responsibilities that went with it: one year after a particularly troublesome rehearsal of *MND* at which the tape-recorder had been playing up and I had taken a flea or two in my ear from LHM-G for failing to produce a Bergomask on cue, I was awarded a house point by SGT "for standing steadfast in the face of the enemy".'

Alison Taylor, a superbly gifted artist, arrived in 1962 and was the inspiration for much excellent art, before leaving as Mrs Robin Milner-Gulland in 1967. Jeremy Carlisle remembers her as 'hilarious, quick, energetic, creative, imaginative, with a brilliant ability to draw, paint, make – inventively and quickly.'

Holly Robinson (1955–70) quickly established herself as indispensable. She was variously described as 'matron' or 'secretary', but neither title begins to do justice to the breadth of her skills. When she retired in 1970 Nan wrote: 'For 15 years (and I suppose there *was* a time when we got along without her) she has been here – omniscient, capable, unflappable; so much a part of everyone's life, so versatile and untiring, that at the moment it is unthinkable that we are really going to have to find the answers ourselves and not just indulge the comforting thought – "Let's ask Holly".' For many nervous new boys she was, as for Matt Mockridge (1966–72), a 'guardian angel'; John Fieldhouse (later Admiral of the Fleet Lord Fieldhouse, Falklands hero) couldn't bring himself to leave his son Mark on his first day, but Holly took charge immediately and he never looked back. Holly herself remembers Cumnor as 'a place filled with caring people having a lot of fun. I recall an end-of-term game of Roccer with all the children and staff and both shaped balls on the pitch, and being sent off with a red card, much to my relief, for breaking the off-side rule which I never understood anyway!'

David Bond (1969–71) is warmly remembered by Matt Mockridge: 'Dave Bond was one of my favourite teachers. He didn't call me a "cretinous moron" or a cuttlefish as others did and he was passionate about games. He ran the evening occupation of "Russian studies" which consisted of half a dozen of us cramming into his tiny room on the top floor and listening to Kenny Ball and his Jazzmen playing "Midnight in Moscow". When we'd heard that a few times, Mr Bond would play a record by one of his friends which had got into the charts called "Yesterday's Gone". I still have a copy of both!'

In 1963 Hal found it very difficult to replace Simon Templer. His notes on applicants give an insight into the problems of staff recruitment:

ES	wrote postcard in green ink, experienced
SRC	15 yrs' exp, I think I've seen him before & was not impressed
ASM	age 23, no exp
Rd'A	age 73, highly exp
DAH	age 17, schoolboy at Worksop
ER	sounds barmy
JS	elderly author – cultured – plays football! Totally inexperienced and might be ragged, but amusing

He eventually engaged Leo Wynne. In a letter to me, teaching for a year at Kent School, Connecticut, he wrote: 'I've signed on two men for next term, Mr Gurd, whose work will be mainly with the D form, and Mr Wynne (French and history) whose wife will also I hope do some art teaching. Old Lord Headley, to whom I tactfully tried to explain that we could now manage without him, misunderstood the gist of what I was saying, insisted that he would be delighted to return, so I haven't had the heart to say no! He's as keen as mustard, just can't keep order.'

I returned to Cumnor for two years (1964–66)

before taking a post teaching Classics at Marlborough College. During this time I was undecided whether my future lay at Cumnor or elsewhere. My father was very keen for me to succeed him, but the situation was complicated by the fact that, probably because of my dithering, he had appointed Patrick Cashell as 'junior partner' with a view to the future, and although Patrick was – and still is – a good friend, I was not sure whether he and I would make a satisfactory partnership. Anxious though my parents were to secure the school's future, they had unhappy memories of their own experience in 1938. Eventually it was amicably decided that we would go our separate ways, with Patrick going on to senior positions at The Hill School, Westerham, and then at Mount House, Tavistock, while I returned to Cumnor in 1969 as 'joint headmaster' with my father. Anna arrived in 1972, after teaching for the Quakers in Madagascar, and we were married three years later.

Leo Wynne arrived in January 1964, and was to stay for 37 years. He remembers his interview at the Union Club: 'Hal was a very thin, dapper man, looking a bit like Jean Cocteau, hunched over his papers in a deep, weathered, leather armchair. I was completely charmed by this diffident, porcelain-like, delicate man who was saying how wonderful was the man he was replacing.' At first the accommodation offered to Leo and his wife Jane, a talented artist and calligrapher, was one room opposite what is now the headmaster's study. The lack of adequate staff accommodation was a real problem for the school for many years, and there always seemed to be more pressing demands on our limited funds.

Poetry was one of Leo's great enthusiasms, and over the years many of his pupils were to win prizes in prep school literary competitions; Hal was soon declaring that 'it is hard to keep track of the many magazines produced by Mr Wynne and his helpers.' Jeremy Carlisle remembers him 'marching up and down, wild, gesticulating, declaiming poetry; living poetry and literature; sardonic, political, argumenta-

Cumnor House, 1965

tive, angry, inspiring, encouraging.' Tom Sherlock (1970–75) felt that 'with Mr Wynne anything was possible, and this made him fascinating, intriguing but also frightening. Fortunately, my one altercation with Mr Wynne passed by relatively harmlessly. I was desperate to read a trashy war magazine but Mr Wynne was on dormitory duty and so a strategy was required! I read it inside a huge hardback book, and when he duly walked past he paused to congratulate me on doing some serious reading. On closer inspection he undoubtedly concluded that a version of the Bible in Latin (and probably held upside down) was unlikely to be my cup of tea. I never saw the trashy mag again!'

Leo got into trouble from one mother when he asked her son to learn 'Tyger, tyger, burning bright'

by heart: 'You can't make a chap learn something that doesn't make sense!' Rosalie Challis, mother of Nicholas Wood, remembers him in the 1980s as 'a dead ringer for a latterday Lord Byron, though certainly not mad, nor bad, but definitely dangerous to know if you were a child and not prepared at least to have a go at reading Conrad aged 11 or, as a parent, not prepared to accept that ANY child, including your own comic strips/TV cartoon/video games-addicted offspring could deal with Conrad at the age of 11.'

Camilla Campbell (1982–85) remembers: 'Leo Wynne set us an essay task, and as I was reading *Swallows and Amazons* at the time, I tried to emulate Ransome's chatty comforting style. As a result I wrote the longest, most boring and pointless essay I think

An aerial view of the school, taken in 1974

Leo had ever had to read. The reason I remember it is because I still have the book in which the essay was written, where you can see Leo beginning to mark it in the margin, and then clearly losing interest as the red pen stops, he turns the pages, and skips to the end and writes at the bottom, "Oh put a bomb in it". A good lesson!'

Ione Meyer (1975–78) has a picture of Leo in the classroom: 'I remember him striding into our classroom five minutes late, swinging his wicker basket that overflowed with our marked books. When he had sat down at his desk he would fling them across the room and we would field all sorts of catches to get them in our hands: "Good catch, Meyer", he would say. His handwriting flourished across the pages if we did good work. He would liberally rule it all out if he thought it was rubbish. He called a spade a spade. When we went up to discuss that poem, or that piece of extended writing, he'd point to just two words in it and say "I like that". I heard him say to one boy who asked for an explanation, "Wipe your own bottom". He was harsh by today's standards but he taught me conciseness and independence of thought.'

Robert Maslen (1970–76) recalls 'Leo Wynne's English lessons, when we recreated the world at his command, rewriting Genesis to incorporate gargantuan kitchens, maleficent fishhooks, and antediluvian automobiles. I've never been able to "walk" anywhere since those English lessons; I've had to "slouch" or "hobble" or "stalk", to "scuttle" or "sidle" or "squirm"; and I still read Ted Hughes in Leo Wynne's voice.'

Nick Illsley (1982–88) remembers a much later incident: 'Leo Wynne was teaching an A1 English lesson in his own style and eventually tired of Harry Dobbs' persistent chatting. "Dobbs, go to bed, now, I've had enough." "But sir, I'm a day boy!" "Borrow one then! Who can lend Dobbs some pyjamas?" Needless to say, no sooner had Harry been suitably kitted out and his head had touched the pillow of the borrowed bed, surrounded by an astonished class, than it was time for the next lesson, for which he was late, with the oddest of excuses.'

Sophia Bentley (staff 1990–95, née St John Parker) remembers meeting Leo when she came for a job interview: 'After the interview, I was shown into the office to meet the bursar and be reimbursed for my train ticket. From behind an amazingly untidy desk, I was greeted with the cheerful words "What do you want, darling?" by the lovely and eccentric Leo Wynne. I rather wondered about this all, later on the train, deciding that surely life could only be made richer by working in such a wonderful and unusual environment.'

Boys

Meanwhile the school was lucky in its pupils. Mike and Chris Bridge were the only two brothers to score centuries for the 1st XI, as Chris (1956–61) describes: 'Mike's century in 1959 was a skilled, elegant affair. His cover driving, as he used to remind me, was "more Tom Graveney than Ted Dexter" whilst his footwork was immaculate, which is rare in a prep school cricketer. More of his runs were scored on the more difficult off side which must have been a joy for Hal umpiring at the other end. Mike's ton was scored against Grove Park of Crowborough who were only, I would later rib him, the Bangladesh of the Sussex prep school cricket circuit; so his timing was superb in more ways than one! My effort against Sharrow of Haywards Heath in 1961 was a much cruder affair. Everything tended to enter the area that even the Aussies denigrate as "cow corner" which means I must have regularly transgressed against Hal's patient hours of net coaching. Decades later I now realise he must have umpired that match in a cocktail of mixed emotions because any coach, if only to justify his own efforts and salary, must surely prefer the purist to the pugilist. The one emotion that I can never erase from that innings, however, came later that evening when Hal suddenly took from behind his back a brand new Gray-Nicholls cricket bat still in its wrapping. To a small boy, it was the ultimate gift from just short of paradise.

'I can still clearly recall Hal's coaching methodology beside that lovely rose garden. He would silently watch everything from behind the two nets as we batted self-consciously in front of him. Then suddenly he would appear in your net and take the bat from your hands and demonstrate with a stylish, wristy flourish the shots that you had failed to perfect for the past 20 minutes. All this was done on hot summer afternoons in his bow tie or cravat; his immaculately white, long-sleeved, MCC woollen sweater; and an evil cheroot clenched between his lips. Moreover, he would put the whole cricket team into his great black Rolls-Royce and drive us down to Hove to see Sussex play the Tourists. I shall never forget watching Gupte, the Indian leg spinner, bowl a ball just outside the off stump to Ted Dexter, soon to be England's captain. Although we were over a hundred yards away, that ball was hit with the ferocity and sound of a very bad car crash. At that very moment every dumbstruck Cumnorian cricketer knew for evermore what was expected of him if he wished to prosper. It was classic Hal

Hal's second Rolls-
Royce, sold in 1963
for £305

Richard II, 1964:
Adrian King
(Bolingbroke), left,
and Philip Snow
(John of Gaunt)

psychology – hands off and learn for yourself – and I
have never stopped thanking him for it; for
introducing us to the bigger stage.'

Audrey Williams, piano teacher from 1964 to
1978, recalls a quaint encounter: 'I always remember
a dialogue which took place during a lesson with Ben
Wilson in about 1970. I was giving him aural tests
and when we came to the conducting, he mentioned
casually that his grandfather was a conductor. Me
(somewhat condescendingly): "Oh yes, and what's
his name?" Ben: "Sir Adrian Boult".'

In 1964 Philip Snow had written two five-act
plays by the age of 12; Robert Gussman had started
Russian and was 'stretching the new maths towards
Mr Straker's own limits'; and Christopher Spooner
was acting *Oliver* around the USA. A landmark was
reached in 1966 when Basil Earle ceased to be a
Cumnor parent after 28 years, on the departure of
Joe, the last of the Earle boys; four of his six sons were
scholars, and he himself had umpired 20 Fathers'
Matches. Three grandchildren were to follow.

Christopher Pegna (1964–69), aged 10, wrote a
moving piece in the 1966 magazine entitled 'Papa':
'When I was young my papa went diving in the blue
sea. He told me about the sea bushes that open and
shut and he told me how he fought the tiger of the
sea, and how he broke his spear and fought the tiger
bare-handed. He told me many a thing but now he is
not and he lies in his golden box in peace.'

Nine-year-old Dominic Lawson, a future editor
of the *Spectator*, asked, on arriving at the beginning
of one term: 'Mummy says will you kindly confiscate
my comic?' A few years earlier Tom Tickell
(1952–56), future Economics editor of the *Guardian*,
wanting to be as adult as possible, had asked his

mother to send him the *Beano* and the *New Statesman* each week.

Cyril Ray recounted a story about his son Jonathan (1967–73), aged seven: 'At a new boys' party, guests had been asked what they would like to drink: some chose milk, some squash, the more raffish Coca-Cola. Young Ray – not, I like to think, showing off, but recalling vaguely what he had heard at some parental saturnalia – thought perhaps a glass of claret. "Of course," said Hal, disappearing into the cellar and emerging with a smile, hospitable murmurs and a specially opened bottle …'.

Jonathan's mother Liz remembers his start at Cumnor: 'When we came to live in Kent with our young son we searched through several (of many) prep schools within reach without finding what we thought was the right one. Then two very different friends, one very academic, the other more sporty, each told us of the school their boys were at and where they were very happy. We thought a school that could be right for two such different families might be the one we were looking for. Then someone else said "Cumnor House? Oh yes, that's the school that turns out amiable eccentrics." That decided it. Jonathan settled in well, we thought, until one of his weekly letters, written in his inimitable handwriting, arrived not with the usual "Dear Mummy and Daddy I am very well we had a match yesterday," but "I am being bollinged by a Lecher." We looked at one another – was this the amiable eccentricity? We went to visit the next weekend and found J well and happy. "What about your last letter?" "Oh that was about Leuchars, he was being a bit of a bully last week." "What have you done about it?" "Well nothing, I was a bit of a bully this week. He's all right." So that was that, and we came to love and admire the school – and the Milner-Gullands – as much as he did.'

In 1971 our head boy Ross Cooper (1966–71) acted the part of Ronnie in *The Winslow Boy* in the West End opposite Kenneth More, and Anthony

D Form, 1973

Murphy (1965–70) was cast as Tom Brown in the BBC TV serial. Tom Sherlock recalls that through his excellence as a batsman he 'achieved a huge amount of "street cred" at Cumnor, and I have since realised how important this was in securing my status at the school. Cumnor strove for excellence, the ethos demanded excellence, and whereas academically and in areas such as music and acting I was nothing to write home about, by succeeding in a sport I was able to feel deep down inside that I was the best at something. Competition was tough and there was a danger of falling by the wayside, but I had an easy-going, laid-back personality that could be too inclined to accept mediocrity, and I needed somewhere like Cumnor to push me forward.'

Neil Canetty-Clarke (1970–75) remembers: 'I loved Cumnor. It is hard to remember any really miserable moments. On the whole, the place sang with happy sounds – trumpet practice, end-of-term songs, dashing down corridors, chattering lunch queue (do they still do hand inspections?), French vocab, learning Shakespeare lines, cheering a goal. Even the food wasn't too bad; for some reason I remember the mince curry as being particularly delicious. Boys' faces still grin out from the 1970s – Bex, McKenzie-Smith, Sherlock, Wharton, Dean,

Pearson-Gee. It feels very much "our" school but of course it belongs to the hundreds before and after us, who were also lucky enough to be there. The staff were surprisingly patient and encouraging, even with those of us in A2. Many of them helped us to refine our sense of humour, whilst guiding us into our next school. I also seem to have picked up one or two other useful life skills – knowing the best way to get into a freezing swimming pool, how to jump into and rake beautifully a long-jump sand pit, and how to sing carols in Latin. Lots of words spring to mind about the place and the people there. Courteous. Curious. Cheerful. Thirty years on I still get the odd flashback that helps to nudge me in the right direction.'

David Mullins (1966–72): 'We had one master who used to read the political column from *Punch* magazine to us seven-year-old boys and the dare was to climb out of the classroom window and do a complete circuit of the school and return without being noticed – a task which was surprisingly easy to achieve. If you misbehaved during the night in the dormitory, you had to stand under the clock on the landing outside X's study door, sometimes for hours at a time. At a certain point in the evening you could detect the faint whiff of cigar smoke coming up the staircase and then X would appear, normally with a comment like "Lordy Bill what a crew!" as he surveyed that evening's miscreants.'

Sport

With boys like the Bridge brothers representing the school, it is not surprising that sporting results remained excellent. During this period we won 85 of our 132 soccer matches played, with six unbeaten 1st XIs. In 1960 Wilf Sobey opened the new rugby pitch ('the far pitch'), which gave a great boost to the sport: our teams in the 1960s and beyond had a series of very good seasons, even though the weather (in 1963) and illness (in 1969) caused two entire seasons' matches to be cancelled.

Chris, left, and Michael Bridge

Cricket was more variable, though in 1970 and 1972 Matt Mockridge easily topped both the bowling and the batting averages. (He was later, when at Marlborough, to win the Public Schools Rackets Championships, both singles and doubles – 'an efficient killer, with the nicest possible manners' – *The Times*). In one 1st XI match Richard Vinter (1959–62) took all 10 wickets for 39, including a hat trick. Simon Templer was in charge of the non-cricketers, for whom a 'Z XI' was devised. Stephen White, the captain, recalls one of their matches: 'This match was played against Ashdown House, a school with a specially high standard of games playing. They managed to get most of us twittering with nerves even before we got to the school. They used a form of psychological warfare, ringing up and happily announcing that the whole school would be watching us, and that since they had no other

John Verney's picture of Cumnor, with Hal and Nan in the foreground. David Duvall remembers Hal's explanation of artistic licence when, aged 10, he had pointed out that the sun was in the north.

Below: Unbeaten 1st XIs, 1967 and 1971

A memorable goal ...

Adam Ogilvie recalls in a letter to his father a memorable goal scored for the Under 11

Dear,

In the last under eleven match I scored a goal although you would not believe it. I scored it from a corner kick like this:—

(a goal from a corner kick is the most difficult place to get a goal from)

I felt very embarrased when I scored the goal because all the boys shouted and cheered.

Brakelands has a lighting conductor (thank heavens), so we will never be struck by lighting.

In carpentry I have made something for the house. Mummy got some things for the kitchen yesterday. Lots of Love from Adam XXXX 0,0 0 0

opposing captain said proudly, but with resignation, as if it could not be helped: "I'm sorry we dismissed you for so few runs." "He led his team to defeat with admirable sang-froid," my report read; "for other aspects of cricket see acting report".'

Annual cricket matches against the Fathers and tennis against the Mothers would be accompanied by gargantuan parties at Newnhams Rough, where David and Tibby Mockridge would regale the teams and their families with strawberries and cream. Fathers' soccer matches however came to an end in 1966 as they were deemed too dangerous. Bruce Walker (1963–68) remembers the final game: 'I have a mental picture of the contrasting figures of Nigel Lawson, spotlessly clad in the very latest soccer kit, including new low-slung boots with white stripes down the sides, trotting onto the pitch, and the craggy, tall and tousled Judge Bazil Wingate-Saul in his splendidly dubbined boots, well above the ankle, complete with toecaps and leather studs; his entire outfit must have been made in the early 1930s ("I last played soccer 46 years ago").'

Neil Canetty-Clarke: 'I have a vivid memory of being driven by NG to away matches in a rather dilapidated old red van. I think you could see the road through the floor in parts. These were always jolly occasions, particularly if we had won. Additional fun came when NG would switch off the engine and freewheel down hills on the way home in order to save petrol. When the engine burst into song again at the bottom of the hill, a cheer usually went up.'

Tennis was more a recreation than a competitive team game, and Hal always insisted on calling it lawn tennis to distinguish it from real tennis, the game he used to play. Nicholas Heath (1966–69), himself now a real tennis enthusiast, remembers: 'Real tennis explains a perplexing conversation I once had with X after prep. When I asked for permission to play tennis that evening he replied that he was too busy to drive me to Petworth – which seemed more than usually eccentric at the time but makes perfect sense now.'

matches we would be using their 1st XI pitch, and their 1st XI games master. When we arrived I was asked if I would like to inspect the wicket, since it was perhaps "a trifle sticky after the rain". I solemnly jiggered myself along to the wicket and inspected the thing. I would have loved to use a bit of psychological warfare on them, by pulling it out of the ground and muttering with a shake of the head "No, this will never do." But if I had been asked why it would never do, or what could be done about it, I would not have known. So I just wobbled back to the edge of the pitch. When we all were out, and some pathetic score in the 20s was stuck onto the board, the

Coeducation

It was in response to parental demand rather than a falling-off of demand for boys' places that in 1970 the first two brave girls, Lucy Artus and Louise Gibbon, slipped in, almost unnoticed. Louise (1970–74), now Joanna Dodd, remembers: 'My parents had no qualms at all about me becoming one of the first two girls to attend Cumnor. This world-shattering event was arranged in what seemed a typically relaxed Cumnorian way. Apparently Hal mentioned that the school was thinking of taking girls and by the end of the day my parents had signed me up. The uniform for Lucy and me was concocted by Nan in conversation with our two mums. It didn't feel that strange to me either – my elder brother Mark was already there and enjoying it. I certainly didn't feel like a trailblazer. In fact it felt totally natural. On the first day of term, Lucy and I met up in the entrance hall, held hands and skipped off into the sunset.

'My memories of Cumnor are very similar to my brothers' – polo mints on your birthday, midge cream for school plays, my first part in the play and holding up the interval sign (perhaps my finest stage moment?), singing, music, bell-ringing down in Danehill church. At least I did get my own set of Cash's nametapes: by the time my younger brother Piers arrived at Cumnor he just got Mark's cut in half. Overall I remember a sense of freedom that certainly disappeared as soon as I moved on to an all girls' school.'

Matt Mockridge too remembers: 'In my final year I would spend the next half hour plucking up the courage to ask Louise Gibbon if I could hold her hand. I never managed it in three terms of adoring her from afar.'

In 1974, by becoming our first girl scholar, at Roedean, Louise conferred on coeducation, if it were necessary, an academic as well as a social respectability. Coeducation had an effect on some teaching and text-books, and we dropped the Latin

Reports

A book could be written about reports alone. Here are some curious examples of the genre:

> She is developing into a very competent sewer.

> Draws neat maps and flags.

> His frog was particularly good, showing great patience and determination.

> Emma's work continues to go up and down like a pendulum.

> She looks quite a promising athlete but she's still finding her feet.

exercise book which asked pupils to translate the sentence: 'Where are the girls' tunics?'

Sarah Jane Sherlock (1972–77) recalls one of the reasons for coming to Cumnor: 'My own first link with the school came when I was about six years old and living with my family in London. My father, an Old Cumnorian who has never lost touch with the place, had invited friends to dinner – I think it was Jack and Margaret Straker. I was in bed and supposed to be asleep. Instead, I was listening to the grown-ups talking about my school (a local state school). My parents were worried about the lack of information the school gave them about my progress. For

Jack Straker and Sarah Jane Sherlock

example, there were no end-of-term reports. Jack Straker asked why this was so. Before my parents could answer, I piped up "Because they don't teach us anything, so there's nothing to report." Fortunately, the grown-ups were so amused by this precocious intervention that I didn't get into trouble.'

At first, fearing that we might be overwhelmed by an unstoppable tide of girls, and then abandoned by boys from more traditional families, we decided to limit the number of girls to a certain percentage of the total; then, when that didn't work, to girls whose brothers were at the school; then, when no system of limitation seemed either fair or workable – or legal – we abandoned the attempt. Neither of our fears was justified.

It took a little time for the implications of coeducation to sink in. In 1970 the children's contributions to the magazine were still entitled 'Boys' contributions', and for several years the staff continued to be listed with the men first. 'Big boys' walks' were not renamed. Girls' sports were a problem which we hadn't quite thought through, as Sarah Jane recalls: 'Having two sports-mad older brothers inevitably gave me an interest in their games. I grew up playing football in the street (in London: not possible now) and bowling and fielding for them in the garden. So it seemed natural to me to carry on playing cricket and football when I got to Cumnor, and to play for the (boys') Under 11 sides. I had a strong left foot and eventually played left back for the 1st XI football team. X taught us, and he used the old 'W' formation for the forwards: left wing, inside left, centre forward, inside right, right wing. He told us it was the same shape as Cassiopeia. We weren't a very strong side, but we had our moments. Herman Siemens once scored a spectacular goal: an overhead kick, with his back to goal.

'I also played 1st XI cricket, but with less success. I actually preferred playing for the 2nd XI, because Oscar Nieboer and I had quite a good opening partnership going, before we were both promoted. I once scored 36 with him before running myself out

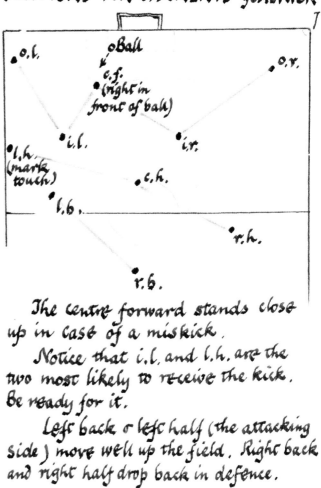

The Cassiopeia formation

going for a second run which wasn't there. Peter Dean was our really good batsman. In one match he scored 43 before holding his bat the wrong way round and getting bowled. Nick Milner-Gulland was umpiring and said he'd never seen anyone get himself out like that. I think he was quite cross, because it was a waste of a wicket and might have cost us the match. My parents suspected that NG

Teapot stands with
Mr Baxter

Out of school

Stephen White has memories of carpentry which must be shared by other makers of teapot stands: 'Carpentry was not very productive: the main trouble was that it took so long. For instance the standard teapot stand consisted of five pieces of wood stuck and screwed together, and it took me a term and a half to make. The reasons for this were my incompetence and the number of people who learnt carpentry when only one man was there to teach it. I would take a piece of wood and ask where it was to be cut, then after a lot of difficulty in sawing it I would show it. "No, it's too small." Having sawn up another one or two and got it right, the task of planing would begin. A line would be drawn for me and I would go off and happily plane away. When shown, it was bound to be too much or too little. After waiting and waiting I would win another audience and be given another line to plane to. This would happen several times more until my wood diminished into a tiny thing hardly worth looking at. Nevertheless after hours of wasted time this miserable piece of wood became a teapot stand. It surprised me most of all.'

Sarah Jane remembers bell-ringing: 'It was one of the occupations you could do on a winter's evening. We went down to the church at Danehill. We were too small to reach the bell-ropes, so the tower captain stood us on boxes and showed us how to hold the sally. This was all great fun, until the day I broke a stave. I thought I'd done something terrible, but everyone was very calm about it and said it didn't matter: it was better than being carried up to the roof of the belfry and being left with an interestingly shaped head. I think they presented me with the old stave, signed by all the ringers. Best of all, they encouraged me to carry on ringing.'

Rhoddy Voremberg recalls that when cubs were abandoned in 1963, 'thereafter one afternoon a week was devoted to something hilariously named (by Leo Wynne, I think) 'C-TA' which stood for Cub-Type

never intended me to play cricket for the 1st XI because he thought it would be unfair on opposition fast bowlers to feel they couldn't bowl at top speed at a girl. But when someone was injured and I had my whites with me, there seemed no harm in giving me a go. The person who was most put out by all this was probably Mrs Leuchars, the games mistress, because my playing "boys' games" meant I was less available to play netball, tennis and rounders – which I enjoyed, but regarded as inferior to cricket and football.'

Activities. A notable C-TA team exercise, which I have always felt should have developed into an Olympic sport, consisted of a combination of orienteering and Chinese whispers on a circuit around the CHS grounds: how it worked perhaps someone else will remember.'

Robert Maslen, now a distinguished author and academic, recalls the play: 'I remember nothing very precise about acting except how important it was. One moment of humiliation, when I had to speak six words in *Much Ado About Nothing*, and was told off for overacting. Otherwise, only the audience-filled dark and the mosquitoes and the tune of "O mistress mine, where are you roaming?". But I can still recapture the sensation of being possessed by a Shakespearian spirit, who pronounced brilliant musical sentences which I thought I must have understood a moment ago, but whose sense had somehow escaped me. I've been seduced by those sentences, and searching for their meaning ever since.'

When he was cast as Pistol in *Henry the Fifth*, Stephen White felt at last able to show his worth: 'Pistol was the part, a large, boasting coward. He was a character, a funny character, and I was him. It brought about a change upon me: I became far less inhibited and self-conscious, indeed I almost became the part in life. It took me some time after the play to adjust my walk again: the Pistol walk was bent-kneed with a stick-out belly. I loved the play and everything to do with it and I looked forward to each rehearsal, and finally the play itself. I discovered how splendid it is to be able to make people laugh.'

Mark Wilson has less happy memories of an onstage attack of hiccoughs as Juliet, and Nick Humphrey as Puck catching his skimpy costume on a nail and having to retire from the stage backwards. Hal's last Shakespeare play was his eighth production of *A Midsummer Night's Dream*, the play which he had first produced 33 years before. In his last few years he had branched out into new territory – *Julius Caesar, The Merchant of Venice, Much Ado*

Mark Wilson as Juliet, 1962

About Nothing – but it was surely appropriate that his final production should have been of the play he loved so much. (Incidentally, before the 1957 performance of the Dream Adam Ogilvie revealed in a letter home the reasons for the choice of play: 'Mr Gulland has just told the school that the play is going to be called "Midsummers Night Dream", he says that he always chooses it when we are short of actors which we are.')

When I arrived in 1969 as joint headmaster with my father until his retirement five years later, I was determined to revitalise the music, which had suffered something of a decline since Bert Chappell's time. In my first year I organised 35 expeditions to concerts, invited many of my musical friends to give concerts at the school, increased the number of instrumentalists and created opportunities for the school chorus to join other groups to perform real music.

Bill Maslen (1969–74) has many memories of the school during this period: 'I remember my first nights at CHS, upstairs in the junior dormitories on the first floor, with Anthony Murphy our dormitory captain. Full of character even then, he cut a dashing figure for us newbies, and on our first night climbed up the tree outside and then through the dormitory window, ostensibly to make sure we were "being good" but in fact for sheer entertainment. Of course dormitories were a special institution at Cumnor – when I moved to the next junior dormitory, still on the first floor, I used to spend hours sitting behind the curtains on the deep window sill next to my bed, watching the amazing starscape and losing myself in the depths between the stars. As I grew older, I and my peers moved downstairs to the former barracks, now semi-legendary among Old Cumnorians, that housed 20–30 children each. With elderly bar heaters fixed to the lofty ceilings, they were often colder inside than the weather outside. So cold were the dormitories that inevitably certain kids, the true chancers, would stay in bed for as long as possible, apparently still asleep. When irate teachers started to chastise them for being late for breakfast they would fling back their bedclothes to reveal that they had been surreptitiously sneaking their garments under the covers from the bedside chairs on which they had been folded, and were in fact fully dressed and ready to go. I remember Mr Tasker in particular being reduced to red-faced incoherence by Eddie Collier and Robert Williams, masters of this particular art of undercover dressing. I remember the camps we used to build in the dormitories as B formers, by pulling the beds slightly away from the wall and using bedspreads and pillows to build walls and draped ceilings. I also remember how hastily we had to dismantle them when a soft-footed master arrived to do his rounds of the dormitories. I remember whizzing along on my pillow under the iron bedsteads, the linoleum providing a perfect surface for high-speed travel. Often the torches of the dormitory captains would become Nazi search-lights seeking us out as we dared to flout the bedtime rules, but we also became very good at concealing ourselves in corners, pretending – by stillness and posture – that we were simply a bundle of clothes that had fallen from a bedside chair.

'I remember the sheer variety of the school grounds and how awesome they were to eight-year-old eyes. There were elegant bits (the pitches, the rose garden), and almost alarmingly mysterious or scruffy bits. There were so many beautiful, mature trees, many of which had their own names (Frank's Caravan, the Camouflage, the Monkey Walk …) and were climbed by generations of schoolchildren. In particular, there was the bamboo grove at the front of the school, infested by nettles which I, as a recent arrival from the tropics, had never seen before, and into which I plunged before realising my folly. And, of course, the rhododendrons, which were especially magnificent, and were the location of many a challenge for newly arrived children. The Crucifix in particular was a terrifying challenge, because in order to traverse from one forked branch to the next you had to hang from one hand and swing your entire body over an enormous gulf until you could grasp the forked branch on the next tree along.

'As a newbie, I was, I suppose, sometimes homesick and lonely – certainly I became a voracious reader in my early years at Cumnor, and for that reason remember the dormitories and the library with particular fondness. Even the junior dormitories had a good selection of books in shelves or between book ends on the window sills, and I can still remember a number of firm favourites that I read over and over again. Of course some of my most influential memories are of teachers. The extraordinary Mr Wynne, saturnine and volatile though he could be, managed to imbue us all with his passion for language – by encouraging us to play with words, to neologise, to recombine, to hunt for rhymes and rhythms, to abandon too-frequent adverbs for more carefully constructed expressions, by taking us out into the fields to look at things, touch them, explore them, and then later, back in the classroom, to write about them as if they were other things, other worlds, and build new experiences in our imaginations on the back of the real things we had just seen. He was also capable of the most remarkable sensitivity in his dealings with individual children, as I discovered on a number of occasions, but especially while staying at the Wynnery in my later years at the school.

'I remember the erudite Mr Middlehurst, with his meticulously prepared brief sheets on everything from the Magna Carta to the English Civil War. I remember his debating society, and his unconcealed delight at our manifestations of intelligence. He was one of the very few teachers I have known who allowed his sheer joy in the bright minds of children to show in bursts of enthusiasm and encouragement. I remember Latin classes with NG, who managed to enthuse me for the language and its structures even though he was by far the most disciplinarian of our teachers (with the possible exception of Messrs Straker and Arkley). I remember Mr Straker's impatience with those who were less gifted at maths than he. I remember Mr Arkley's slim form – he was the first genuine vegetarian most of us urchins had ever encountered – and the gruff, occasionally volatile but usually entertaining Mr Tasker with his rats and his snakes and his Burmese cats. I remember the unkempt Mr Bond, who was always good-natured, would take children for motorbike rides across the school grounds, and allowed himself to be beaten up regularly by hordes of screaming urchins without losing his temper or indeed his essential authority.

'One of the highlights of the school year was the publication of the *Cumnor House Magazine*, in which, if you were lucky, you might be mentioned – indeed, in which a piece of your work might actually appear! It's difficult to overstate the pride felt by many a young heart on seeing that a poem, or short story, or even just a funny remark made to the headmaster had been published in the magazine. Being mentioned in a parent's or teacher's review of a play or concert, or else in a summary of sporting achievements, was also a source of enormous pride. Even now, long after leaving Cumnor, I still feel a glow of pleasure when I see my or a family member's or friend's name appear in the Old Boys section.

'Smells are something I remember, too. The maturity and sheer variety of the trees and bushes in the grounds, and the adjoining farm, with its well-saturated cow fields and invasive geese who would occasionally march down the drive terrorising kids with that astounding self-confidence that only geese seem able to radiate. The smell of mown grass as Mr Bates finished preparing the fields for cricket. The pervasive smell of mud as we played football and, in particular, rugby on pitches that had been churned to something resembling the fields of Flanders. I remember times when the ground was hard with frost and the puddles had frozen over, so that anybody stupid enough to do a proper diving rugby tackle (and I was, because my grandfather had been capped for Wales and I had been taught to admire him as man and athlete) could cut their hands and knees on the sharp ice. I wasn't a 1st team athlete (except in rugby, where I played in the 1st XV simply because of my tackling ability), but sports and physical activity were an important part of school life, and the smells of linseed oil and the various unctions used to whiten cricket pads and gym shoes are still very evocative for me today. I remember the smells of the sick room, of which I was an occasional resident, and the smells of the surgery. I remember the smell of the flowering rhododendrons, and the marshy expanse of the old swimming pool, and of the dusty branches behind or beneath which we would lurk as we played soldiers (or "armies", as we called it) for hours, until our jeans were so stiff with grime and mud that they could stand up by

Peter Hankey, youngest
member of the National
Youth Orchestra, with
Dame Ruth Railton,
1962

Above: *Noyes Fludde*, 1974

Right: Bill Maslen as Lancelot Gobbo, 1972

bicycles to home-made go-karts. I remember Jeff Mockridge hurling himself and his bike into the "new" swimming pool, ostensibly by accident but in what could only be described as suspicious circumstances. I remember the amazing throws with which his brother Matthew used to win the "throwing the cricket ball" competition year after year – he could hurl a ball further than many grown adults. I remember sporting visits to other schools, which often featured equally beautiful grounds and even more impressive athletic and other facilities, but were also frequently marred by what I can best describe as a "public school" atmosphere, which is something that Cumnor House never had. In winter months, I remember NG's constant exhortations not to run in the corridors.

'I remember the huge Christmas tree that used to appear in the front hall as December drew near. I remember the "sing-songs" that took place at the end of every term – initially quite rowdy affairs under the benign governance of Mr Straker, but later governed with a firmer hand by NG himself, who clearly indulged in these sentimental celebrations of English popular music with considerable reluctance and refused outright to play what he

themselves. I remember the smell of shoe polish that pervaded the changing rooms in the mornings after we had finished polishing our "good" shoes in preparation for church on Sunday morning.

'I remember some of the more manic and fearless characters who loved to hurl themselves down the steep banks that bordered the sports pitches on any kind of vehicle at all, from elderly

clearly considered to be the more vulgar favourites. I remember Mrs G and other grown-ups joining in the crossed hands of "Auld Lang Syne", a tradition that even NG didn't dare to overturn.

'Then I remember the food – and Mrs G's repeated exhortations to appreciate how lucky we were to eat fresh food grown in Cumnor's own garden. We certainly appreciated the small, many-legged residents of the fresh food, especially the lettuce – they formed a significant proportion of the protein intake so vital to young, growing bodies. I remember the amazing curries, alternately green or yellow, replete with squashy raisins and other unidentified ingredients. I remember the porridge – sometimes thin and anaemic but more often robustly lumpy, and the mysteriously colourful puddings – pink, green or blue. I remember the sheer noise that permeated the dining room when meals were in full swing.

'I remember so much music – not just the classical music appreciation sessions with NG, but the many practical opportunities to make music offered by the school, especially after NG's arrival. I was lucky enough to have a good treble voice, and was the soloist at many school choir performances. The ones that I remember best are all by Benjamin Britten: his *St Nicolas*, which we performed several times at various locations, the *Missa Brevis*, and of course *Noyes Fludde*, in which I played Sem, one of Noah's sons. I also remember the high-calibre performers who used, at NG's behest, to come and make often startlingly good music in performances both for the school and with the school. I still remember the sheer good humour they would display in response to the curiosity or admiration displayed by us urchins.

'Performing was, of course, one of the things that we were encouraged to do at CHS in all sorts of ways: in debating societies or in plays and concerts arranged by teachers, but also on our own behalf – I was one of a group of children who put on regular

performances of what we fondly imagined were "spy thrillers" on a kind of "Addams Family meets James Bond" theme, and teachers and fellow pupils were very generous in coming along to watch, applaud and generally make us feel special. But the chief highlight of the school year was the summer play, and I was fortunate enough to be chosen for a number of key roles – Lancelot Gobbo was my very first opportunity to shine, in *The Merchant of Venice*, followed by Dogberry the Watchman in *Much Ado About Nothing*, with my brother Bob playing Verges, and finally, in my last year at Cumnor, as Bottom in *A Midsummer Night's Dream*. I remember X, as rigorous a director as any I have worked with in subsequent productions at college or in amateur

Performances involving CHS children

1971	Britten *St Nicolas* (with Adrian de Peyer) at Ardingly College
	Purcell *Dido and Aeneas* (with Angela Hickey) in the Open Air Theatre
1972	Britten *Missa Brevis* and *St Nicolas* with Michael Hall School
1973	Haydn *Nelson Mass* with the Fayrfax Singers
	Mozart *Coronation Mass* with the Fayrfax Singers
1974	Bach *St Matthew Passion* (two performances)
	Britten *Noyes Fludde* with five local primary schools

theatre, sitting at the very back of the auditorium, obliging all us young thespians to throw our voices effectively so that he could hear us. And finally, dressed as Bottom – one of the most satisfying roles a young person could possibly wish to play – I remember standing in the summer dusk, behind Cumnor's unique outdoor stage, making ready for an entry and gazing up at the star-filled sky with the heavy scent of rhododendrons in my nostrils. I remember then thinking: "This is the last time you'll do this, and you'll remember this for ever." And I do.'

CHAPTER 8

HAIL AND FAREWELL

1974

CUMNOR HOUSE SCHOOL, DANEHILL

16 May '55

Dear Martin,

We were all delighted to read in the Times of your success with the Winchester Reading Prize: many congratulations. I remember James Mason & myself going in for a similar thing when we were up, but I think it was only a college prize. We were presented with a piece of J. Bunyan to read, containing the word 'quag' (i.e. quagmire). Nobody knew how it ought to be pronounced. Anyway we were both also-rans.

Miss May, always a one for saying the right thing, declared that your prize was entirely my doing, basing this on memories of plays long ago. If she is right, no doubt you will shortly be forwarding the appropriate rake-off!

Please excuse the odd appearance of this letter: as you may guess it is an experiment. Love from all.

Yours ever

HMG.

Exegi monumentum aere perennius

HORACE, *ODES* III.30

Hal's retirement

Nigel Lawson wrote in 1976: 'That Cumnor House was a very good school – and I use the past tense merely because it is seven years since I was a Cumnor parent – is obvious to anyone who looks up its academic record, and the credit must doubtless be shared among all those who taught there. But it was also a very special school, and for that the credit goes entirely to one remarkable (and slightly eccentric) man, Hal Milner-Gulland…. However vague and distrait he could at times appear, he always knew exactly what he wanted – and also what he did not want, in which context he could exploit his own deafness ruthlessly. He knew that real freedom is to be found only within rules of order, and that tradition is something alive and binding, rather than dead and oppressive. But, as if to underline his deter-

mination to go his own way, he instinctively adopted (at least in public) the manner of a shy and somewhat dandified aesthete, the polar opposite of the stereotype of the hearty prep school headmaster. Cumnor House was also a very happy school. This stemmed partly, I think, from the strong sense of family with which Hal was imbued; but, above all, credit here must go to Nan who – in the best possible sense – was everything that Hal was not.'

When my parents retired in 1974, they had been running the school for 36 years. It was their personal qualities more than, say, the reputation of the school or its scholarship record that attracted parents to the school, and many Old Cumnorians have deep and lasting memories of them. Cumnor was at that time a boarding school, with no half-terms or home weekends, and pupils regarded Hal and Nan as their

OPPOSITE PAGE

Above left: Nan at the 50th anniversary dinner at the Savoy, October 1981, with Tony Curtis, left, and Geoffrey Lovegrove

Left: Hal directing

Dear Mummy and Daddy,

        Well, here we are back at school. I'm in A1. There are 13 of us (which in case you don't know is the square root of (1)..... It also happens to be the sum of two squares (2)..... and (3)..... Add another square number, which is (4)..... and you get the number of letters in Cumnor House School. Here's a funny thing; that number is also the sum of two squares (5)..... and (6)..... It's also the sum of a square and a cube, which of course are (7)..... and (8)..... Also the sum of two cubes and a square, (9)....., (10)....., and (11)..... You can't make it the sum of two prime numbers, but it can be the sum of three primes in various ways, such as (12)..... + (13)..... + (14)....., or (15)..... + (16)..... + (17).....

        We're going to do a good deal of French I believe, so next time we go to France I'll be able to say a lot more than just (18)..... ('thank you') or (19)..... ('please'). I'll be able to say things like 'I want a cake' (20.....), or 'How much money?' (21.....), or 'Give me a newspaper' (22.....) or 'ten litres of petrol' (23.....). Then I'll know things like the feminine of nouveau (24.....) and beau (25.....) and vieux (26.....), and adverbs like 27..... (well) and 28..... (badly).

        Don't know what we'll be doing in English - maybe reading some poets like the authors of 'The Ancient Mariner' (29.....) or 'Ode to a Nightingale' (30.....) or 'Richard III' (31.....) or even 'Edward II' (32.....), or that chap with the funny name (33.....) who wrote 'Summoned by Bells'. Now I'm going to give you six spelling mistakes: seperate - embarassed - parralel - Portugese - fushia (the flower) - parliment. Can you do them? They ought to be (34)..... (35)..... (36)..... (37)..... (38)..... and (39).....

        Wonder what our soccer team will be like after everyone's been watching the World Cup! It certainly was a wonderful Final when England beat (40)..... by (41)..... goals to (42)....., and it was good to see (43)..... score three goals. I'm glad they made (44)..... captain. His club, (45)..... , must be proud of him. Cricket seems far away, but anyhow (46)..... won the last Test Match; about time when they had lost (47)..... out of the other (48)..... test matches. I think it was because they made (49)..... captain for that last match.

        What more news is there ? Well, the new Head Boy (also difficult to spell) is (50).....; there's a new master called Mr.(51).....; there are (52)..... new boys altogether. The oldest of them is (53)..... years old and his name is (54)..... The youngest is (55)..... and his name is (56)..... There's one day boy called (57)..... Each house has (58)..... boys in it; I notice there's a picture of (59)..... on top of the h.p. board this term.

        It was funny; at high tea yesterday I said 'Pass the sodium chloride' and nobody knew that meant (60)..... Then I said 'Pass the H_2O' and of course all I wanted was some (61)..... Good job I didn't ask for H_2SO_3, or (62)..... !

        In evening occupations I'm going to do bellringing. Did you know the heaviest bell is called the (63)..... and the lightest the (64)..... ? Also Chess; did you know that '0 - 0' means (65)..... , and that KNP means (66)..... ? And maybe pottery, making a jar or something on the wheel, what they call (67).....

        Hope I don't fall ill, and that my temp. stays normal or (68)..... °
Miss Wright's dog, (69)....., is as lively as ever. Mr.Cashell's baby seems well; she's called (70)..... Wonder if Mr.Templer will be doing a play this term; this time last year he produced (71)..... by (72)..... Nicky Gulland's gone to teach

surrogate parents. Richard Tapper remembers Hal as 'possibly the most formative and positive influence on my life. I can't imagine myself, any good qualities I may have as an academic or a human being, as anything other than a product of his early guidance and example. For years I would respond to challenges by asking myself, how would X have dealt with it.'

The name 'X' derives from wartime, when Hal was asked by what letter he should be shown on the timetable. Peggy Garrard already had G, so Hal nonchalantly suggested X. It stuck.

Kindness seems to be the quality for which Hal is best remembered. Indeed when the poet Yevtushenko visited the school and was asked how he liked it, he said, after a long pause: 'When the gardener has kind eyes, the plants grow well.' Sarah Jane Sherlock remembers 'once trying to help him repair the leather bindings of some old books. He carefully explained that the mixture we were about to use was very precious and needed to be used only in very small doses. Within minutes, I had knocked over the bottle and lost half the contents. I was very upset, but he was so nice about it, assuring me he had plenty more etc, that in the end I really believed it didn't matter.' Ranald MacDonell recalls the occasion when 'a nasty stomach bug was sweeping the school, causing the boys to wake up at night and vomit copiously and messily. The matrons (Miss Chard and Mrs Layard) were exhausted from spending night after night being called to change beds and mop up, so Hal offered to be on duty for a night. The following notice appeared on the door of Mrs Layard's room:

IF YOU'RE DYING, SICK OR SCARED,
DON'T APPLY TO MRS LAYARD.
PLEASE REMEMBER, WHATE'ER YOUR WOES,
THE MATRONS NEED A NIGHT'S REPOSE.
IF VIOLENT ATTACKS OF NAUSEA
FROM BETWEEN THE BLANKETS FORCE YER,

UPSTAIRS AND COME TO ME -
FIRST ON THE LEFT, LHM-G'

'He was incredibly perceptive,' writes Vanessa Hawkings (née Gabriel, 1974–79) 'and spotted that I was a very nervous unsure eight-year-old who had made friends with the only girl in the form above. With characteristic kindness, he moved me up to be with my friend, and although I struggled with the work, I felt secure for the first time.'

Jeremy Carlisle remembers an eighth birthday present from Hal in July 1962: 'a pocket-sized drawing box. Miniature pencils, crayons, sharpener, eraser. All cut to size and carefully arranged in the box. How did he know I was going to make a career out of art?'

Oliver Jory (1976–77) recalls Hal's teaching: '"Perhaps there were lessons too?" asks Simon Williams, citing a long list of extra-curricular interests for which Cumnor was justly famous. Well, it is the lessons that I remember best, particularly the ones unique to Cumnor House. How many 11-year-olds today learn ancient Greek, or italic handwriting, or Roman history at 7.30 am in a French farmhouse? "Each of you is an expert," Hal Milner-Gulland assured the sea of blank faces before him. It was my first week at school. "Each an expert in one particular field." Intrigued, we looked around the room trying to imagine what. "H, he knows a good deal more than most of you ever will about pets; S is something of an authority on English hymns. And you, you are an expert on the French language." So that was it, the benefit of a bilingual upbringing. A year later I would have been happier to be recognised for my brass playing (continued to this day) or starring role in *The Two Gentlemen of Verona* (the zenith of a lamentably undistinguished stage career). Hal though proved more insightful: 15 years later I was chasing French clients of a major investment bank for a living.' Oliver's father Gerald admits that it was against the inclinations of his French wife that Oliver should

OPPOSITE PAGE
A typical Hal jeu d'esprit: A1 test paper, 1966

board, but they were both delighted when he won the top scholarship to Westminster.

Robert Footman (1961–66) remembers 'one summer evening being woken to go to the stage, where LHM-G had prepared a terrific barbecue, with the most delicious sausages.' Elizabeth Maslen has happy memories of Hal's dealing with homesickness: 'There was Hal's magic touch when Jess was homesick on her first night: finding her in tears, he woke up her two brothers, bundled them all, in their pyjamas, into his car and drove to the local pub. There, in the car park, he treated them to soft drinks and crisps. There were no more tears after that, and there was always a sure sense that the headmaster was a fellow human being. Jess recalls how Hal, tired at the end of term, came to say goodbye to some little girls who were packing up their last things, fell asleep on one of the beds and was watched over solemnly by the girls, who sat quietly waiting for him to wake up.'

'One summer term,' Andrew McKenzie-Smith (1972–75) recalls, 'I was playing cricket during break time with Philip Artus and Tim Cashell, and I received a message to report to X in the Common Room. I went in fearing the worst, only to be told that I had been seen playing with a very straight bat! That summer all three of us made the 1st XI while still in the B form.'

But he could also be fierce. Matthew Williams (1968–72) remembers: 'He reduced me to tears after my first six-goal performance for the 1st XI when he took me to task for putting the c before the t in etc and suggesting – rather forcefully – that my extraordinary stupidity was the result of misplaced complacency brought on by my sporting success. But he could be kind and so could Mrs G. I knew that X knew that the ages of eight to nine were the best years of all because he told me and then commiserated sadly when I turned 10, making it clear that I had now embarked on a slippery slope with little if any hope of recapturing the halcyon days of

Hal and Nan

innocence. I doubt that X was ever motivated by money. He cared about knowledge, skill, the qualities of children, civilised behaviour, civilised activities and tastes, and he cared about doing things well. We all knew he had a broad view and that his basic premise was that this was available to all of us; we were never patronised.'

Richard Sinclair (1964–69) writes: 'Hal was quite a frightening figure but I enjoyed his art and pottery lessons very much. I do remember once inadvertently jabbing his hand with my pen while pointing at my work. He instantly jumped up and ran screaming out of the classroom. That left us all bewildered, not knowing what to do or what might happen next. Quite soon he was back, completely wrapped up in bandages around his head, shoulders and both arms. He then proceeded to take the rest of the lesson dressed up in this ludicrous attire. He might have been a figure of authority to us but he also knew how to create the absurd and enjoyed children's sense of humour and fun.'

Tyler Butterworth (1966–72) has similar memories of unpredictable buffoonery: 'It was a long, hot, lazy summer term. Rehearsals for the play were underway, and as would occasionally be the case, our lesson was a little late in starting as X was having to make his way up from the stage. It was a French class, and we were to be tested on our verbs. I was nervous; I wasn't good at French verbs. Suddenly, accompanied by the customary waft of Hamlet cigars, the door swung open, and X's familiar, slightly stooped figure came round the door topped with the largest backcombed, brassy blonde wig I'd ever seen. It was a monstrous confection of shocking nylon, it went off in every direction like a giant Roman candle. He walked quickly and quietly to his table and settled down. We were stunned. Our headmaster had wandered into class looking like Diana Dors after a bad weekend and we weren't expected to notice? Should one of us draw his attention to the stork's nest on his head, in case he

didn't know it was there? Only a complete fool would open his mouth and tackle the subject. "Sir …" I heard myself say. X looked up, his face stony. He raised just the end of an eyebrow. "Sir – about – er – the verb parler …". I fizzled out, I lost my nerve. The wig had won. Eventually the lesson ended; he collected his books and strode out with his usual elegance topped by his backcombed, brassy blonde wig. He never mentioned the wig, ever. It was a professional performance. Pure X.'

In the 1950s Nick Humphrey (1952–56) found his discipline perplexing: 'Experimental homosexuality was rife among the boys – and I'm sure harmless, at least when it was just between us little boys. LHM-G, when every now and again he caught wind of it, came down in a rather heavy-handed way, threatening us with the slipper and possible expulsion. But LHM-G's methods in general were definitely old-fashioned. When some boys were found smoking, he locked them in a small room where they were obliged to smoke cigars and cigarettes until they were sick. I was often in trouble over food. I got beaten on one occasion for not eating my fish, and beaten on another for taking an extra banana. I well remember LHM-G's jingle at Boarders' Feast: "No more Turner, no more Krish, no more fussing over Humphrey's fish", and then to rub the point in "No more Bottom, no more Quince, no more fussing over Humphrey's mince". Funny, only up to a point. He didn't know how I would long to get a letter from my parents, so that at breakfast I would have an envelope in which to hide and remove the rancid margarine. Still, the bottom line for me was that I knew Mr Gulland loved me. He – and Nancy and Mr Straker – made those years at Cumnor House in many ways the best years of my life. I was greatly privileged to have been in the care of such an extraordinary teacher and role model. He even once, in 1955, took me and Simon Barnetson on a bicycle trip to Rouen. I remember staying in the Hotel de la rue du Gros Horloge, and after breakfast practising our Greek unseens at the café table (to the maître's amazement). Who nowadays gets any such chance?'

Philip Snow (1961–65) wrote about 'the way X used to enter the classroom and open the lesson with some outrageously irrelevant question ("Which barbarian leader overthrew the last Western Roman Emperor?"). He had the most extraordinary gift of arousing one's curiosity and reminding one that the oblique approach to life is often the most rewarding.' David Duvall thought that 'he could teach anything and make it fascinating: there was one morning when the arrival of Dr Sibley in his Standard Vanguard led to a lesson on Roman battle formation.' Stephen White, aged 13, recalled: 'If there is a Latin lesson, there is no guarantee that we shall be taught Latin. X may get carried away into the Common Market, Communism, history or geography. "Did you know that America receives the largest amount of immigrants a year?" he might begin a lesson. Or through the Latin lesson, into Chaucer and Bunyan, Thackeray and Dickens. "When did Dickens die, I can't remember?"'

Holly Robinson, secretary, who ran the 'shopping list', was amused to receive this spoof request from Hal for a notoriously unpunctual member of staff

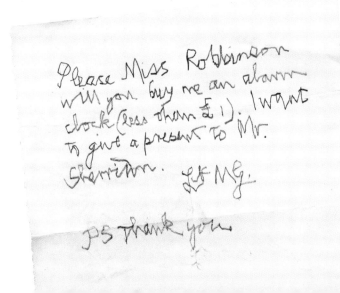

Approachability was one of Hal's characteristics. Sarah Reardon, as a new girl aged eight, told her father Martin, 'He is so interesting and easy to talk to. He doesn't talk like other grown-ups. He talks about what I'm interested in.' Graham Butler, father of Nicholas and David, wrote: 'I still remember distinctly my first visit to Cumnor. Hal was standing in the drive. I thought that he couldn't be the headmaster because the boys were going up to talk to him – unheard of when I was that age. Hal wasn't very interested in Sheila or me, just in Nicholas. We didn't bother to look at any other schools.'

After he retired from the joint headmastership he continued to teach a little and to help with the plays. Ione Meyer recalls: 'A favourite place was the Pink House, where we would visit X. There we would rehearse parts of the summer play, receive his wise tutelage in French or Latin and sometimes come out richer with a few words of advice on learning: "Writing a sentence down is like reading it twice." A smell of polos, which he always had handy as well as house points to reward eager students, hung around him. We were always eager to learn; those horrible words "geek" or "boffin" had not yet invaded the student's vocabulary.'

Janet Canetty-Clarke, music teacher from 1966–75, remembers Hal's deafness: 'Dear Hal would often sit in a big comfortable chair at the back of the library, reading his newspaper, while I battled beside him with class recorder lessons. What true devotion to music, I thought, and I mentioned this to the boys afterwards. "Not really," came the reply; "haven't you noticed, X always turns off his hearing aid the moment we start blowing!"' Rhoddy Voremberg recalls how Hal's cigars 'not only provided generations of Cumnorians with pencil boxes, but also enabled him to be tracked around the school.'

He also wrote a series of home-produced books: Simon Williams (1956–60) remembers what a privilege it was 'to be given one of those meticulously made little volumes of useful Latin phrases (I've never had any trouble with my ramparts or my cohorts).' Though Hal encouraged all pupils to aim for excellence, he was concerned with every pupil, not just the brightest; indeed he was fond of quoting Van Gogh's dictum: 'One must begin by having some respect for the mediocre – it is only reached by great effort.'

Combalou

In 1963, after their sabbatical term in the Dordogne, Hal and Nan bought Le Combalou, a small and picturesque farmhouse near Montignac where for more than three decades they spent as much time as they could spare. They loved the house dearly: above the fireplace Hal inscribed these lines from Horace:

ILLE TERRARUM MIHI PRAETER OMNES
ANGULUS RIDET
(This corner of the world smiles for me more than any other)

Le Combalou, 1977: Oliver Jory, Herman Siemens, Tim Cashell, Philip Stedman, Philip Artus, with Nan and Mlle Marie-Patricia Demoulins de Rochefort

A House in Périgord

Dick White wrote about Combalou:

Lucky that Combalou has found a friend
In Scottish Hal;
Ten years ago he found this little house
Sad only to be empty,
Bought it with fifty hectares of land
And made a second home in Périgord.
And now we could imagine Combalou
Filled by the interests of our two friends,
Who every springtime bring their scholars here
To study Classics in their final year.
Children on holiday, to study … Greek!
It sounds a contradiction, yet I speak
Of things that I have heard from my own son.
Perhaps there clings about this country place
The airs and echoes of an antique grace;
I only know young scholars seem to thrive
Where it is such a joy to be alive,
And revel in those pleasures we could see
Belonging to a cheerful company:
The children in the kitchen crush for food
By talk and laughter all the more enjoyed,
Excited to be there, a strange new sense
Attaching to the French experience;
Or off on expeditions with their lunch
To eat upon a willow patterned bank;
Then lying in long grasses in the sun
Simple and silly in the afternoon,
Till prehistoric caves arouse their zest
And painted animals their interest,
Ancestral hunting scenes that make you see
And feel the shock of great antiquity.
Then home again to country food and wine,
An evening gossip underneath the vine,
A game of chess until it's time for bed
And happiness dissolves each tired head.

Thus we imagined life at Combalou,
The empty house re-peopled by our friends,
A life of zest and schoolboy sentiment
Where all are learners, yet are all content;
A new and most enlightened kind of school
Where age presides and no-one needs to rule.

Above left: Reading Party in the Dordogne, 1963. Left to right, Richard Rees, Christopher Dewing, Sebastian Tombs, Mark Wilson, Peter Argles

Above: Helping to repair the roof of Valojoulx church

They were attracted by the prehistoric caves, the gastronomy, the churches, the countryside, the language and the people; and Hal got to know the novels of Eugène le Roy, the Périgordin Thomas Hardy, several of whose works he translated. It was his translation of *Jacquou le Croquant*, at a time when it was being serialised on French TV, that earned him the award of La Médaille Eugène le Roy 1974, presented at a huge banquet with all due ceremony and much cordial speech-making. It saddened him that he never succeeded in finding a publisher for *Jacquou*.

For many years Hal and Nan ran Easter holiday reading parties at Le Combalou for prospective scholars, and over the years about a hundred boys must have benefited from these. They tended to work in the morning and visit a cave in the afternoon, as well as attempt some French with the neighbours; one year a group helped a local workman to repair the terrifyingly steep stone roof of the village church.

Nan

Nan's interests were many and diverse, and mostly complementary to Hal's. David Duvall writes: 'Her swan swam perhaps less serenely than his, but still confidently, and confidence-inspiringly, whatever might have been going on beneath the surface. And her real affection for the boys matched his, as did ours for her.' When Hal once asked her if she thought they were too arty-crafty, she replied: 'Yes, you're arty and I'm crafty.'

Out of school she was much involved in the WI, where she rose to be County Vice-Chairman, and in education, being a governor of several schools and colleges. Hal used to say that she was the educationalist, he a mere teacher. In the school she was closely involved in the welfare of every child and communication with parents; she oversaw the matrons, gardeners and kitchen staff. In 1980, with the gardener, John Bartlett, she provided in the kitchen garden a 'vegetable sanctuary' to help preserve varieties of vegetable threatened with extinction, in

Katie Stewart with her son Andrew Leask

association with the Henry Doubleday Research Association. She also acted as part-time bursar, which normally meant a few scribbles on the back of an envelope on a Sunday evening. In a speech to the Boarding Schools Association in 1977 she spoke of her 'consistent, obstinate – well, even aggressive – stand as a buffer between the male chauvinists, who are normally in the majority on the staff of a boys' school and who seek to dominate what they regard as their domain, and the female element, without whom the whole place would instantly collapse in ruins.'

Katie Stewart recalls: 'When I was a parent in the 1970s I was working as food correspondent for *The Times*. Nan always took a keen interest in my recipe columns. One of her favourites was chicken paprika and another the lemon sorbet. Nan always had a stream of visitors at the Pink House; I know that my recipes were cooked up many times and maybe in a small way I helped smooth things along!'

Nan chaired the very popular Discussion Group, which Charles Snow likened to 'going into the Savile Club'; his son Philip remembers that 'Nan sometimes chose recondite subjects for Discussion Group – Retail Price Maintenance wasn't an easy one for a 10-year-old. I was always attracted by her mildly radical politics and her abiding social concern.' Jeremy Carlisle found these sessions rather terrifying: nothing was left unchallenged, unquestioned. Nan herself described what went on: 'They sit or sprawl on my drawing room chairs or carpet, about 10 or 12 of them, eating Rowntrees fruit pastilles. I have heard more home truths in these hour-long sessions than at any other time, and we discuss everything from nuclear fission to the best way of doling out sweets after lunch. On one occasion everyone was giving his opinion as to whether he was more encouraged to work hard by praise or by blame. An absent-minded type called Henry was, as usual, staring into the middle distance. When his turn arrived, I asked "How about you,

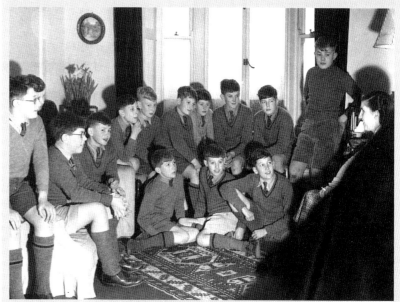

Above: Discussion Group with Nan, 1951

Left: Nan at the 21st anniversary dinner at the Hyde Park Hotel, April 1952

117

Simon Williams
with Hal, above,
and below, at the
CHS May Ball,
1988

Henry?" "Oh," he replied, "when a master criticises me I just think he's mistaken." Lucky boy! – and this enviable, if somewhat arrogant, philosophy probably helped earn him his subsequent scholarship.'

Piers Morgan has strong memories of the Discussion Groups: 'They were endless heated debates with the likes of Quentin Curtis, James Lovegrove and Matt Byam Shaw, perfect practice for *Question Time* with William Hague, George Osborne and others; Nan was of course the David Dimbleby, teaching us to speak our minds, have opinions, not to be afraid to change our view and always to be courteous in battle – very wise advice that I have always tried to follow, though not without difficulty. Those Discussion Groups were free-spirited, energetic, dynamic, occasionally furious, always great fun, and they had a huge effect on me.'

Simon Williams, who in later years became one of Nan's dearest friends, as a boy found her alarming. This is how he recalled her at the commemoration of her life: 'Hal was always a piece of cake: in the event of a transgression he would simply register a terrible sadness. He would open his mouth to speak … and then close it again with a pained world-weary disappointment in one's fallibility. But not so Nan. If we were sent up to the drawing room for a dressing down our fervent prayer would always be "please let it not be Mrs X".

'It was from her we learnt an early definition of what "rhetorical" meant. There you'd be in the Monkey tree reading a comic, say, and eating a bar of illicit chocolate and out of a cloudless sky you'd hear that most dreaded of questions: "What do you think you are doing?" As if there was some difference between what one was actually doing and what one imagined one was doing. She was scary. Picture Nan's silhouette in the doorway of the dorm interrupting a perfectly planned midnight feast (at about 8.15) – that was scary. Sensing Nan standing behind you as you struggled with the cold roast beef at Monday lunch. "Is there something wrong with it, Simon?" My alter ego answers, "You mean apart from the fat and the gristle, Mrs Gulland?" The real me says "No, Mrs Gulland – it's lovely." Imagine hearing the sound of the dreaded wooden-framed Nanmobile, screeching through the gravel to catch you and your gang looking for newts in the pond – during "Rest" and in "the wrong trousers" – that was to know real fear.

'When I announced that I wanted to withdraw from the cubs because the knots were just too irritating it was suggested that as an alternative I could spend the time weeding the terrace under Nan's supervision. I was back the next week working away at my half clove hitch as if my life depended on it. She was canny too. When it became clear that there was no way I would get into Harrow on academic grounds I suspect it was Nan who dreamed up the scheme to get me in on a sporting ticket. There were only two football teams at Cumnor in those days but for one match only they created a third football XI and made me captain of it. We had one fixture against Temple Grove and won it 9–0. My prospective housemaster was subsequently thrilled to read Hal's character reference of me, especially its mention that "Simon had captained an unbeaten school football team."'

When Anna and I moved into the Pink House in 1984, Nan and Hal moved to Park Cottage, from where they continued to take a close interest in everything that went on at Cumnor. Though the school became very different from the one they had run, they understood the reasons for change and were always supportive. The only event that Nan refused to attend – indeed, even refer to – was the opening of the Sports Hall in 1984, taking up as it did half of her beloved kitchen garden. They came to every play, after which Hal would (for a few years at least) send me copious notes about how it might have been done differently. Hal made a series of hilarious speeches at the annual Cumnor House Dinners held in the Barn, revealing his masterly

acting skills, particularly in timing. He also designed the CHS logo, used to this day, and the attractive medallions which are given out as prizes on Sports Day. Hal died in 1994, and Nan in 2005.

Anna

Anna Froud joined the staff in January 1973, and her mother Barbara describes the curious but lucky chain of events which brought her to Cumnor: 'Just before Christmas 1972, Anna came home from Madagascar. She had been teaching as a Quaker volunteer at the FJKM, a protestant school, and had chosen a troubled time to work there. The Malagasy people were restless under the pro-French administration and student riots had led to their imprisonment and the withdrawal of the volunteer teachers from the schools. Luckily she was soon befriended by Alfred Vestring, the German ambassador, and taught his three children. But this was a temporary respite and she had to come home. I remember her disgust at the Christmas shoppers in Chichester after the simplicity of her life in Ambatomanga. She had bequeathed most of her clothes and possessions to her friends and brought home raffia cloth, drawings, simple toys and embroidery made by her pupils. On her return she was hoping to find a teaching post in one of the underprivileged areas in the East End.

'In her impatience to start teaching, she saw an advertisement in the *Times Educational Supplement* and applied for a post at Cumnor. Not the type of teaching that she had in mind, but she discovered

Hal at the CHS
Dinner, 1985

Nick and Anna at the wedding of Joumana Es-said, Lebanon, 1999

very quickly that children in the Sussex prep school needed her too, and for the next 18 months she was happy again, but always with the prospect of going back to her dear friends in Madagascar. And so it was that with an air ticket for Madagascar in her handbag, she suddenly realised as we drove home from leaving Cumnor that it was there her heart truly belonged. Thus began what Leo Wynne once described as her "roller-coaster life with Nick", until she left Cumnor 28 years later.'

Later Anna admitted that she had never planned to stay more than a term, and that the job at Cumnor would do until she found a proper post in a deprived inner-city school, or else was able to return to Madagascar. Leo Wynne claimed to remember that Anna 'used to walk up and down behind the parents on Sports Day watching them all and muttering to herself "This is a disgrace – all these privileged people", and as Nick was speaking to the parents she would be muttering "Absolute rubbish!"'

Certainly I remember her expressing a proper Quaker indignation at my inviting a naval officer to talk to the school about careers in the Navy. When

Anna retired (finally!) from Cumnor in 2001, Leo spoke at her leaving party: 'The roller-coaster started when she married the headmaster, founded the pre-prep, brought up three children of her own and the dozens of others entrusted to her care, and played her crucial part in making this brilliant school. Of course we all know that the greatest people in history are all teachers. Anselm was a teacher. When he was made Archbishop of Canterbury by the worst king England ever had, William Rufus, he was honoured but refused; he had to be dragged up the nave of Canterbury Cathedral to be consecrated. He did not want to be yoked to that fierce young bull – the king. It was a bit like that with Anna when she was proposed to by Nick. She was honoured but she disapproved of herself. She's a rebel, a Quaker at heart, won't doff her hat to anybody. The Mother Theresa in her wanted to go back to teaching those really deprived, who didn't have shoes or glass in their windows, had dust for their floors, no books, no television. She wanted her pupils in her beloved Madagascar. She did not want to marry the head of a smart school for a privileged élite in Sussex.'

Nevertheless we were married in the Friends' Meeting House in Chichester in November 1975. For the next quarter-century Anna was to be as essential to me at Cumnor as Nan had been to Hal. Kate was born in 1977, Jamie in 1979 and Toby in 1986. Paula Arkley (staff, 1977–85) remembers 'the day Kate Milner-Gulland was born. School was closed for the afternoon and we all moved out onto Ashdown Forest for jollity and celebration! Bonfires, barbecues and fun. To me now, as a head myself, that highlights the gap between life at CHS then and school life today. Now my staff worry about fitting everything in if they deviate from their plans for even one lesson!'

Rosalie Challis (Wood) remembers Anna as 'the epitome of calm, practical, level-headed, often amused interaction with all ages and all personalities around her – fussing mothers, boys in a scrap, sulking girls, temperamental toddlers, owners of badly parked cars, overplayful dogs, etc etc.'

David Anderson, retired headmaster of Pridwin School, Johannesburg, remembers his first visit in the mid-1980s: 'The one enduring picture I have of Anna is of her organising and serving meals in the CHS kitchen and dining room. Unflappable, incredibly busy, ever-cheerful – and producing a jolly good meal! She was the epitome of what a head-master's wife should be – a Jack (or should it be Jill?)-of-all-trades – friendly, caring, yet with a no-nonsense approach when required, totally supportive and having that unique Cumnor House welcoming warmth.'

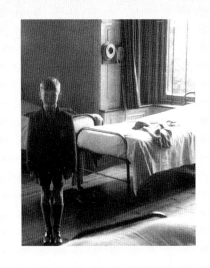

CHAPTER 9

HOME FROM HOME?

Robert Saunders reads
The Eagle as he waits for
the school train,
September 1953

Like a winged seed loosened from its parent stem

C DAY LEWIS, *WALKING AWAY*

OPPOSITE PAGE

Above left: David
Mullins in his
dormitory, 1966.
Note iron bedsteads
and Davey fire escape

Left: End of term

In the wake of the student upheavals and unrest of 1968 new attitudes to boarding began to emerge. Maybe, parents thought, the continentals are right, and boarding really does produce emotionally stunted and deprived adults? Should we allow schools to usurp the parents' role? Should my child be subjected to possible misery, bullying, heartiness, conformity, unthinking obedience, homosexuality, obsession with rules? Is it right that for 36 weeks in the year children should be removed from their families and be under the complete control of others, however benevolent? Is it healthy that an Old Cumnorian, for instance, should remember Hal as 'possibly the most formative influence on my life'? Even if such a system may have suited the days of Empire, is it necessary or desirable today?

These were serious concerns, and at Cumnor we were not unusual in experiencing a slackening of demand for boarding and a sharp increase in demand for day places. All over the country, boarding school heads were asking themselves where they were going wrong. Perhaps conditions were too spartan. Perhaps punishments were too harsh. Perhaps scarce resources should be allocated to advertising – anathema to a previous generation, and until recently banned by IAPS, the prep schools' organisation, but now vigorously promoted. Perhaps alternative sources of boarders (Hong Kong? Thailand?) should be explored. In the past, boarding need had been clear-cut: in 1939 it was because of evacuation; after the war many parents worked overseas, a number in the Services or the Foreign Office, where local schooling was unavailable or inadequate; others felt

that boarding school, though tough, was character-building. Now, a new role for boarding was needed.

One cannot pretend that boarders were happy all the time. Ronnie Pilbeam (1954–58) described in 1958 the bewilderment of the young boarder: 'I arrived in the school bus, deciding to go and see the "headmaster" at once. When everyone had got off, I was still sitting in my seat, taking stock of my surroundings. I descended and looked dolefully around. A rosy cheeked boy came up to me and announced that he was Hunter, and presuming that I was R J Pilbeam, was going to look after me. He took me up to the dormitory and told me to deposit my case, and took me down to the form room, where he explained to me about house points. Just then up storked a big chap who asked me, "Who's your house captain?" I had been told but could only remember that it began with an M, and said so. He said that he was my house captain. I only found out his name four days later. When, after tea, we were read to, I was staring round the room, until we went to bed, not listening to the story whatsoever.'

Stephen White expresses his first impressions as an eight-year-old boarder in 1961: 'As we came down the drive, I saw cars, with myriads of people getting out of them, people running, shouting, jumping. It was all so bewildering. I walked into the hall. It was too large; everything was larger than it had been before. They were all looking at me – the new boy. I went to see my dormitory with my mother. It seemed agreeable enough, perhaps a little too prison-like, with black iron bars on the beds: I was very fussy about rooms I had to live in.'

Patrick Sherlock (1968–73), although his brother and sister were happy boarding, and although he wept inconsolably on leaving, expresses his misery more forcefully: 'Alas, my memories of Cumnor are not, overall, happy ones. I can vividly remember arriving very early for my first day at school and looking up at this imposing brick building. I thought, "Oh, no – I have been sent to prison." On going inside I saw some boards on a wall with people's names on them, and, instinctively, I knew I would never appear on one of them. I was correct. Cumnor is miles from my then home (Islington, North London) and I knew nobody there. Various members of staff that I thought were Patrick-friendly all left after a short time – people like Patrick Proffitt, Holly Robinson and David Bond. I spent two years in D form coming last or second-to-last in virtually everything. Julian Cornwell was a chap, like me, who rarely got hps and trying to beat him provided a sort of a challenge. Unfortunately, he too left after a while. Being happy is what a lot of contemporary Cumnorians seem to remember about me, which doesn't really ring true. When I left in July 1973, I cried quite a bit as the coach left the school – which is something I shall never forget. After all, how could I be so unhappy at leaving a place where I had so many miserable memories?'

In 1979 a nine-year-old said of his parents: 'I've forgotten what they look like, but I remember the car.' Christopher Winnington-Ingram, aged eight, was not happy with the school meals: 'In the Dinning room there is a defening sound, knapton's

Little boys' dormitory, 1953

manners are disgraceful he puts his knif in his mouth.' E J Milner-Gulland (1975–79) remembers 'tomato soup and cornflakes for our first tea after the parents went – the taste of desolation.'

So much for the negative side; but it was much outweighed by the positive. For example, John Turner has rosy memories of boarding in 1947: 'I think I had just turned seven – maybe I was six – when I first became a boarder. People are horrified when I tell them that I boarded at that age – and then I find out that they have few happy memories of their early schooldays. Conversely mine are of an almost mystical experience – due entirely to the culture of the school created by Hal, Nan and the staff they chose. I found a letter amongst my mother's papers (written at the end of my first week at Birch Grove) in which I pleaded for her to take me away – but that 'misery' was quickly replaced in

Eightsome Reel with Jack Straker, 1951. In front of Jack is Rod Meikle, then (clockwise) Charles Metherell, Nigel Stainforth setting to Ian Frazer, John Dutton, David Wright, Graham Hornett, Ian Smith

subsequent missives by an evident feeling of well-being. She too had chosen with foresight.'

A little later Simon Williams has happy memories: 'Nowadays people suck their teeth at the idea of eight-year-olds being sent to boarding schools, but to us baby-boomers Cumnor House wasn't Colditz, say rather Butlins – it was the place you could get everything done: unharried by testy parents you could get on with your model plane, your hamster, your patch of garden, the Tarzan rope, marbles, your trombone, conkers, highland dancing, your part in *The Tempest* – perhaps there were lessons too.'

Later still Emma Pinkerton (1983–89) remembers the family feeling: 'What was it about Cumnor that made it so special? For me I think it was the feeling of being part of a huge extended family, and that was very special. What do I remember most? Probably the things that other people can't believe, at least not from someone who went to boarding school in the 1980s (rather than some time in the 1940s!): sharing baths and flooding the bathrooms; sitting in the old library in our dressing gowns and pyjamas while NG read *The Wind in the Willows* (with sound effects) to us all; midnight swims; building dams in streams and rafts on the old swimming pool; feeling part of something; the friends I made.'

And Roger Charlesworth (1951–59), aged seven, enjoyed the end of term festivities:

Bordse Fest

On bords Feast in the wnter in the arfnoun wc had games in C Form with Mess Tisington and ferst we had muskol bumps. After the gams we went to woshed and sat down in oure clars room. Wen we wer told we went to have a goud big tea. After we hade the prisis the sheld went to the blue House. Then we had cundring by the boys and at the end we saw a rabit then we had a sig sog.

David Guilfoyle writes: 'I have just recalled something that happened on the last day of one

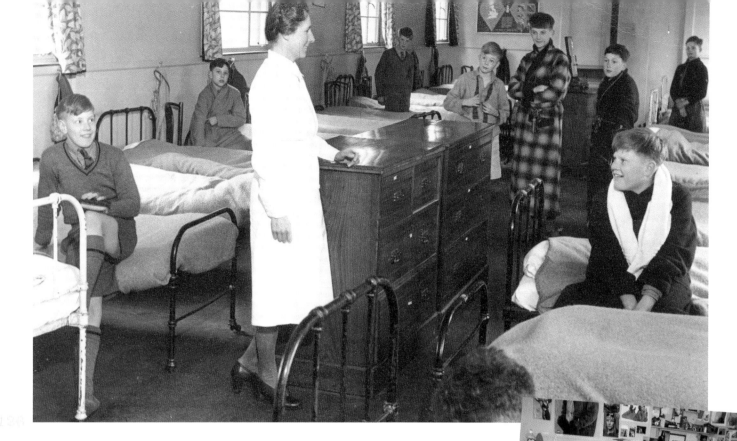

summer holidays. We were all gathered in the kitchen sorting things out when our daughter said, "Oh good, I'm going home tomorrow." Maureen and I burst out laughing. It was good to know that she regarded Cumnor as a home from home.'

Una Dean, mother of Peter and John, both of whom boarded, writes: 'I don't know what makes today's parents tick. I think most of them can't bear the thought that their children may have to board. I don't think Geoffrey would have survived if the boys had been at day-school.' And Ben Bray, as a seven-year-old boarder in 1981, remarked during his first home weekend: 'Since I've been boarding, Mummy, *you* seem so much nicer!'

Anne Morpeth writes about her grandson: 'Andrew recalls initially distinguishing himself by being the youngest boy to get the furthest distance from school without the use of public transport when he ran away in his second term – a record he believes may stand to this day. Andrew's calligraphy career was short-lived when X spotted him flicking ink at a classmate (in retaliation, he assures us). The strangely obligatory Morpeth brush with expulsion at Cumnor had its beneficial effect as Andrew

became head boy four years later. He tells us that industrial quantities of polo mints played a part in his rehabilitation.'

At Cumnor, as elsewhere, we needed to think very carefully about who our future pupils were to be and what sort of school we wanted to run. I made two rather unsuccessful overseas recruiting trips, but my heart was not in them, and more and more I came to believe that, much as we welcomed pupils from abroad, the main raison d'être of an English school must be to serve a largely home-based clientèle, which tended to travel by car. If this meant more day children, the school would need to expand in order to balance the books; and we recognised the probability that traditional parents seeking boarding at eight would look elsewhere. Indeed the dwindling number of eight-year-old boarders tended from now on to be sent to the few all-boarding schools such as Ashdown House, Cottesmore and Windlesham House. I was however very anxious that boarding should continue at Cumnor: the timetable was built around it, the play

Top: Bleak House: Peggy Chard in the Red Dormitory, 1951

Above: Girls' dormitory, 1990-style. Left to right: Keira McColl, Amelia Stewart, Clare Straker

and evening occupations depended on it and the staff and I believed strongly in its value.

Gradually we found that parents wanted a longer period of day education, although they were happy for their children to board later, often for their final year before going on to board at their senior school. Thus the parent body became more local; fortnightly 'home weekends' and week-long exeats were introduced, which would never have been possible before, and parents became much more involved in the school. Although this was not always to their children's advantage, in general we welcomed parental interest, and a closer partnership developed between school and home. Regular parent evenings were started in 1977, and when the Barn was opened in 1980 parents were invited to a large number of concerts, talks, plays, quizzes, wine society meetings and parties,

including the annual CHS Dinners. At the same time there seemed to be more parents expecting instant access to me or to other members of staff. How different from the occasion that Clive Williams recalls at Ashdown House some years ago when a parent rang up and asked if he could speak to Billie Williamson, the headmaster. 'Certainly not!' said the headmaster's wife, slamming down the receiver.

With skiing trips and foreign sporting tours, which many parents joined, mothers' tennis mornings and, after the building of the Sports Hall, fathers' soccer evenings, the school seemed to have become the centre of a sort of social and sporting club. The important thing, as I saw it, was to ensure that this proliferation of activity did not deflect us from our primary responsibility of providing a first-rate education for our pupils.

Dads' Football

Richard Maxwell-Gumbleton writes about a popular activity: 'The sound of a football thumping against the wall of the Sports Hall late on any Tuesday night in the year does not mean there is an after lights out kickabout by the children. The reason for this is an institution called "Dads' Football", a weekly gathering that has been ongoing since September 1995. Having been beaten in the previous year in a match against the staff, the fathers decided some practice was needed when the September 1995 fixture was upon them. The resultant session in the Sports Hall was so enjoyed by one and all that arrangements were made to continue playing on a weekly basis. This has even developed into the Cumnor Dads playing matches not only against the staff but also against Brambletye Dads and Stoke Brunswick Dads. Still playing from the first gathering in September 1995 are David Clancy, Michael Johnstone and Richard Maxwell-Gumbleton. Other long-serving regulars include John Dyball, Hugh Johnson, Robin Pritchard, Peter Scaramanga and Robin Turner. A recent influx of younger fathers is helping to keep the ball rolling – long may it continue!'

Dads' football, 2006. Back row, left to right: Chris Goddard, Robin Turner, Jim Mann, John Dyball, Charles St John, Hugh Johnson. Front row: Simon Lloyd, Robin Pritchard, Richard Maxwell-Gumbleton, Cameron Hatrick, Richard Evans-Thomas

CHAPTER 10

OWNERS AT LAST

1975–89

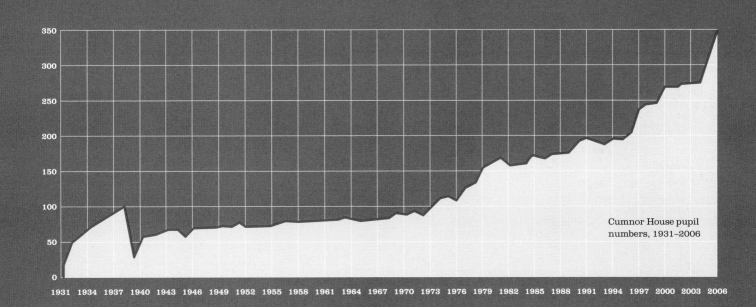

Cumnor House pupil numbers, 1931–2006

Enterprises of great pith and moment

SHAKESPEARE, *HAMLET*

When I took over as sole headmaster I had no idea that the next 15 years would bring such exhilarating and far-reaching development. I could see that numbers must increase as the balance of boarders to day pupils changed; I could see that new buildings were required but couldn't see how we could afford them; I was keen to develop coeducation, which had started well, but after four years there were still only 13 girls in a school of 109; the school was still running on a shoestring; and there was the niggling worry that in 1983 the lease would be coming up for renewal.

Out of the blue came two unexpected opportunities which were to give the school a security that it had never had before. Supported by a massive wave of generosity and benevolence from parents, friends and OCs, we at last bought the freehold in 1977 after numerous previous requests to do so had been turned down by the Macmillans; and in 1988 we became a charitable trust and bought the adjacent Woodgate Farm and the 50 acres surrounding the school. Roddy Gye, a governor since 1988 and Old Cumnorian (1960–64), explains with clarity and understanding these developments and the reasons behind them:

'It is said that between the wars there were more than 30 prep schools in Eastbourne along the sea front alone. Most were tiny, no more than private tutorial establishments run by couples in their own homes with a handful of boarders – and by today's standards most of them were pretty grim. And, of course, most of them disappeared. The picture was repeated around the country; most such schools

Sketch plan of a proposed 'Globe Theatre' for Cumnor House School,
drawn at balcony level.

Harley Sherlock's plan
for a Globe Theatre

aftermath, about which you will have read elsewhere in this book. 1950s Cumnor was, in business terms, not untypical: Hal Milner-Gulland was a proprietor headmaster; he and Nan ran it completely as a joint enterprise, really as an extension of their own family. And it ran on a shoestring. When I joined as a child in 1960 there were 74 boys and the fees had just risen, with sincere apologies from Hal, from £68 a term to a dizzy £72. By my calculations the school's annual turnover was slightly less than £16,000 a year (plus a few extras for those who wished to pay for an extra boiled egg or apple each week). Whilst staff salaries were modest, even accounting for inflation, it seems a remarkable feat that the school was able to exist on such a sum.

'But exist it did, and grew. Hal and then Nick made do and mended, so much so that in 1977 they were able to buy the freehold of the school from the Macmillan estate. Nick was by this stage the major shareholder, with a couple of trusted long-standing colleagues taking minority holdings. Leo Wynne, who had arrived in 1964 to teach English, became bursar and tackled the finances with a panache that left bank managers running for cover and, one suspects, Nick with a few sleepless nights. But between them their achievements were remarkable; pupil numbers grew and the premises gradually grew with them – an extension over what was known as the New Wing (currently the dining room) and a succession of prefabricated buildings often picked up by Leo for a song at some sale or other.

'As every Cumnorian knows, drama had a central place from the outset and the open air theatre, constructed soon after the school ended its wartime diaspora and the boarders finally settled at Woodgate House, was at its heart. But Hal had always hankered after an indoor theatre as well, and in the mid-1970s an ambitious plan emerged to build a miniature Globe theatre in the grounds. It was an exciting idea that fired everyone's imagination, and a sketch even appeared on the cover of the school magazine. But it

withered away, and a good thing too. But some didn't, and evolved into "proper" schools that flourished and grew, still under the ownership of their founders or their heirs.

'Some of the most enduring images of prep school life were forged in the 1950s, immortalised by two rather different schoolboy icons – Jennings and Molesworth. Linbury Court and, we assume, St Custard's had much in common with many real life schools; all-boys, all-boarding communities of some 70 or 80 souls run by a headmaster who was also its proprietor. They often had makeshift facilities, dedicated but generally unqualified teaching staff, and were run on vestigially militaristic lines which inmates would later recall either with a shudder or with nostalgia or, perversely, both.

'It was in this climate that Cumnor grew, from the peripatetic chaos of the war and its immediate

Above, the Barn at Horsted Keynes and, right,taking shape at Danehill, 1979

was far beyond the school's financial reach, and that was when the idea of the Barn Theatre was born. Martin Hilton, a parent, came up with the idea of buying a tumbledown barn in Horsted Keynes, dismantling it and re-erecting it at Cumnor as a theatre of real character. It was still financially well beyond the school's reach – the project would cost £50,000 – but it might, just might, be possible to fund it from an appeal.

'A firm that specialised in school fund-raising was approached, and after bringing the weight of their experience and expertise to bear on the problem announced that, for a school of this size, a realistic expectation would be about £10,000 – of which their fee would be £6,000. So Nick and his colleagues decided they could manage without outside assistance and, in what seemed like an astonishingly short time, raised £50,000 from Cumnor's generous community of parents, former pupils and friends. The Barn Theatre, designed by Old Cumnorian and former Cumnor parent Harley Sherlock, was opened in 1980

and quickly became a completely indispensable part of school life; indeed, it is difficult to understand quite how they managed without it before.

'An event in 1982 was arguably the catalyst for much of what was to happen in the development of Cumnor in the two decades that followed. Nick was awarded an English-Speaking Union scholarship which involved a month in the USA studying an educational topic of his choice. That his choice was drama was in some ways incidental, for he came back from a trip which took in a number of schools charged with fresh ideas about Cumnor's future direction. One idea common amongst American independent schools was a system of peer review, in which teachers from non-competing establishments would be invited to inspect each other's school. In Britain the Independent Schools' Inspectorate had yet to be invented.

'Nick asked three friends – two distinguished senior schoolmasters and one quite undistinguished Old Cumnorian – to spend two days in the school and to take it apart, leaving no teacher unmonitored, no meal untasted, no mattress unsqueezed, no cupboard unopened, no changing room unsniffed. It was a fascinating experience, and whilst the three of us met both with and without Nick, Anna and his colleagues, we were ultimately asked to submit three separate reports. I still have them. All three were overwhelmingly positive; it was clearly a fine school doing a fine job for its pupils. But we didn't pull our punches where we had concerns, and they were largely about the future.

'One weakness those reports identified was the shortage of indoor exercise space, and in a rapid reaction to our recommendations the school embarked on the construction of a new Sports Hall. That it was a huge asset immediately became clear. The one regret, particularly for Nan Milner-Gulland, was that it had to be built in the kitchen garden. Those of us who had spent balmy summer evenings as children podding peas on the terrace

might have had regrets too, but in truth home-grown vegetables had long ceased to make economic sense.

'Other small developments continued, but it was clear that Nick was starting to think about the much longer term. How was the school to survive and prosper in a changing economic and political climate? How could it improve its facilities to match parents' ever increasing expectations? And what was to happen when he retired? It's always fun to imagine that one was present at the very instant a momentous idea germinated. I have a clear memory of walking round the grounds with Nick, speculating on where and how the school buildings could be expanded. We stood and looked at the wall of the near derelict barn that marked the boundary with the tired dairy farm next door, and wondered whether it would be possible to buy or lease the barn or a bit of land. A year or so later the farmer finally retired; the milk quota was sold, and the Macmillan estate which owned the farm decided to dispose of it and the 50 acres or so of land attached. There was one small obstacle: £250,000.

'It was an opportunity that the school could not afford to miss. Equally, it was an opportunity the school on its own could emphatically not afford to seize. It became clear to Nick and Anna that now was the time to turn Cumnor into a charitable trust. It would bring a number of advantages, not least the tax benefits of charity status, all the more valuable during the inevitable appeal for funds. Whether at the outset Nick regarded the other major change as progress or a necessary evil is less clear: the need to create a board of trustees whose employee he would become. But at least he was able to invite friends whose opinions and expertise he valued to become trustees, no doubt crossing his fingers that their first decision would not be to hand him his P45.

'In 1989 Cumnor House School Trust Ltd was born, under the chairmanship of Hugh Bennett QC (later Sir Hugh). Nick and Anna ceded the school to the new trust on remarkably generous terms. Its first responsibility (apart from deciding to keep the headmaster on) was to oversee a hugely ambitious appeal, masterminded by Peter Wigan. He set about it with vigour, aided by a great outpouring of goodwill towards the school. We kept our emergency plan up our sleeves: if the appeal fell significantly short of our expectations (well, wildest dreams, really) we would sell the farmhouse and keep the rest. Of course, we needed far more than the quarter of a million for the farm and land; there was the small matter of converting what could be converted and flattening and rebuilding that which could not be reused.

The West Building before conversion ...

... and after

'Donations and covenants poured in, including several of five figures. Then, in a huge boost to the morale of all of us, Peter announced that a trust that administered the residue of a former girls' school in Lewes had given us £130,000. The science and computing block was named the Southover Manor Barn in grateful recognition, and a handsome plaque was designed for it by Michael Renton.

'During the decade that followed the Farm development was completed, step by step, helped by a well-supported top-up appeal. Two buildings, the North Block (classrooms) and the Music Block, were entirely new, replacing ruins that were not worth salvaging: these were opened in 1997 by the Rt Revd Michael Vickers OC, retired Bishop of Colchester.

Southover Manor Barn
before conversion ...

    ... and after

E Form (Reception)
classrooms

The Saga of Erik Nobeard, 1988

All the other buildings around the two quadrangles are in the most part original, with the conversions being expertly overseen by the architects Rod Whittaker, David Tetley and Gareth Wright.

'It would be idle to pretend that the Farm complex was the result of a clear vision in 1988. We didn't know how many pupils we would be catering for, how much we could afford, how parental demand would change. Rather, it evolved. The western quad has become the pre-prep. The building at the northern extremity of the original Cumnor site, which in the 1960s was the gym and the garage for Hal's vintage Rolls-Royce, later art room and pottery, ended up changing its aspect to become the southern component of that pre-prep quad. And in due course several generations of children have come to assume that the Farm site has been there since the beginning of time and it looks established and firmly part of the landscape.'

The Barn

Many kind people helped us to build the Barn, not only our extremely generous donors. Charles Snow spoke at the launch of the 1978 Appeal, memorably saying how much he disliked institutions, with the three exceptions of Christ's College Cambridge, Leicestershire CCC and Cumnor House School. The ever-generous Harley Sherlock not only refused any payment for his designs for the Barn, but also donated the gallery when it looked as if we might have to save money by leaving it out. Roddy Gye produced the appeal brochure. Katie Stewart edited *Cumnor Cooks*, a book of recipes by friends and parents. Ann Lock masterminded the appeal with great determination and efficiency. Richard Lewis (tenor) and his wife Elizabeth (contralto) generously put on a fund-raising concert. John Hubbard designed and gave the weathervane showing a group of musicians with me on the

Mak the Sheep Stealer, by Herbert Chappell, 1980. Principals, left to right: Jeremy Goulden, Elizabeth Ibbott, Andrew Mitchell, Edmund Price, James Edsberg

Dragon Scales, 1984: an illustration by the author, Robert Maslen

harpsichord. Finally Dame Margery Corbett Ashby, aged 99, who had been brought up at Woodgate, cut the ribbon in February 1980, as the culmination of three years' planning, fund-raising and building, which involved transporting the ancient wooden frame from the Western Hemisphere (Horsted Keynes) to the Eastern (Danehill). Of how many buildings can this be said?

There was an immediate burgeoning of concerts, operettas, exhibitions and parties, for which the Barn proved an excellent and characterful venue. A series of annual joint orchestral days began with the orchestras of Brighton College JS, Great Walstead and Worth JS, for which we commissioned new compositions by William Godfree, Kenneth V Jones and Tony Smith-Masters. We had talks from the poets John Agard and Roger McGough, and workshops with the composer Paul Patterson and the trumpeter John Wilbraham; lectures by Paul Reid, author of *Colditz*, who allowed us to touch the very rubber that he had used to forge German passport stamps, and by Stephen Venables, mountaineer, who was soon to make history by being the first Briton to climb Everest without oxygen; recitals by Tamas Vasary, Adrian Thompson, Roger Vignoles, Elizabeth Bainbridge, John Dobson and John Hancorn; operas by Almaviva Opera; and much home-grown entertainment such as *Mak the Sheep Stealer*; in the presence of the composer Bert Chappell, *Dragon Scales*, a hilarious romp written for us by OC Robert Maslen, *The Demon of Adachigahara*, starring Francesca Faridany, and *Spell Me a Witch*, written for us by Barbara Willard with music by Tony Smith-Masters.

Woodgate Farm

Roddy Gye has explained the purchase of Woodgate Farm and the establishment of the trust in 1988. In announcing these plans to parents I said that the number of pupils would inevitably rise 'but only by 12 to 15'. May I be forgiven. Peter Wigan, who had arrived in 1978, immediately showed an extraordinary talent for fund-raising; I had thought that he was too nice, but I was delighted to be proved wrong. He supervised both phases of the appeal, for which he raised over three-quarters of a million pounds for the school.

The first trustees were Hugh Bennett (chairman), Richard Baldwin, Mary Flecker, Roddy Gye, Ann Longley, Alex Maitland Hudson and Martin Pavey. Hugh, knowing the school well as an old friend and father of four Cumnorians, as well as husband of our excellent secretary Liz, steered the trust with great sensitivity through its first five years, before being appointed a High Court Judge and handing over the chairmanship to Martin Pavey. Hugh's seven-year-old daughter Rosamond (1983–89) wrote about him in the 1983 magazine: 'My daddy has blackey browney hair he has blue eyes and he likes reading the newspaper and he is tall and he likes watching the newes and he likes brinking cider so he can stay asleep for a long time he goes to work in Chambers to get some money and he has got a very big room with too desks.'

By this time the job of bursar had become vastly more important, and Leo Wynne was as colourful in this role as he had been as a teacher of English. There had been a 37-fold increase in NI and PAYE contributions between 1962 and 1979, the payroll and turnover was much larger and there was ever more government intervention and legislation. In 1985, in an article titled 'A Bursar's Day', Leo wrote in his characteristically robust style about his job: 'I go into Prayers with the orchestra approaching the triumphant end of "Full in the Panting Heart of Rome" or is that the wrong sect? Anyway heads are

Leo Wynne

turning and there are smiles so they're obviously enjoying themselves. Prayers now, then the soloist. The melody is simple and pure. A lovely way to start the day. Like the juice of an orange at breakfast.

'Now I can see how we did last month. The meat bill is up a bit. We shouldn't really have had those nets for the Sports Hall. We should have waited. When interest rates are so high and inflation so low it pays to wait. But nobody can wait nowadays. All instant gratification. Anna breezes in. "We could all do with having a little less round here. We've all got far too much already." I long for Anna's cultural revolution. Does this mean we shouldn't have decided to have the nets after all?

'Mr Wynne, you're already late for our lesson. What, later than everybody else? Can't have these young people sitting on me. What's the lesson? Poetry. Got to be kind to the little darlings these days. Can't ask them to exert their blotting paper minds any more. Learn a poem? The mothers will be up in arms. What's all this silly nonsense? Anyway poetry should be fun, not hard work. Blake doesn't make sense and Chaucer's not even English, Yeats is just weird, maybe unhealthy. Poetry should be bouncy and rhyme…. My little darling has got to be bounced through his entire school, not come across anything real. Experience it all, even Belsen, through the soft and comforting flashes of the television screen. All life to be once removed … some children do have 'em. Don't seek out a real experience and explore it, and you won't have to learn; you'll pass by on the other side. But there are still some who observe with a striking clarity and use words with a lyrical beauty.

'The drive needs resurfacing. But the potholes slow people down, and nothing's uglier than a great slab of black. Looks bad, as if we don't care. But the cost is £9,000. Must we pay out huge amounts to please people whose priorities we may deplore? Yes, a stitch in time … let's compromise and wait a bit and see if we can do it ourselves at half the price. So arguments are not won or lost: they are resolved as events overtake them. We had no choice but to resurface the drive in the end and the leaves are covering its raw blackness this autumn. And we did it ourselves for half the price.

'Now my stint for the government. I spend a third of my day working out what to give the government or getting permission to have something done, often something which another government department has told me we have to do. I once had a fire escape we were ordered to build by the Fire Authority turned down by the Planning Authority. Concentrate instead on keeping the boat afloat. A bursar has to be a no man. There is no shortage of brilliant ideas on how to spend money we have not got. The best part of the job is when I act as "minder" and "fixer". I mind the buildings and the people and the money. I fix the finance and negotiate the prices for the big things. I enjoy the calculated risk. I enjoy planning and adjusting plans and seeing how it all pans out. But all independent schools are businesses however much some might dress themselves up as charities.

'But, of course, the best thing about the job remains the teaching, even after 20 something years.

Acting as amanuensis (and waste paper basket) for those fresh glimpses of the real world we adults have no time for. I'm not like St Paul; I never put away childish things. That's why I think it's worth keeping the old ship afloat.'

Academic

Meanwhile we were running a school, and I was anxious that so much change should not affect the way we operated. An Old Cumnorian, who was also a prospective parent, wrote to me saying 'Please, please, do not let size or ambition change the intimate specialness of Cumnor'; throughout this period I had this plea in the back of my mind. It was a great disappointment to me that we had to abandon Greek as a timetabled subject, not through lack of interest but because other subjects were clamouring for inclusion; furthermore we found that after two years of Greek at Cumnor pupils were often at a disadvantage at their senior schools, where they were frequently taught in a set of beginners. One subject I did introduce was 'I and You' (from Martin Buber's 'Ich und Du') for the A forms. I was keen to plug what I thought were several gaps in our curriculum, and wanted to cover such topics as relationships, sex education, parenthood, siblings, the police, courts, Civil Service, and national and local government, including much discussion. I suppose it was a combination of 'civics' and PSHE.

There was an obvious demand for an E form (pre-prep department), and this was started in a small way in 1977, with Caryl Fisher and Aileen Stevens in charge; within two years we were turning people away. Ann Thirkell, who taught the four-year-olds for many years, writes: 'My time in the pre-prep has rushed by, helped enormously by the endless fun, enthusiasm and loyalty shown by the staff, parents and of course the children. It was very liberating to join a two-class unit where I could arrange my own timetable, my own syllabus and my own way of teaching. In the summer it was

Opposite: Reading under the old oak

Aerial views of Cumnor House: Main image, *c.*1966, with groaning kitchen garden. Inset top, *c.* 1962; Pink House just built. Inset above, *c.* 1989; Woodgate Farm purchased but not yet converted. Right, *c.* 1998; farm buildings, except Hovels, completed

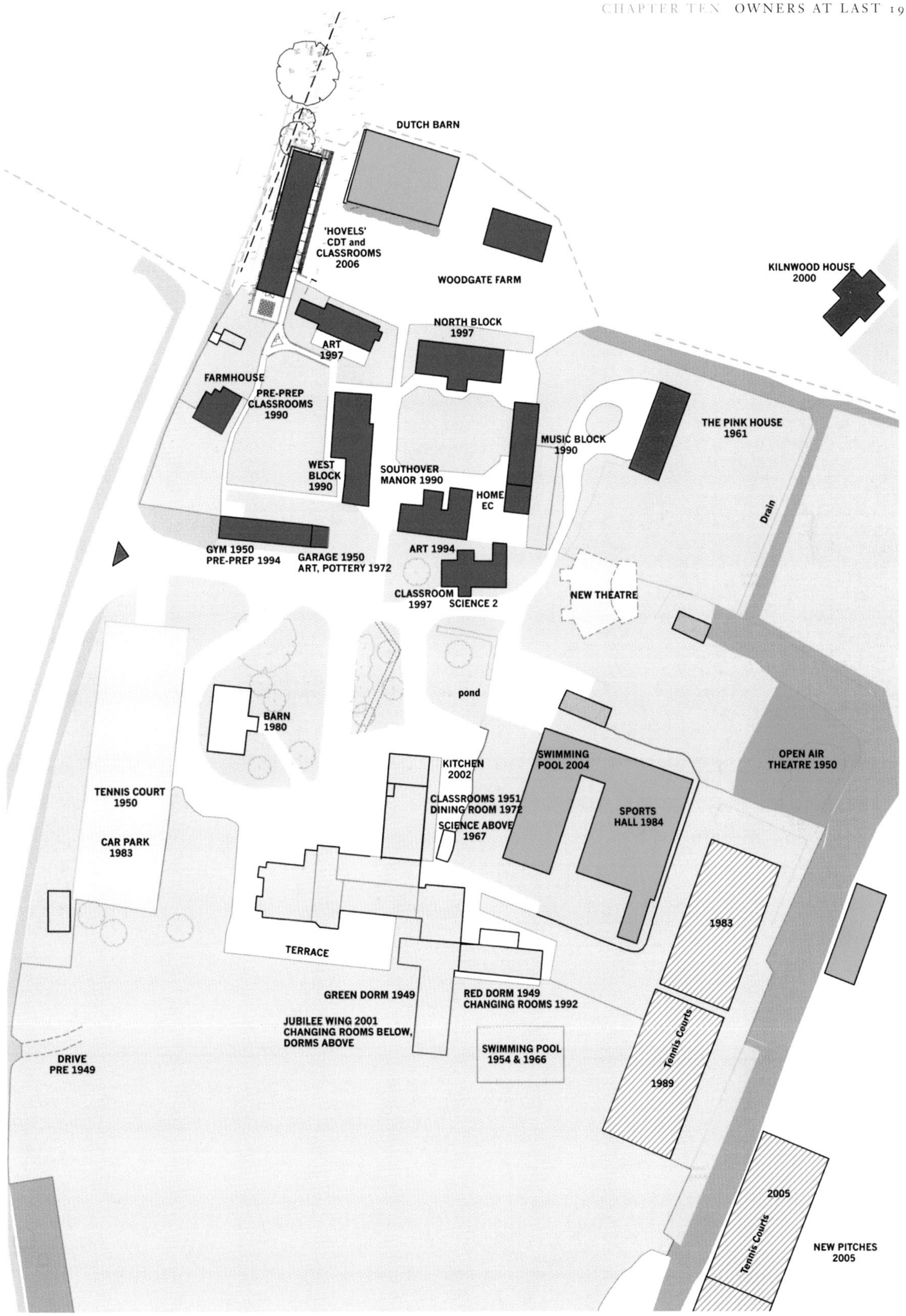

How the site has developed

DUTCH BARN

'HOVELS'
CDT and
CLASSROOMS
2006

WOODGATE FARM

KILNWOOD HOUSE
2000

NORTH BLOCK
1997

ART
1997

FARMHOUSE

PRE-PREP
CLASSROOMS
1990

THE PINK HOUSE
1961

MUSIC BLOCK
1990

WEST
BLOCK
1990

SOUTHOVER
MANOR 1990

HOME
EC

Drain

GYM 1950
PRE-PREP 1994

GARAGE 1950
ART, POTTERY 1972

ART 1994

CLASSROOM
1997   SCIENCE 2

NEW THEATRE

pond

BARN
1980

KITCHEN
2002

SWIMMING
POOL 2004

OPEN AIR
THEATRE 1950

TENNIS COURT
1950

CLASSROOMS 1951
DINING ROOM 1972
SCIENCE ABOVE
1967

SPORTS
HALL 1984

CAR PARK
1983

1983

TERRACE

GREEN DORM 1949

RED DORM 1949
CHANGING ROOMS 1992

Tennis Courts

JUBILEE WING 2001
CHANGING ROOMS BELOW,
DORMS ABOVE

SWIMMING POOL
1954 & 1966

1989

DRIVE
PRE 1949

2005

Tennis Courts

NEW PITCHES
2005

Above: Ben Holmes-
Attivor in home-made
coracle

Right: On the old
swimming pool

that often even the four- and five-year-olds would
accompany their parents to see the proper showing
in the evening, being allowed to bring sleeping bags
in which they could lie, warm and comfortable, in a
semicircle in front of the stage, absorbing the
atmosphere, the drama and the language. I think
they were referred to by William Nicholson as
"baglings". It was a wonderful introduction to live
theatre.'

By 1970 we were able to attract first-class
qualified staff, and no longer the oddities who
sometimes slipped through the net in previous years.
Gavin Tasker came in 1969; my niece E J Milner-
Gulland remembers 'his python and its untimely
death from cold when its lamp went off, and the

particularly joyous because we could move lessons
outside at will, making great use of the shaded area
by the little pond. Here we could have stories, poetry
and superb interactive nature lessons. Every year we
would have some frogspawn donated to us and
became expert at rearing it into tiny miniature frogs.
At this point we would float a ruler in the tank and
the children would rush in in the morning to see
how many froglets were sitting on it. When most of
the tadpoles had changed into frogs we would
release them into the little pond and the children
would watch fascinated as they swam vigorously
away to find a reed or leaf where they could land and
survey their new home. On subsequent visits they
would look out for the new residents and were
always certain that the little frog they saw was the
one that they personally had released.

'One event I looked forward to with great anticipation was the summer Shakespeare play. We used
to tell the pre-prep the story each year and often
produced a plethora of art work. Sometimes in good
weather Nick would invite us to come down to the
open air theatre with him to watch rehearsals. These
times were magic and Nick was very good at
explaining what was going on to the usually very
attentive audience. What was so good about this was

damp musty sandy smell in the dark pet room under
the science labs.' Nick Daniel (1976–81): 'Mr
Tasker's study was like a tropical rainforest, crawling
with plants and hazy with pipe smoke – condensa-
tion dripping from the windows, yellow and green

crawlers creeping over bookshelves piled heavy with books on Darwin and ecology. There were even orchids hanging in wooden pots above the sink. In the middle of this encroaching greenery, in a frayed armchair with a sunken seat, sat Mr Tasker, gently puffing pipe-smoke into the air and listening to Mozart with a faraway look in his eyes.'

Fiona Darroch arrived in 1974. E J remembers her 'speaking firmly about the evils of Enid Blyton, and banning her in D form – hence ensuring an avid underground fan club for her books.' Fiona herself remembers: 'I cared very intensely for the classes that I taught, in the D form (eight-year-olds). I have been told, in recent years, by some of my victims, that I was considered to be a stimulating teacher. But at the time, Leo kept asking me, whilst curling his lip, when I would be introducing them to Proust. I also failed to understand why, as the only history graduate in the place, I wasn't allowed to teach history to the A forms. Leo and I would share buckets of cheap whisky and packs of No 5 cigarettes over his big wicker basket, as we considered more and more exciting "occupations", and I negotiated budgets with him for such things as the Dark Room for photography and frontline cookery in the classroom. He was for everything, encouraging a limitless intellectual approach.

'After Prayers one day J lisped into my ear in the D Form: "B told us in the dorm last night that she had heard of a man whose penis stretched one and a half times round the room. Is that true?" This was at the start of a first-of-the-day maths lesson, so after some reflection I reprogrammed the lesson plan. I thought it would be awful if anyone would think in such predatory terms about a penis for one more hour. I spent the hours between prayers and break that day teaching "the facts of life" to the D form, having set out the terms for the class discussion. I imposed one condition: no sniggering, on pain of exile from the classroom. Only one person sniggered, and then successfully renegotiated

Gavin Tasker

his exile out of his desperation to stay in the discussion. Everyone got a good grounding on the issue, from a Christian perspective, but then J's mother (a member of staff) castigated me a few days later in the Common Room for even discussing the facts of life with J, which she said was her job. She was of course right, but I took the view that if she put her daughter in a dorm with B, then there would be consequences which she should have anticipated.'

Judith Miller, piano teacher at Cumnor since 1976, has a poignant memory: 'One little boy came in and said "Something very sad happened at half past four yesterday: my Grandpa died." Having said I was very sorry, we carried on with the lesson. As he was leaving, Tom said he was sorry his playing was not as good as it usually was but his heart was too full of sorrow. Quite profound from an eight-year-old.'

Tyler Butterworth was a pupil at Cumnor from 1969 to 1972, and joined the staff in 1977. Mike Mills came in 1976. Nick Daniel: 'There was the comic duo of Tyler Butterworth and Mike Mills. They were Little and Large, a Laurel and Hardy act, a Cumnor House Morecambe and Wise. In a classroom together they were unstoppable – hilarious, irreverent, gut-achingly funny. In the middle of a geography class, between tectonic plates and tidal waves, they would break into spontaneous acts of comic genius – imitating voices, dancing the tango, leaping onto tables or re-enacting Mr Milner-Gulland's sports day speeches.' Annabel Virtue recalls Tyler's 'class about the coffee bean. His drawings on the blackboard will stay with me for ever.' E J again: 'Mr Butterworth taught us everything there was to know about the Wash one term in geography, which was fascinating, and there was an extra frisson at the end of term when he said we'd learnt far too much by mistake and we should forget it. It was my best term of geography ever for that reason, and I still know more about the Wash than I ought.'

Mike Mills: 'In the summer of 1976, newly qualified as a teacher, I found that I did not, after all, have the teaching post with Humberside LEA that I thought I had. In a hurry for a job I was attracted by the prospect of working down south and saw, in the *TES*, that there was a need "at a sane Sussex prep school" for a teacher of French with boys' games. Never believing that any school would describe itself as sane, I applied to "The Headteacher, Cumnor House School, Sane, Sussex". The application (miraculously) got there. I (even more miraculously) got the job, stayed for two glorious years and made many friends in a school whose sanity still, for me, shines like a beacon in a mad, mad world.'

Jack Straker, who was running the Cumnorian Society, retired in 1979 and died in 1987; his old friend Bishop Mervyn Stockwood gave the tribute at his memorial service in Horsted Keynes Church. Meanwhile John Arkley had taken over the maths, having previously taught science. John himself recalls: 'They say that schooldays are the best days of your life. This is applicable not only to childhood: I came to CHS as an adult and I have many, many happy memories. There were some less-than-happy periods, but these were few and insignificant compared with the enjoyable times. The place was special. There was a lot of hard work but at the same time it was easy-going and relaxed.'

Left: Leo Wynne with Mike Mills behind, 1976

Below: Jack Straker

E J remembers 'feeling terribly sorry for Mr Arkley as he ate his veggie cutlets every night – always the same, always foul – almost (but not quite) enough to put you off being a vegetarian for life. There was also his fireworks display in our last chemistry lesson of term – particularly the volcano and setting fire to phosphorus – surely not allowed these days.' Julian Marsh (1980–84) recalls 'using an old tea chest to collect methane from the old swimming pool. This was part of a science experiment under Mr Arkley's guidance to demonstrate that decomposing material does in fact provide energy. We collected the gas in a glass beaker and then set fire to it later.' Sarah Jane Sherlock remembers: 'John Arkley taught me science, and he had a hard task of it. The only time I remember getting a half hp from him was when he decided to try to teach us thermodynamics. He began by asking if anyone in the class knew the First Law. To his surprise, I put up my hand and said "Heat is work and work is heat". When he said that was right, the whole class turned round and stared at me in astonishment. He then asked if I knew the Second Law. I thought I did, but was too embarrassed to say any more. What they didn't know was that I had recently become a Flanders and Swann fan.'

Penny Mussell arrived in 1982, and was still at Cumnor 24 years later. She has memories of her initial interview: 'These days finding a new member of staff involves a formal advertisement in *The Times Educational Supplement*, interview panels, sample lessons and demonstrations to show that the applicants have mastered technological teaching aids such as Smartboards. Twenty-four years ago my interview experience at Cumnor was a little different. Hidden amongst the advertisements for second-hand furniture and puppies in the local *Friday Ad* could be found: "Enthusiastic teacher for a class of 9- to 10-year-olds required. Must have good sense of humour". My interview – I use the word loosely – was more of an informal chat. Nick did put

in an appearance at one stage, but was rushing off to London, so my interview panel comprised Anna and the school cat which sat on my lap and assessed my pastoral care. Using the timetable as a guide, Anna then showed me around the school. She took me to several classrooms to show me lessons in action, but to her embarrassment most of the rooms were inexplicably empty. The teachers had obviously decided to make the most of the fine weather! Apologising profusely, she took me instead to the dormitories where, to her further embarrassment, we found a small boy hiding under a bed. He had hidden there when he heard us coming to avoid getting into trouble. A few kind words from Anna saw him quickly on his way to his next lesson.

'They say these things come in threes. As we walked through the area that is now the library, the handyman, George, was standing on a ladder changing a light bulb. I passed underneath as carefully as possible but managed to emerge with a

Top: John Arkley

Above: Arkley's Morris Men, 1980. Left to right: Edmund Price, Michael Horlock, Martin Read, Ben Radcliffe, Ben Burdett

Noreen Ford with
Sophie Tarnoy

lampshade on my head. More embarrassed apologies! Much to my amazement, Anna rang me the next day and offered me the job. She later told me that she did not expect me to accept in view of my "unusual" interview. Little did she realise that it was the homeliness and lack of formality that was most appealing! Twenty-four years on and that original advertisement is as applicable today as it was then. The fabric at Cumnor has changed substantially over the years, but enthusiasm and a sense of fun remain at the heart of life at the school, and long may it remain so.'

In 1983 Noreen Ford came to teach French, having been teaching in a Sheffield comprehensive. 'Like stepping out of Coronation Street into Mansfield Park' was how she put it. She was worried that her move was a 'sell-out', but it was a great boost for the intellectual life of the school. Her wit, her chuckle, her indignation (for instance when a girl told her that she was going to New York in the holidays 'to go shopping'), her *bons mots* (a social climber was 'au dessus de sa gare'; when she learnt that her successor was called Barrie Waterfall, 'après moi le déluge') made her a popular addition to the Common Room. Noreen retired in 1991 and very sadly died four years later.

When John and Paula Arkley left to teach in York in 1986, Anthony Bagshawe took over as resident housemaster in charge of maths; Aman Chandra (1987–91) remembers 'Maths with Mr Bagshawe – one of the best teachers I can remember from all my school days at CHS and Lancing.'

In 1988 Martin Godber arrived to take charge of science: a remarkably gifted all-rounder, he went on to establish computing at Cumnor, with a new computer network throughout the school in 1998, as well as play the oboe, horn, violin, double-bass and piano, and speak Italian and Russian. Martin organised the sound and lighting for all our plays, helped with orchestral, cycling and canal trips, and went on to become director of studies, a post he held until his departure to teach in Rome in 2005.

Another 1988 newcomer who made a big impression on the school was Jeff Lowe, who taught CDT. He also constructed an adventure playground, designed and planted the gardens at Woodgate Farm, built water-wheels, planted trees, repaired the old swimming pool, made a score box and mower shed for the Farm pitch, organised paper-making days, and with Barbara Clements ran Raku days, when children would camp out, rise at 4am to stoke the kiln and spend the whole day producing

Far left: Sue Calver, our much loved secretary, who retired in 1976

Left: Jill Daniel, who, as Head of English, continued Leo Wynne's enthusiastic encouragement of creative writing

Below: Jeff Lowe

147

wonderful pots. Barbara, pottery teacher from 1983 to 1996, remembers: 'Each summer, with the excellent assistance of Jeff Lowe, we organised a Raku firing day for all the pupils and often some teachers, glazed and fired all day, involving most of the children. Jeff had a rota for six boys to collect the necessary sticks of wood required for heating the brick kiln and I saw to it that each child's pottery was individually carefully glazed and raku-fired in the outdoor brick kiln. It was always an exciting day, invariably very hot and usually extremely exhausting!' Barbara herself was responsible for many pupils' successes in national competitions.

Andrew Rose OC (1967–72) arrived in 1989 to be head of English and coach of the 1st XV; after my retirement in 2000 he would also produce the annual Shakespeare play. Amy Arthur (1993–96) declares: 'the wonderful Mr Rose was the main inspiration behind not only continuing to write, but also going into teaching.' As a boy Andrew had been a memorable Shylock in his last term, about whom Charles Snow had written: 'Andrew Rose made an impressively effective Shylock. He is said not to have done much acting, but he dominated the stage, and he more than took advantage of it.' Matt Mockridge remembers this production: 'I wished I had been a

Above: Barbara
Clements

Right: Nat Cockburn
and Raku firing

Below: Oliver Wills

better actor for the cast's sake as I was given the role of Bassanio (probably because I had been head boy for three terms and X felt he had to give me a main part!) in *The Merchant of Venice* and I was opposite a superb Portia (played by a boy, Ian MacNeil, despite the fact we had girls in the school; but I think X felt they hadn't been there long enough to warrant a main part) and a brilliant Shylock in Andrew Rose. Andrew has come back to teach here and there are now four of us Old Cumnorians here, Mark Dickens, Mark Prescott, Andrew and me.'

I hope it won't seem immodest to print some memories of my own teaching contributed by some ex-pupils. Matt Mockridge: 'Having been caught smoking in the bamboos at the end of the old tennis court, I and a few others were understandably rather apprehensive about what punishment we would receive. NG took us up to his father's study and showed us a film of William Franklyn walking solemnly, clad in a black cloak, around a hospital oncology wing and then down to pathology where we were shown pictures of diseased lungs and dead bodies. The impression worked and I managed to steer clear of the smoking brigade at Marlborough for the next four years.'

Sarah Jane Sherlock: 'I remember Nick for instilling in me a love of music and of Classics. He introduced me to the piano and violin, and I practised away, sometimes in stationery cupboards, sometimes in slightly grander surroundings. The piano obviously made a better noise, but the violin, however terrible, gave me access to the school orchestra, and that was well worthwhile. I'm sure Nick wrote special parts for us beginners, with lots of long notes on open strings. Our horrible noise would be drowned by the better-sounding brass and wind instruments, so we could feel we were contributing to something tuneful. Best of all, Nick introduced me to Bach's *St Matthew Passion*. I was part of a CHS chorus which sang the treble part twice at local concerts, usually with the Fayrfax

Left: *The Merchant of Venice*, 1972: Matt Mockridge (Bassanio) and Andrew Rose (Shylock)

Below: Nick Abrahams (Caliban) in *The Tempest*, 1987

Singers. It remains one of my favourite pieces of music. Nick once said that the two bars "Truly, this was the Son of God" were arguably the best two bars of music ever written. I wouldn't disagree.'

Aman Chandra, now a doctor, recalls being taught Latin 'to a level well above Lancing scholarship, earning me top marks in the Latin scholarship paper at Lancing and the title of "top Classics scholar".'

Robert Steel (1978–83): 'One year the CHS orchestra had joined up with a couple of other schools to play at Brighton College. NG and the composer agreed to make a small alteration at the end of the last movement with a cymbal clash. There was no time to practise, but I do remember it being a very long movement and my mind began to wander. Needless to say I suddenly found I had lost my place. Ever the optimist, I thought I would detect the right moment. So as the movement neared the end, I stood up and waited for my big moment, when all of a sudden the music stopped! I thought what do I do now? Oh well, I had better sit down.'

Stefan Cucos (1977–81): 'I enjoyed being read to by Nick on Sunday evenings. He read us *The Odyssey* over at least a couple of terms which was a special treat. As was P G Wodehouse. Whenever I reread the Bertie Wooster stories I always hear his voice for Jeeves. It's the best rendering. Stephen Fry's isn't even close. One particular event sticks in my mind from about spring term 1978. We were called in to the old library for what was supposed to be a singing practice. Nick played "The Old Hundredth", which in the final chord miraculously became the hit "Summer Lovin" from *Grease* and the opening number of a wonderful comedy revue by the members of staff.'

Ione Meyer: 'Nick Milner-Gulland was my Greek teacher and introduced me to acting Shakespeare. The rehearsals began in NG's home when we read the summer play by parts. Then when rehearsals got serious we would – oh joy – cut

Ione Meyer in Beijing
Opera costume, 1993

lessons to rehearse in the outdoor space that was the stage in the school grounds, and Sarah Wallis and I recited our lines together, sitting on the steps outside B2. I recall when I had just auditioned for the part of Julia in *The Two Gentlemen of Verona* Nick took me aside in the school hall and told me the story of his first part in the same role, when Cumnor was boys only and as in Shakespeare's own time cross-dressing was the norm. The next year he produced *A Midsummer Night's Dream*, a play I have always enjoyed for its humour and celebration of fairies and the fairy world. The outside stage was a perfect location. Bathed in the early evening light the audience believed in Titania's flowery bower, not put out by marauding midges. His passionate enthusiasm for Shakespeare was contagious to all! We longed for those summer days, and in later life the Cumnor idyll lived on in my mind. It served as inspiration in my acting career. Years later during my apprenticeship at the Beijing Opera School in China, I went back to playing dual-gender parts like Julia. Yang Ba Jie, a noblewoman of the Song dynasty, dresses as an itinerant general to spy on the Mongol enemy when China feared invasion from across the Wall. I wrote a letter to Nick to tell him, which he subsequently printed in the school magazine. On my return to the UK in winter 1993, he invited me and my theatre company, Painted Faces, to perform for Cumnor on Guy Fawkes Night. Our first paid job! We performed both in the Barn and on the lawn in front of the school, with Chinese drum and Irish pipes, fire juggling and Beijing Opera costumes. Always a champion of the arts, where most people would have discouraged me from choosing such a hare-brained career, Nick gave me encouragement.'

Sport

Keen as I was to promote the arts, I did not want this to be at the expense of sport. So it was unfortunate that 1974 was the first of several weak years for boys' sports, although cricket improved dramatically with the arrival in 1978 of Peter Wigan, ex-captain of Eton. In 1977 Piers Pughe-Morgan (later plain Morgan) headed the bowling averages with 5.6, taking 10 for 9 against Copthorne, a feat which had been achieved at CHS only twice before; Piers was again top of the bowling averages the following year. Rugby improved dramatically, with the 1988 XV being our best ever (points for 350, points against 4). Peter Bonetti, ex-Chelsea and England goalkeeper, came in 1984 to coach soccer and PE. It was an enormous help to have a new Sports Hall, opened by the Sussex captain John Barclay in 1984, and new pitches at the farm in 1989.

The girls meanwhile were achieving consistently excellent results under the expert care of Jane Leuchars; several previously boys' schools were now taking girls, and by 1978 we were playing rounders, athletics, tennis and netball against six other schools. In 1989 the netball team won 18 of their 19 fixtures and were finalists in the National Tournament.

Angela Morpeth recollects a curious exchange between her son Richard and Anna. Anna: 'What position are you playing today, Richard?' Richard: 'Over the far side, by the pavilion.'

Clive Williams, retired headmaster of Ashdown

Right: Piers Pughe-Morgan (now Morgan), CHS cricket captain, 1978

Far right: Six-a-side competition in aid of John Barclay's benefit, 1986: left to right, Oliver Clayton, Mihai Cucos, Henry Price, JRTB, Patrick Wigan, James Barron

Below: Peter Bonetti instructs Tarquin Southwell

House, recalls another incident: 'I have known Cumnor House for 50 years as boy and man. As a boy at Ashdown we loved our matches against CHS. They were always fun, often exciting and occasionally surreal. I recall a delay of some minutes years ago in a 1st XI cricket match when the ball had been smitten out of the ground into the back of a passing truck. A replacement ball was eventually discovered. Then there was a memorable occasion when Nick M-G had turned out very smartly in shorts to referee a 1st XI soccer match. Before we got going he wandered over to me for, I thought, the exchange of a few pleasantries while the boys warmed up. "Clive," he said, "have you got a coin by any chance?" I had a coin; the toss over, ends having been changed, the teams lined up. Nick came over again. "Er, got a whistle by any chance?" No, I hadn't got a whistle on me. So a boy was despatched to NJM-G's study with the instruction to rummage around in the bottom left hand drawer of the headmaster's desk and come back with the whistle.'

Music and drama

My first Shakespeare production was *Twelfth Night* in 1975, a play which my father had never produced, partly, as Elizabeth Maslen recalled, 'because he disliked the ease with which one twin could be taken for the other; quite simply, such a casual confusion of identities was against all he believed in', and partly because he couldn't bear the cruel treatment of Malvolio. I tried to soften the latter by including Malvolio in a final dance, reluctantly at first then with

A Midsummer Night's Dream,
1982: Claire Packman (Hermia),
Edmund Price (Lysander)

Performances involving CHS children

Plays

1975	*Twelfth Night*
1976	*Romeo and Juliet*
1977	*The Two Gentlemen of Verona*
1978	*A Midsummer Night's Dream*
1979	*Richard II*
1980	*The Knight of the Burning Pestle*
1981	*The Tempest*
1982	*A Midsummer Night's Dream*
1983	*Macbeth*
1984	*As You Like It*
1985	*The Two Gentlemen of Verona*
1986	*Henry the Fifth*
1987	*The Tempest*
1988	*A Midsummer Night's Dream*
1989	*As You Like It*

Outside Concerts involving the CHS Chorus

The Chorus performed in a large number of concerts with the Fayrfax Singers and Orchestra:

1976	Vivaldi *Gloria*, Handel *Ode on St Cecilia's Day*
1977	Bach *St Matthew Passion* with Michael Hall and at Ardingly
1979	Britten *Missa Brevis* at Worth Abbey, Haydn *Nelson Mass* at Ardingly, Britten *St Nicolas*
1981	Orff *Carmina Burana* with Worth JS
1982	Mozart *Coronation Mass* at Ardingly
1983	Haydn *Paukenmesse* at Ardingly
1985	Bach *St John Passion* at Ardingly
1986	Handel *Messiah* at Ardingly
1987	Stravinsky *Symphony of Psalms* and Bach *Cantatas 50 & 51* at St Swithun's, East Grinstead
1988	Dvořák *Te Deum* at Ardingly
1989	Bach *Cantatas* at Ardingly

St Nicolas, 1979: left to right, Andrew Mitchell, Crispin Flower, Tom Maslen, Jeremy Goulden

increasing assurance; but I don't think Shakespeare would have approved, even if Hal did. I much enjoyed producing the plays, even though they were rehearsed in only four or five weeks; to this day I have occasional nightmares in which I am at the stage, parents are beginning to arrive for the opening performance and I am anxiously wondering which play to put on: can I get away with the Dream yet again?

In 1987 onwards we were helped in the make-up department by three generations of the Tormé family – Daisy, her mother Jan Rademaekers and her grandmother Dame Thora Hird. Dame Thora was later our guest of honour at Sports Day 1993, when she spoke warmly about her 'second favourite school in the world'. During this time Margaret Durrant, who taught dancing in the school, produced a number of excellent shows, both in the main school and in the pre-prep, and had a remarkable facility for turning out appropriate and effective Elizabethan

Left: 'Three Boys' with
Patricia Rosario in Kent
Opera's *The Magic Flute*
(1987). Left to right,
Rebecca Toms, Gabi
Cotton, Rufus Cotton.

Below: *As You Like It*,
1984, a sketch by
C Walter Hodges,
Shakespearian scholar
and illustrator; inset,
Sarah Geere (Rosalind)

dances for the play at a moment's notice. In 1975 we
were invited to provide some children for Jonathan
Miller's Glyndebourne production of Janácek's *The
Cunning Little Vixen*. David Wilson was the frog and
James Lovegrove the grasshopper, with Felicity
Braham and Miles Balfour taking the same roles in
the 1977 revival, with Jeremy Goulden and Tim
Mather as fox cubs. Ten years later Gabi and Rufus
Cotton and Rebecca Toms played the three boys in
Kent Opera's production of *The Magic Flute*.

James Lovegrove as
Grasshopper in *The
Cunning Little Vixen* at
Glyndebourne, 1975

A popular tradition was started in 1980 with the
first summer orchestral trip. Elizabeth Muir-Lewis
recalls: 'My husband and I took the school orchestra
to St Cyprien in the Dordogne, leading a convoy of
cars, instruments strapped to the top, boys and girls
packed in the back, head-counting every evening and
morning to check that no-one had got lost. Finally
reaching our destination, was it a holiday? Hardly. I
and several other mums cooked for everyone in the
farmhouse lent to the school for the trip by Michael
Horowitz, father of Brook. What fun we had playing
in Haydn's *Toy Symphony*, Nick assigning me to the
triangle, and going down to the village to hear the
orchestra play in the tiny square. I remember
venturing into the cafés to exhort the locals to come
and listen.' Subsequent trips were to Chilcombe,
Dorset, at the invitation of John and Caryl Hubbard
(1981–84), Gloucestershire (1985), Monnickendam,

Above, the orchestra, 1985, and below, at Springhead, 1989

Holland, at the invitation of Lies Schokking (1987) and Springhead, Wiltshire (1989).

Out of school

In 1979 the seven-year-old Michael Paterson (1979–85) was impressed by the facilities:

> *The things what you can do here*
> At this school there is a salt corse it has a Tarzan rope, a trye that swings, a cat walk, a pole with noches in it and when you get to the top you have to walk across a rope and theres a scary way up too. There is a big tarzan rope too it goes over the old swimming pool (a german plane crashed in there in the Would War II). There is a death slide down a hill, there is an underground camp.

Two Old Cumnorians have memories of the hurricane which terrified the boarders and claimed 12 trees in the grounds in October 1987. Nick Illsley: 'As dorm captain (self-appointed or otherwise) I decided that the windows in the red dorms were unsafe and corralled as many as I could into the loos and by torchlight read extracts from Mr Shepherd's *Daily Mirror* to keep minds away from the smashing glass and groaning portacabins.' It was Aman Chandra's first term at CHS. He found the hurricane 'terrifying, yet exciting; there were incredible winds, and the back door of the green dorm was blown open, yet still hanging on to its hinges. Looking back, I am particularly impressed with the leadership of the dorm captains with organising everyone into the corridor of the dorm out of the cubicles. I am not sure if there was any adult supervision of this; if there wasn't – what leadership! After that hurricane, NG suggested that I stay with the Cottons in the immediate aftermath, as I wouldn't be able to get to London to my guardians. If it wasn't for that suggestion, the lifelong relationship I have had with the Cottons (including being godfather to Olivia's son and best man to

Far left: Hurricane damage, 1987

Below: Summer holiday projects: quilts by Jo and Harriet Charlesworth

Rufus) most probably wouldn't have blossomed! Marvellous foresight!'

Anna and I took the CE candidates for several holiday reading parties, once to the Hubbards' home at Chilcombe and another to the Wye Valley, thanks to John and Ros Edsberg, in imitation of my parents' French trips with prospective scholars. We had three exchanges with the Lycée International at St Germain-en-Laye, through the good offices of Rosalie Wood and Isabel Lawson; and in 1989 Anna and Noreen Ford took a group of 12 children to the Dordogne as guests of the local Rotary Clubs. In the summer holidays 1981 we asked children who were about to start their final year to produce a project on a topic of their choice. This system, shamelessly stolen from Great Walstead, still operates today, and is responsible for some of the most wonderful work I have ever seen our pupils produce – even if it is often done with help from parents. Another happy and long-lasting tradition which we started at this time was 'Staff Supper', at which groups of children in their final year were invited to supper with the staff on Monday evenings. In 1982 Michael Likierman ran his first Cumnor ski party (to Châtel): these parties were an increasingly popular annual event for eight years.

Summer visits in the early 1980s from Rein Sillart, from Tallinn, Estonia, were the start of an interesting connection with School no 7 in Tallinn, which was to bear fruit in 1989 with the first of two fascinating exchanges with a country that was still a Soviet satellite, in the heady days leading up to independence. One of the Estonian boys who came to us in 1989, Andreas Veispak, was subsequently accepted at Eton, where he did well and in time won a place to University College, Oxford. His ambition at the age of 11 was to become president of independent Estonia. In the following year we invited a group of Estonian teachers of English to England under the auspices of the British Council and with the generous help of several Cumnor parents.

One of the teachers, Kristi Tarand, remembers her impressions: 'How Nick Milner-Gulland managed to do it, I do not know, but ten teachers of English from our school were invited to be guests of Cumnor House School in the summer of 1990. For us it was a very bad time economically, the Soviets did not allow us to exchange any money, and we were a real burden on the school and the parents for the week we spent there. Everybody was kind to us. It was the first visit to the West for most of us and we were definitely not ordinary visitors. I lived in the Pink House, at the Milner-Gullands, and got a rather good idea of the buildings and the school. I was delighted with many things, especially the summer theatre, the library, the staff room, the grounds and the garden, the pottery room and the kiln. I must confess I was not suitably impressed with the cricket grounds (sorry!) and I was secretly horrified seeing the spartan dormitories, especially those of boys. I am sure our children would have protested at the hard beds and rather cold rooms. Having read Delderfield (*To Serve Them All My Days*) and some other authors I thought I knew the system of independent schools pretty well but I still got several pleasant surprises. One of them was the support Mr Milner-Gulland got from the parents of his pupils in entertaining us. I liked the beautiful rooms in the main house and even when the pupils were not there in this last week of July, there was an atmosphere of studying but also having a childhood and a good time.'

This period was an exciting time to be running a school, and it is much to the credit of the trustees that the change of management went so smoothly.

Although we were answerable to them, they allowed the previous team (Anna and me, Leo Wynne and Peter Wigan) a very free hand. Andrew Brand (1979–81) writes: 'My recollection of the school during that period is of a winning formula that produced excellent results. In retrospect I think that this was because the school's unifying philosophy seemed to be the design of a single mind – or a group of very similar minds. Implementing this design via a leadership structure based on benign dictatorship meant that there were virtually no internal contradictions in method, style, or format. Nowadays this would be called product consistency and it resulted in a system that gave the overwhelming impression of being somehow eternal – as if education had always been done this way and always would be.'

Estonian visit, 1989:
Eva-Maria Keskküla
and Rachel Barnes

CHAPTER 11

TO THE MILLENNIUM

1990–2000

Sweet childish days, that were as long
As twenty days are now

WORDSWORTH, 'TO A BUTTERFLY'

The Old Oak, 1995

OPPOSITE PAGE

Top: Jonathan, left, and
Bobby Dickens, 1990

Left: *A Midsummer
Night's Dream*, 1994:
Elves (left to right):
Alex Furness-Smith,
Jonathan Atkinson,
Freddie Cole, David
Arnold, Forbes Henley

'Mothers,' Leo wrote in 1995, 'seem younger than ever: that must be a blessing. Precautions are more obtrusive. Trees aren't climbed these days. Things generally are safer and more comfortable and less eccentric. There are more treats, a wider choice of games and pastimes. Everyone rushes about doing more, busier than ever.' However when Jackie Sampson (Rosling) joined the pre-prep staff in 1979, she was pleasantly surprised at our freedom from regulations: 'Imagine my delight, having come from the rules of state schools and others, where every child must be protected from every imaginable danger (which often means spoiling their fun), to find the children disappearing into bushes and up trees where I couldn't see every single one of them all the time. I had to grab a passing member of main-school staff to find out if this was really allowed, as the children had assured me it was! I soon learned that here was a school where children could have a real childhood building camps and getting muddy. Playtimes are a joy in such an environment and great discoveries can be made while digging or climbing. This enthusiasm and questing is to be seen carried on in the classrooms in many ways. In common with the multitudes who have now left Cumnor House, I remember it with a mixture of fondness and gratitude as a place of endless opportunities for new beginnings and unimagined experiences, where children can learn, grow, laugh and play in a wholesome and nurturing environment.'

Part of this environment, and one of the school's landmarks, the Old Oak, sadly died in 1995, possibly aged 800 years, and had to be cut down.

A job which gave us great soul-searching and heartache and sometimes created much ill feeling was the appointment of house captains. I saw 'leadership' more as service to the community than as bossing others: there was a danger that we were making little gauleiters of the chosen few and reinforcing a sense of failure among the others. At the same time house captaincy seemed to confer status but no real power; and in any case the exercise of power by 12- and 13-year-olds needs to be supervised with great vigilance. We therefore abandoned house captaincy and devised a system whereby every child in his or her last year would assume various responsibilities in turn, although we continued to appoint a head boy and head girl. Thus every pupil would learn the skills of 'leadership'. Several children surprised us by their positive response to this challenge; others, who might have become keen gauleiters, were not so good at checking that the lights were off or that the chickens had been fed.

As day numbers grew and boarding numbers dropped, the system of evening occupations lost some of the central importance that it had maintained since 1948; in those days the occupations were looked forward to with great enthusiasm, and were for many pupils the beginning of a lifelong interest, for some even a career. By the 1990s some occupations were not much more than time-filling exercises, and were optional for day children.

Julia Doherty had two pet hates: 'Can I nominate "Pom-Pom Pets" as surely the world's least imaginative "occupation", closely followed by the "Decorated Brick Doorstop" craft activity? I recently hurled Daniel's masterpiece out of his bedroom window in cold fury, having stubbed my toe on it just once too often.'

In 1995 we had an inspection from ISJC, newly set up as the independent schools' inspectorate, which was extremely complimentary. We had a series of very good CE results, and a huge number of awards (17 in 1996 alone). During this decade we gained scholarships at Eton (Albert Cheung) and Winchester (George Howe), and four at Westminster (James Fairbairn, Tom Jelly, Clem Naylor, Ned Naylor): these three schools continued to be the gold standard of academic achievement, gratifying as other awards might be. Elsewhere award inflation seemed to have taken place, with a huge increase in the number and scope of awards: as a typical instance, Oundle offered 61 awards in 2006, whereas 50 years previously they had offered 12.

Right: Peter Wigan

Below: Matt Mockridge

Bottom: Andrew Keith, left, and Martin Godber on board *Lady Daphne*

casualty of the Gulf War; and in 1999 Sarah Cheung (1992–96) died of leukaemia at the age of 16. Just after her cancer was diagnosed, she had written:

Life's Blood
    silent as night
    and black,
    black as fields of coal-dust,
    hidden
    unbidden
    in streams of deep, sickly red

    betrayal
    bribery by the dark side
    to a world of slow
    body-consumers

    a civil war,
    weighted heavily against
    the good guys –
    started without their knowledge,
    seething like a mountain of magma

    the longer they get
    the surer the victory

'League tables' were introduced in 1996, with all their inaccuracies and erroneous simplifications. Prep schools were mercifully exempt, but our colleagues in senior schools felt obliged to supply their data, since opting out would imply that they wished to hide poor results. Richard Morgan, Warden of Radley, wrote: 'When a parent asked whether Radleians ironed their shirts well, I found myself replying that we had come fifth in the shirt-ironing league. To my horror, she believed me.' At Cumnor we held a parents' seminar to discuss the question of prizes: it was a fascinating exchange of views, with widely differing ideas expressed by the three speakers, Donald Fowler-Watt, Bill Nicholson and Stephanie Thornton.

People

Peter Wigan, a popular and much respected figure, became deputy headmaster in 1990, and it was a relief for me to know that the school was in such safe hands in my absence, particularly in January 1998 when the trustees kindly awarded Anna and me a sabbatical term.

The deaths of two Old Cumnorians brought great sadness: Wing Commander Nigel Elsdon (1958–64), a Tornado pilot, was the first British

Sue and Andrew Keith joined Cumnor in 1992, Sue as secretary and Andrew in charge of maths; he was also (and remains) a fanatical cyclist, taking children on holiday expeditions to Skye, Ireland, Wales, Norfolk and Devon, often accompanied by Penny Mussell.

Matt Mockridge, who joined the staff in 1994, explains his family connection with Woodgate: 'My great-grandfather, Charles Corbett, Liberal MP for East Grinstead in 1906, owned Woodgate, which stood on land which was later to be owned by Harold Macmillan and part of which would then come back to Cumnor where I would be both pupil and master. My two brothers were also lucky enough to be at CHS and my sister was constantly envious of us as she slogged down to school in Bexhill, while we skipped across the valley up to CHS.

'My return to CHS came when I had been running my golf club business for 13 years and my family was starting to grow but the business wasn't keeping up with the rate of growth. I had done some work with the children at St Giles' church in Horsted Keynes and in 1994 decided to ring NG, with whom I'd kept in touch, in order to get a feeling as to whether and how I should consider teaching as my next career. The "interview" was pure Nick and Cumnor (informal and immensely trusting on his part as was the case with so much of the Cumnor charm) and I found myself hearing that he could find a job for me somewhere soon. Within a week of starting I knew I had found a profession that suited me, and after a year Nick seemed to think so too, as he made me head of games. I was back where I felt I belonged, having had not too shabby a sporting career at CHS 25 years earlier. I taught my first lesson in my great-grandfather's study in the south-west corner of the main house, standing in front of the now redundant fireplace and imagining a fire blazing on a cold Sunday morning as he stood beneath some shooting painting.

'In September 1998, Nick made me deputy headmaster, as PW "with characteristic grace and understanding" stepped aside to become senior master. Little did we know then that Nick would become ill in 2000, Peter would take over for a one year interregnum and that he too would become ill on an otherwise splendid cricket tour of Sri Lanka in the spring of 2001. I think therefore that as I stepped

Rosi Robinson's batik of CHS life, 1969–2000, in aid of the Royal Marsden Hospital. Scenes include the orchestra trip, the art room and Penny Mussell's 2CV; the children's gardens; sketching bluebells in Kiln Wood; the play; the Old Oak; ropes over the old swimming pool; Leo Wynne on Sports Day; the orchestra with Nicola Beddy and Martin Godber (horns); Hal and Nan; the Barn and the Tulip Tree; Nick and Anna; and 'Under the Clock'.

First impressions

It is always interesting to know what motivates parents to send their children to us. Here are two parents' accounts:

Rosalie Challis (Wood): 'The first contact with Cumnor left an indelible memory. Having visited an exceedingly orderly school, with well-scrubbed, rather subdued children and a decidedly spartan ambience earlier in the morning, it was with delight that, on reaching Cumnor and opening the front door, we were greeted by a blazing log fire, a not particularly tidy pile of wellingtons pressing through the cloakroom door and a well-fed ginger cat draped round the front hall radiator. The first pupil we spotted wore the trademark bright scarlet blazer, though this blazer had definitely seen better days and its wearer had a toothbrush visible in the top pocket. Such details, together with the relaxed and friendly reception we were given by the staff and the pupils we met, confirmed irrefutably the impression of warmth, humanity and concern for civilised values given by the Cumnor information pack.'

Edward Faridany: 'When Nana and I were looking at schools we ended up looking at two on the same day through bad management. First was a certain institution on the road into East Grinstead. It was all shiny surfaces, echoing corridors and precision, inside and out. All seemed impeccable – we were impressed, but not sure. Next, on to Cumnor. Only five miles on the map but worlds apart. There was no-one around when we arrived. In we went through those awkward front doors. Still not a soul anywhere to be seen. The only signs of life were the distant sound of a piano being played somewhere and, there in the middle of the hall floor, a pair of crumpled red games socks. They were oddly comforting. We had a good interview and school tour, but I think it was those socks which really clinched the decision for us.'

in to be acting headmaster for the summer term of 2001, I became only the second ex-pupil of CHS to act as headmaster.

'My overwhelming feeling as I write this is one of happiness and the empirical and perfect foundation that CHS has given to my being: knowledge, the ability and confidence to question, caring, understanding, successes achieved, failures faced, friendships. Cumnor remains a first-class prep school: thriving,

bold, unusual in many ways and a wonderfully friendly community in which to spend one's formative years or those taking one to retirement.'

In 2000 Kiln Wood House was built as the deputy headmaster's house at the south-eastern corner of the farm pitch; this was the almost single-handed work of our marvellous resident builder, Wayne Martin.

Several enjoyable staff excursions took place, once to Calais for lunch, once down the Thames on Mark and Caroline Tower's sailing barge *Lady Daphne* and once at Bore Place, where we made mallets and bricks in pouring rain. Sheena Broughton, member of the kitchen staff, is fondly remembered by George Howe 'for her ability to boil an egg with her bare hands. When asked what was for lunch, she replied "Food"; on a request for clarification she then narrowed it down to "School food".'

In 1998 Stephen Cockburn took over as chairman of trustees from Martin Pavey. Stephen reveals how his son Nat (1987–92) had come close to destroying the school: 'November 5th 1990 had seen the usual CHS firework display but the following morning Nat and another boy had discovered a large firework which had not gone off. Digging it out of the ground they carried it unseen into the changing rooms where they hid it in Nat's locker. After a few days the other boy announced to Nat he didn't want anything more to do with it and he was accordingly giving Nat his half share in the trophy. On the Saturday of the first home weekend in December Nat said he had something to bring home and staggered to the car with a large and heavy object wrapped in an anorak. On reaching home in Cuckfield he revealed this giant firework. It was certainly unexploded but the fuse was either very small or had been lit and gone out before setting off the contents. Nat had the bright idea, despite the very late hour, of trying to set off his firework. Cautiously, with everyone standing well back, with a long taper I dangled a flame where the fuse appeared

to have been. With a splutter of sparks as I beat a hasty retreat the thing started up. It was amazing. For what seemed like ages the blue and red Roman candles, whizzing rockets, showers of silver and gold and great bangs filled the garden. Tension broken, we all giggled helplessly. If it had gone off in the CHS changing rooms the whole building would undoubtedly have burned down. Next day Nat's mother had comments from neighbours. "Did you hear those terrible yobs last night setting off fireworks in the recreation ground?" (our garden backs on to it); "wasn't it awful, so late in the evening too!" She simply smiled and nodded.'

Art

Rosi Robinson, head of art since 1987, continued to produce wonderful work, notably the large batik in the hall depicting different aspects of CHS life. The opening of new specially designed premises in 1996 greatly enhanced the provision for art, and we were extremely grateful to Stephen Windsor-Clive for designing and constructing the magnificent mosaic on the outside art room wall.

Above left: Stephen Windsor-Clive's mosaic

Above right: Kate Cuppage, left, and Olivia Cotton, 1990

Right: *A Midsummer Night's Dream*, 1994: Lachlan Nieboer (Lysander), Philippa Chatterton (Hermia)

A Midsummer Night's Dream, 1999: Camilla Johnson (Titania), Ned Naylor (Bottom)

Drama

Rebecca Hall (1987–95), who was to go on to be a wonderful Miranda, Helena and Beatrice at Cumnor, starred in her father's TV production in 1991 of *Camomile Lawn*; some years later, after leaving Cambridge, she embarked upon a promising stage career. At our performance of *Macbeth* in 1992, we were pleased to ask Dr Robin Moffatt to take a bow: he, as Theseus in 1941, had uttered the first words of the first Shakespeare play ever produced at Cumnor House. In 1998 our performance of *The Two Gentlemen of Verona* was watched by two previous Silvias, Camilla Campbell (1985) and Michael Feaver (1944); in this year we had two plays, with Andrew Rose producing *The Comedy of Errors*, exploiting two sets of identical twins, Robin and Tim Jackson and Anna and Lizzie Jones. We had specially commissioned music by Tony Smith-Masters for *The Tempest* and *Much Ado About Nothing*, Joshua Cunningham provided incidental music for *A Midsummer Night's Dream* ('an energetic and melodious score') and three girls – Amy Arthur, Sarah Cheung and Madeleine Sumption – composed the music for *The Old Wives Tale* in 1996. The choice of this strange Elizabethan play by George Peele was perhaps a mistake: one member of the audience was heard to remark after the performance, 'It makes you realise how good Shakespeare is.'

Performances involving CHS children

Orchestral trips

1991, 92	Dieulefit
1994, 96	Siena
1995, 97	Berbiguières
1999	Château du Livet
2000	Carcès

Open air plays

1990	*Richard II*
1991	*Twelfth Night*
1992	*Macbeth*
1993	*The Tempest*
1994	*A Midsummer Night's Dream*
1995	*Much Ado About Nothing*
1996	*The Old Wives Tale*
1997	*Twelfth Night*
1998	*The Two Gentlemen of Verona*
1999	*A Midsummer Night's Dream*
2000	*Macbeth*

Ned Naylor (Valentine) in *The Two Gentlemen of Verona*, 1998

Chorus concerts with the Fayrfax Singers

1990	Kodály *Missa Brevis* (Oliver Wills, treble)
1991	Mozart *Requiem* and *C minor Mass* Charpentier *Messe de Minuit* (with Stoke Brunswick)
1992	CHS 60th Anniversary concert at the Purcell Room (with John Wilbraham, Adrian de Peyer, Bert Chappell) Britten *Noyes Fludde* in Lancing College Chapel (IAPS Centenary concert)
1993	Puccini *Messa di Gloria*
1994	Haydn *Paukenmesse*
1995	Purcell *King Arthur*
1996	Handel *Coronation Anthems* Bach *St Matthew Passion*
1997	Brahms *Requiem*
1998	Haydn *Nelson Mass* (Eloise Irving, soprano)
1999	Gilbert and Sullivan *The Yeomen of the Guard*
2000	Bach *Cantatas*

The Open Air Theatre in summer and winter

Below: Simon Thornton, left, and Geoffrey Pulford on the Old Swimming Pool

Literature

Meanwhile interesting written work appeared in the pages of the magazine:

> 'God made the world and the birds and my Mummy and my Daddy and my breakfast.'
>
> *Robert Condon* (4)

> 'We went to the sheep farm we saw sheep of course other wise it wood not be a sheep farm but a ordinary farm.'
>
> *Emma Tower* (5)

> 'I dont fel very well today. My mummy gave me her cold, Caspar gave me his and I had one of my own already.'
>
> *Orlando Sheppard* (5)

> 'The teacher snorted loudly and rather rudely at the headmaster's joke. It was a laugh just like a piglet scrambling over its brothers and sisters to get to its food.'
>
> *Alice Edwards* (10)

Deafness

Life is, for me, a colourfully jumbled
Mass of sounds coming in
Streams
       and   t
            r
              i
             c
           k
            l
             e
                s of nonsense,
Blaring, hooting, screaming, yelling,
Whispering, tinkling, crashing,
Falling over one another to
Reach my ears;
Weaker sounds getting trampled in a violent rush
Of sonorous buzzings, with fuzzier bits
Put in to confuse my unreliable ears;
I tune in on a particular sound,
At once I hear a million
Words pushing and struggling,
Trying above the chatter of
Words and more words to
Register themselves in my brain,
But failing miserably, to land
In
     a
         heap at
             my
          Feet.

Justin Cheadle (12)

Above: The organ

Opposite page: The orchestra at Dieulefit, 1992

Below: The orchestra performs at the Château de Berbiguières, 1997

Extra-curricular

The Chorus continued to give regular concerts with, among others, the Fayrfax Singers and Orchestra. Orchestral trips in the summer became more ambitious, with visits to the elegant houses and châteaux of various kind friends: Steve and Jo Cotton at Dieulefit, Drôme; Anthony and Sarah Boswood near Siena; Jonathan and Teresa Sumption at the Château de Berbiguières, Dordogne; Clive and Rowena Williams at the Château du Livet, Normandy; and Leo and Nicole Wynne at Carcès in Provence. Anthony Boswood has these memories of the 1996 trip: 'the rapt expression on the face of Dom Marchetti as Henry Irving sang "Marianina"; the fixed expression on NG's face as he played the accompaniment to the same: evidently not his favourite piece; the genuine musical pleasure to be had from Louise B and Eloise Irving singing "Sound

the Trumpet", accompanied by NG and Jamie; NG's lugubrious orchestral setting (reminiscent of Max Reger) of the Sienese anthem "Nella piazza del Campo", and the surprising pleasure which the local audience took in the same; cooking on the barbecue with Elgar 1 etc at full volume on outside loudspeakers; singing the doxology (Tallis' "Canon") in seven parts; the absolute necessity of finding Frank Cooper's Oxford for NG's breakfast.'

In March 1992 we gave a concert at the Purcell Room to celebrate the school's 60th anniversary, with John Wilbraham (trumpet), Adrian de Peyer (tenor) and Bert Chappell (composer of *The Daniel Jazz*). Another anniversary was celebrated later that year, the IAPS centenary, for which 14 Sussex prep schools came together to perform *Noyes Fludde* in Lancing College Chapel.

James Woodhouse, ex-headmaster of Lancing,

and Bill Llewellyn, ex-director of music at Charterhouse, had collaborated on writing a musical version of *The Elephant's Child*, of which we gave a performance in the Barn with the composer at the piano, and starring Amy Arthur in the title role: 'I remember being the Elephant Child and wearing an enormously heavy nose made of grey corduroy which could be pulled out and used to slap people.'

Other memorable concerts in the Barn included Nicola Loud's quartet, with OC Jan Sodderland on the viola, a recital by Anthony Peebles (piano) and a memorable performance of Beethoven's *Kreutzer* Sonata by Dmitry Sitkovetsky and Roger Vignoles. Meanwhile the new CHS hymnbook appeared, and Krystian Bellière christened the Bechstein grand piano, newly acquired in 1997. A new and popular venture was Grandparents' Day, involving a concert, tea and a tour of the school. Finally we enjoyed a lecture on Scott's expedition to the Antarctic by Broke Evans, who showed Ponting's original slides on a real magic lantern, and brought along the silver sugar bowl that Scott had used on the expedition.

The Barn in its first two decades had proved to be an excellent venue for such events, and it was gratifying to read in 1996 the report of Mrs J McLean, HMI: 'The considerable number of outside speakers/performers over the past three years indicates a school very much in touch with the wider community, despite its rural location.' A superb addition to the Barn was the very generous gift from Stephen and Judy Cockburn of an organ. This fine 18th-century English instrument, which had come from Queniborough Church in Leicestershire, was installed and improved by Richard Scothon. I was asked to give the inaugural recital in autumn 2001.

Other examples of this interest in the wider world were our second exchange with School no 7, Tallinn; the arrival for two years of Orsi Farkas from Hungary, thanks to the generosity of Michael Bedford (a CHS trustee) and the Paul Hamlyn Foundation; the gift of a large quantity of stationery

and school equipment to the Ecole FJKM, Ambatomanga, Madagascar; a fête organised entirely by Sadruddin Alexander which raised over £600 for Bosnian refugees; the visit of 21 Chernobyl children from Minsk; a large number of books for the Marondera Children's Library in Zimbabwe; and the sum of £2700 raised at the 2000 Christmas Fayre for the Royal Marsden Hospital.

Roddy Gye took over from Michael Likierman the organisation of the annual skiing holidays, and there were numerous other expeditions, such as Barrie Waterfall's trips to Dieppe and Andrew Gilliam's to Milly-la-Forêt. Sporting tours proliferated hugely during this decade. One wonders what George Howson, headmaster of Gresham's Holt 100 years ago, would have thought: he banned matches against other schools for fear of moral contamination. In 1993 we had our first visit from Pridwin School, Johannesburg, and two years later we went to Zimbabwe, thanks to the generous hospitality of Clive Barnes, headmaster of Prince Edward's School, Harare, and Jennifer Dent, grandmother of the three Kruger children; we also visited Johannesburg, where we were looked after by David Anderson and the Pridwin families. For George Howe this tour 'was quite literally the making of me, and I have been

Above: CHS v. Ruzawi, Zimbabwe, 1998

Below: Sam Downe, left, and Lachlan Nieboer, both not out in a stand of 145 v. Handcross Park, 1991 (U11 record)

Above: 1st XI at Hove, victorious in the Hayland Trophy, with Peter Wigan and James Martin-Jenkins

Left to right, Amy Mansell, Mishka Adams, Emma Furness-Smith

immensely grateful ever since.' We were back in Zimbabwe in 1998. Not to be outdone, the girls went on two netball trips to Jersey, and in 2000 were taken by June Barton to Sydney. In the same year Jane Leuchars retired after 24 years at Cumnor, during which she produced wonderful netball and rounders teams year after year: for instance in 1994 and 1995 the 1st rounders team won all their matches, and the following year the netballers won 50 of their 58 matches at all levels.

Cricket went from strength to strength. Since the school's foundation Cumnor boys had scored only five centuries: in the 1990s there were no fewer than 10, including four in 1995 alone from the remarkable Tom Dowdall, whose batting average for that year was an amazing 116.83. Other centurions were Daniel Comber, Edward Dean, Jamie Gilbert and Johnny Norfolk; and even two Under 11 boys, Jonathan Atkinson and Johnny Norfolk. Undoubtedly pitches are better now, matches are a little longer, and we have excellent coaching; but even so, however technically proficient a boy may be, he still has to summon up a degree of concentration which is rare in boys so young. Meanwhile the Eton team in the 1992 Eton v Harrow match included three OCs (Oliver Clayton, Henry Price, Patrick Wigan).

Another great cricketing success was the memorable day at the County Ground, Hove, in 1992 when we won the Hayland Trophy (for Sussex prep schools) at both 1st and Under 11 level. In 1996 we had an unbeaten 1st XI, and there was a curious incident in a match on the Farm pitch in which the scorebook records 'Flying ants stopped play'. A similar diversion occurred in Zimbabwe when a match was halted while the players lay on their stomachs as a swarm of bees invaded the pitch.

Soccer and rugby had been rather disappointing until the very good teams of 1995, when the 1st soccer XI won each of the two local Sixes competitions and the 1st XV won eight of their nine matches. Manners Makyth Man, it is true, but we had to cure one 10-year-old of an excess of them. His soccer report read: 'C is the first boy I have ever encountered whose initial reaction on scoring a goal is to apologise profusely to the opposition.'

In 1995 a new six-hole golf course, designed by Andrew Rose, was completed; and two sets of kind parents enabled us to have a new pavilion (Bob and Sue Dowdall) and a new floor and ceiling for the Sports Hall (Jon and Julia Aisbitt).

Retirement

In May 2000 I was diagnosed with multiple myeloma, a cancer of the bone marrow, and was treated with chemotherapy and radiotherapy at the excellent Royal Marsden Hospital, Sutton. I asked Des Martin, the school doctor, what I should do; he wisely recommended that I should resign from the headmastership, as the outcome of the treatment was unsure. In any case I had reached the age of 60. I immediately told Stephen Cockburn that this was what I proposed to do, and it was decided that Peter Wigan should be asked to step in for a year to allow time for the appointment of my successor. Matt Mockridge has already described how Peter himself, by a cruel twist of fate, was struck down by Guillain-Barré syndrome, and Matt took the helm for the summer term. It says

Left to right (standing), Jamie, Toby; (sitting) Kate, Nick, Anna, 2005

much for the quality of the staff and the loyalty of the parents that Cumnor weathered these storms so smoothly. Meanwhile my cancer went into remission; we bought a house in Lewes, and were able to spend a blissful fortnight recuperating in Cape Town with our old Pridwin friends, David and Eve Anderson.

After 31 years as Cumnor's headmaster, I was very sad to retire so unexpectedly. They were happy years, during which Anna and I were married, we brought up our three children, saw the school established as a thriving entity and above all made a great number of close friends. We have now made a new life for ourselves in Lewes, where I am involved in much conducting and organ playing, as well as teaching basic skills at HMP Lewes, while Anna teaches dyslexics at St Bede's prep school, Eastbourne. I hope that the wonderful doctors at the Royal Marsden Hospital may grant me a few more years of remission.

At my departure, parents were amazingly generous to us, writing marvellous letters and presenting us with a huge cheque (immediately spent on a car – no more school ones!) and a magnificent Regency music stand. Bill Nicholson, at his own suggestion, wrote and produced a Pageant of CHS life, compèred by Piers Gibbon, which involved every child in the school and a large number of Old Cumnorians. Bill writes: 'On Sunday June 17th 2001 a motley procession filed down to the lower lawns. In the lead was the school orchestra. Behind marched a column of Cumnor boys and girls, each banging a home-made instrument – tin cans, buckets, bricks – to create what was dubbed The Big Noise. The conductor of this mayhem was Nick Milner-Gulland, making his final entrance after his resignation as headmaster, and launching a celebration of the school he had led for 31 years. Nick's resignation was forced on him by ill-health. This day of open-air celebration was threatened by rain clouds. Both were to pass by.

'Over the next two hours an immense gathering of Cumnorians old and new retraced the past. Matt Mockridge and Andrew Rose stood under the clock one last time. Joanna Dodd gave her memories of being the school's first ever girl pupil. Former star actors from Willam Maslen to Clem Naylor presented a Parade of Bottoms from past *Midsummer Night's Dreams*. Nick's marriage to "rubeous Anna Froud" was commemorated. Ten members of 1988's unbeaten 1st XV rugby team paraded in Cumnor strip. There was Cumnorian music, from barbershop quartets to Haydn trios. And at the end, Prospero's words "Our revels now are ended ..." prefaced a farewell speech from the man himself.

'That emotional Sunday in June was a celebration of the spirit of Cumnor – that indefinable quality that caused us, like so many parents, to entrust our children to the school's care. That spirit lives on. *Omnia mutantur, nihil interit.*'

It was an extraordinarily happy and moving occasion, spent in the presence of very many old friends. It was an overcast afternoon; but miraculously, at the very moment that I was mentioning my debt to my father, the clouds parted and the sun broke through with a sudden shaft of radiance.

Anagram Story

Bill Nicholson's *Anagram Story* was recited at The Big Noise 2001 by Ann Thirkell and the E form:

Once upon a time two animal chums, a Mouse and an Emu, went to school at Cumnor House. The Emu was not happy.

ONE SOUR CHUM

He missed his favourite food, which was, of course, scones. The Mouse decided to make some scone dough for him.

CHURN O MOUSE

The prospect of scones put the Emu in a much better mood – what he called his

SCONE HUMOUR

He ate the entire batch, and went to bed happy. The next morning, or as emus quaintly put it

COME SUN HOUR

– the Emu felt quite ill, and regretted his greed.

SOON RUE MUCH

Strange noises came from his belly. The worried Mouse called the school nurse, and described the belly noises.

COO HUM NURSE

'Don't you worry' said the nurse.

SOON CURE HUM

In fact, the strange noises were coming from the next door room, where the Cumnor House senior chorus was rehearsing. Now as you will know, all emus have a passion for choral music. So picture the Emu's dismay when he learned

NO EMU CHORUS

Such was the inviolable rule at Cumnor House.

O CRUSH NO EMU

sobbed the heartbroken flightless bird. I have few talents. I can't spell. All I want is to

HONOUR MUSEC

The story has a happy ending. Today the Emu is a leading counter-tenor, star of the world's

EUNUCH ROOMS

and a credit to

CUMNOR HOUSE.

The Big Noise 2001

Are we to part like this, Nick? Left to right,
Jenny Ohlson, Phoebe Wynne, Lucy Crosthwaite,
Sophie Morgan

Left: "Going to the Palace":
left to right, Amelia
Stewart, Harriet Tarnoy,
Hannah Cotton.
Inset: Harriet (Cinderella)
and the ugly sisters
(Hannah and Amelia)
in 1987

Left: Parade of Bottoms: left to right, William Maslen (1974), Tom Kilroy (1982), Nick Illsley (1988), Clem Naylor (1999)

175

Below: Bill Nicholson

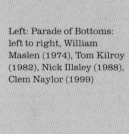

CHAPTER 12

A NEW ERA

2001—06

The old order changeth, yielding place to new

TENNYSON, 'THE IDYLLS OF THE KING'

Nat Wilby, left, and
Piers O'Conor

OPPOSITE PAGE

Above left: Rosi
Robinson with
Genevieve Maitland
Hudson and
Jessica Hoyal

Left: Isabelle Owers,
Ellie Daly, Rosanna
Smith-Langridge and
Grace Gregory

Roddy Gye describes the challenges of the new millennium: 'The new century brought more change, most dramatically in Nick's enforced early retirement through ill health. The trustees, that group of Nick's chums which, with one exception, had seen several complete changes of membership, suddenly found itself in the position of having to appoint a new headmaster, one who really would have to account to us rather than we to him. The chairman by now was Stephen Cockburn, who had happily imagined himself retiring a year or so before Nick, leaving the onerous task of appointing Nick's successor to his own successor. It wasn't to be, but Stephen was the ideal man to conduct an extremely thorough search for the right person to take Cumnor forward.

'And so the development of Cumnor moved on. Another appeal and the fruits of strong demand for a Cumnor education have allowed us to build new dormitories, an indoor swimming pool, new kitchens, more classrooms, a design and technology lab … and car parks, endless car parks. At the time of writing, further, yet more ambitious plans are being forged. For the first time Cumnor has a professionally prepared master plan, a document that examines the site as a whole and the relationship between the buildings, the landscape and the movement of people and vehicles.

'Cumnor has changed, more dramatically than Hal and Nan could possibly have imagined. One hopes they would approve of at least some of what has happened to their school; I have no doubt they would not approve of it all. But equally, one suspects they would disapprove of many of the imperatives that have driven those changes at Cumnor: government regulations, the changing expectations of

parents, the dominance of the motor car, the economic exigencies that ensure survival in a competitive market. What was wrong, they might have said, with spartan dormitories, chalk blackboards, building dens in trees, unqualified but passionate teachers …? And part of me would agree.'

The new headmaster, the 42-year-old Christian Heinrich, was selected from a very strong field of 150 candidates; he had read American Literature at the University of Kent and had taught at Summer Fields, Oxford, for 15 years, where he was housemaster and deputy headmaster. As a member of the Independent Schools Inspectorate, he has a wide knowledge of every sort of prep school; behind his easy and affable manner there lurks a decisive mind and a steely determination to see his projects through.

Having been appointed in November 2000, Christian and Belinda had two full terms in which to familiarise themselves with the school, and visited Cumnor every Thursday in the spring and summer terms. After so many recent changes of leadership, the school appeared to Christian like 'a sailing ship with canvas lowered, drifting gently and safely but without any firm direction. Almost anything done with confidence by a new head would meet with approval.' The staff were behind him: 'I have been blessed in my relatively brief time at Cumnor by the unstinting support of many members of the academic staff who predated my arrival, notably Matt Mockridge, Peter Wigan, Andrew Rose, Chris Cheadle, Ann Thirkell and Martin Godber, and feel equally fortunate to have such a supportive

management team, which as we begin 2006–7 comprises Matt Mockridge (deputy head), Mark Dickens (bursar), Julie Wood (director of studies), Victoria Homewood (head of pre-prep), Di Medhurst (head of junior school), Harry Hastings (director of sport) and Clive Smith-Langridge (head of maths); and thank goodness for the patience, common sense and energy of the houseparents, Toby and Lucy Sawrey-Cookson!'

After 62 years of Milner-Gullands at the helm, Cumnor had settled into a comfortable and predictable routine, and it must have been hard for Christian to implement changes and take the school in the direction that he envisaged. Yet by his second term the Social Services inspectors were reporting that 'the headmaster provides clear leadership, with clear lines of responsibility', and in the following year the *Good Schools Guide* described Cumnor as 'a little gem of a school'. The school inspection in March 2003 was extremely complimentary.

Christian's philosophy is that change is disturbing but constantly desirable: 'only dead fish swim with the tide'. When he arrived he detected a worrying lack of urge to change, as well as weaknesses in other areas: inadequate provision for sport, especially for the girls; patchiness of drama, with a great emphasis on the Shakespeare play not matched by similar opportunities for younger pupils; lack of record keeping and clearly stated routines; no overarching curriculum in the six pre-prep classes, which seemed to function as independent fiefdoms. Relations with Leo, who overlapped with him for one term, were 'doomed from the start: we were simply worlds apart.' Leo's successor, Mark Dickens, an Old Cumnorian, now has an assistant bursar as well as an accountant, while Mark himself has been heavily involved as project manager for the enormous building programme that Christian initiated:

~ the 'Jubilee Wing', the old Green dormitory rebuilt to provide attractive accommodation upstairs, with boys' changing rooms, laundry and linen rooms below (2001)
~ refurbishment of the Pink House (2001)
~ new kitchen and extended dining room (2002)
~ new classroom in music block (2004)
~ indoor swimming pool (2004)

Above: Alastair Seaton and Lucy Scaramanga

Below: Lindsey Martin

- ~ conversion of attic to extend the housemaster's flat (2005)
- ~ three large new pitches on Lower Lawns, involving a huge landscaping operation (2005)
- ~ The Hovels, a two-storey classroom block incorporating a fine new DT workshop and six classrooms (2006)
- ~ extended car parks for more and bigger cars (2006)
- ~ refurbishment of classrooms in the main building and extension of the office (2006)

The next development (Christian writes) is 'the final "keystone" piece in the bricks and mortar structure of the slightly expanded Cumnor – a magnificent new theatre. This will build upon the Cumnor tradition of excellence in the arts, allowing dramatic productions and workshops involving year groups of 48 to have much needed room on the one hand, while on the other offering all pupils at Cumnor the opportunity to learn dramatic skills and the skills involved in sound, lighting and backstage roles in the setting of a purpose-built theatre. The music department will also benefit from a flood of new practice areas – from the light and airy foyer, via changing rooms to the green room, not forgetting the stage itself, large enough for the First Orchestra to perform at ease. The theatre will be situated in the centre of the school (adjacent to the outdoor theatre but not replacing it) and will be the metaphorical heart of the site: children will begin every day there at assembly and Prayers. It is a fitting project to mark the conclusion of Cumnor's 75th anniversary.'

The view over the new pitches. Inset: The landscaping of the Lower Lawns, 2005

Some of these wonderful facilities became necessary as the school expanded, others reflected new expectations for teaching and living accommodation. It is certainly true that a school lacking such facilities would find it very hard to attract pupils or, crucially, first-rate staff; but they come at a cost. Fee rises have been consistently well above the level of inflation. For 75 years we have worried that the next fee increase would price us out of the market; not only has this not happened, but the school is fuller and more popular than ever before.

Christian also introduced many other changes:
~ forms were renamed according to year groups
~ a tutorial system was introduced
~ the staff appraisal system was extended
~ the format for reports was enlarged, to include curriculum statements as well as comments about pupils' work
~ 'trial boarding weekends' were started
~ there was to be voluntary supervised prep for boarders
~ the Kalendar became larger and more detailed
~ the catering was contracted to an outside firm, with greatly improved quality and choice
~ 'Under The Clock', a traditional punishment, ceased

Since 2001 Cumnor has developed a new personality, not only as a result of Christian's vision for the school, but also through staff turnover. Twenty-seven full-time teachers have been appointed, together with new groundsmen, nurses and kitchen arrangements. Peter Wigan, after 25 years as teacher of geography and scripture, cricket coach and deputy headmaster, took retirement and became the school archivist; several other long-serving members of staff also retired: Ann Thirkell, after 23 years, Andrew Gilliam after 13, Martin Godber after 16, latterly as director of studies, and Mick Holland, groundsman for 17 years. Lindsey Martin, our sympathetic and much-loved matron from 1984 to 2002, was remembered by George Howe for her

Top: Model of the proposed new theatre

Above: The Hovels, opened 2006

'novel way to beat homesickness: I was given long sickbay lists to check and then put a large red tick at the bottom. I'm sure the usefulness of this task was nothing compared with the importance I felt – intriguingly I also forgot to be homesick, so absorbed was I in my job.' It was a great sadness when her husband Des, school doctor for many years, died suddenly in 2005.

Art remains very strong under the guidance of Rosi Robinson, and art awards have been won at the rate of two or three a year. Music continues to thrive under two excellent successive directors of music, Alison Wicks and David Brown: by 2002 90 per cent of the school were learning an instrument, and the annual orchestral trip has remained an important feature of the school year. The orchestra has visited Siena once more, thanks to Anthony and Sarah Boswood, the Château de Pléhaut (Mrs Wendy Craske-Binder), the Château du Livet (Clive and Rowena Williams) and, for the last three years, the Château de Sauveterre near Toulouse. Andrew Rose has taken

Above: Tabitha Grainger (Titania) in *A Midsummer Night's Dream*, 2006

Left: Four and twenty blackbirds: trompe l'oeil by Susie Rotberg, 2004

Below: batik by Victoria van Holthe

over the production of the Shakespeare play, having gallantly stepped in to produce *Macbeth* in 2000; at the same time there is more drama for the junior forms.

Sport has been pushed, and it must have been a pleasure for Christian that in his first term the soccer XI was unbeaten. Results have been consistently good, more children have the chance to play in a school team and inter-school fixtures now include swimming, golf, show-jumping and 'Incrediball'; meanwhile the new 25m pool is a marvellous year-round asset, not only to Cumnor pupils but also to the local community. The pool, set in the kitchen garden, with attractive landscaping by Nikola Sly, was funded by the Landmark Appeal which raised £346,000 in two years, then another £27,000 at Martin and Rose Armstrong's Auction of Promises. Yet again the extraordinary generosity of the Cumnor community was essential to the success of the project.

Left: Under 11 rugby

Below: the orchestra playing at Clinton Lodge, Fletching, 2006

Mothers' race,
Sports Day, 2006

Tours have become more frequent: cricketers went to Sri Lanka in 2001, netballers to Jersey in 2003 and there was a combined cricket/netball/hockey tour to South Africa in 2004. Ghislaine Nankivell took Year 7 to the Alps, to the quaintly named Onnion; Year 8 went with Chris Cheadle on an Outward Bound expedition to North Wales.

Three serious road accidents shocked us all in this period: Leo Wynne in France, Sophie Morgan in Scotland and William Tetley in Sussex all suffered very severe injuries. These terrible accidents were the spur for great charitable efforts: there was an appeal for a page-turner and a voice-activated computer for Leo, and large sums were raised for the Stanmore Spinal Injuries Unit and Unstead Park, Godalming. The ever-growing Christmas Fayre, organised by

Above: The cast of *Peter Pan*, 2006

Below: Cumnor House, 2006

Belinda Heinrich, gives an annual opportunity for Cumnor pupils and parents to involve themselves in giving practical help to such excellent causes.

Christian is anxious to preserve the best aspects of Cumnor which, in his words, 'truly does put the children first and fosters the love of learning and the development of relationships founded on mutual trust and respect at all levels.' I am sure that there will continue to be many pupils who will echo the words of Imogen Cox (1995–2004): 'I was so sad leaving Cumnor and everyone we had been with for the past exuberating nine years.' How proud and delighted Martin Wheeler would be to see the thriving state of the school which he founded 'in a spirit of faith and adventure'. Seventy-five years on, his faith has been amply rewarded.

The Heinrich family.
Top: Jamie, Alice, Kate
Below: Belinda, Christian, Georgina

SUBSCRIBERS

Agne Aas and Airi Aas
Mr and Mrs A.L. Abrahams
Michael A.P. Adams
Arabella Allcock
Oliver Allcock
Sophie Allen
George Allison
Tom Allison
David Amos
Clemmie Anderson
David and Eve Anderson
Thomas Andrews
John and Paula Arkley
Patrick and Pamela Arnold
Robert Arnold
John and Hilary Arthur
Herry Ashby
Barbara Ashcroft (née Jack)
Mr Hubert Ashton
Pix Ashworth (née Bennett)
Kate Atkinson
Mike Atkinson

Anthony W.N. Bagshawe
Natasha, Duncan and
   Christopher Baird
Anna Baldwin
Claire Baldwin
Graeme Baldwin
Dr and Mrs Richard Baldwin
Sebastian Banwell and
   Arabelle Banwell
Ross Barnetson
The Bartons
Daniel and Harriet (née Potter)
   Bastide and family
Sue Bayley
Aisling Beddy
Mark and Nicola Beddy
Niamh Beddy
Nic Bellatti
Benenden School
Hugh and Liz Bennett
Violet and Clementine Bennett
Sophia Bentley (née

St. John Parker)
Michael Bex
Wendy J. Binder
Lesley and Peter Boase
Katie Goodson and
   Angus Bolton
A.R. Boswood
Audrey Bowes
Nick and Rozzie Bowlby
Kat Bowness (née Waglé)
Louise Bradley
Andrew Brand
Peter and Ronald Branscombe
The Bray Family
Christopher Bridge
The Britton Family
Mr and Mrs A.
   Brotherton-Ratcliffe
Sheena Broughton
C.R. Brown
David Brown
Oliver Buchanan
Patrick Buchanan
William Buchanan
Patricia Bullard
John and Pamela Bunney
Gillian Burdett
Rose Burton
Sophie Burton
Nicholas Butland
Mary Butterfield
Tyler Butterworth
Justin Byam Shaw
Matthew Byam Shaw

Jonathan Caffyn
Ginny Calver
Hugh Campbell
Mrs S. Campbell
Janet Canetty-Clarke
Neil Canetty-Clarke
Mrs J. Carlisle
Jeremy Carlisle
Patrick Cashell
Tim Cashell

Mrs Rosalie Challis
Angus Chalmers
Nigel and Jane Champness
Dr Aman Chandra
Herbert Chappell
The Charlesworth Family
James Charrington
Justin Cheadle
Lady Ursula Cholmeley
Chong-Wha Chung
David and Joanna Clancy
The Clayton Family
James Clayton
Leo Clayton
Mia Clayton
Ollie Clayton
Sallie Clayton
Barbara Clements
Wg Cdr and Mrs P.D. Cliff
Stephen and Judy Cockburn
John and Jane Coke
Nicola Colchester (née
   Rocksborough Smith)
Penelope Coleing
J.P.W. Coleman Esq
Lady Collum
Luke and Ben Colyer
Sieona and Richard Cooper
Mr and Mrs A. Cope
The Cornes Family
Nick Corrie
Hannah Cotton
Olivia Jo Cotton
Rufus Cotton
Mr G.A. Cowley
Georgie Cox
Imogen Cox
Crane Family
The Creamer Family
Andrew Simon Crosby
David Crowley (ex T.G.)
Mrs Brenda Mackenzie and
   Mr Robert Crowther
Mihai Cucos
Stefan Cucos

Mrs G.M. Cuppage
Anthony and Sarah Curtis,
   parents of Job, Charles
   and Quentin
C.Z. Curtis
Mr and Mrs Ian Curtis
Job Curtis
Quentin Curtis

Chris M. Dalgarno
Ben and James
   Dallimore-Symonds
Jill Daniel
Susanna Daniel
Benedict and Luke Davenport
Mrs Diana Davy
Prudence Dawes and Ruby
   Dawes
Mr and Mrs A. de Peyer
Edward C. Dean
Peter Dean
Peter and John Dean
Hannah Dennison
Jennifer Dent
Rayad Denyer-Green
Hugh and Fiona Dibley
Richard Dibley
Bob Dickens
Joff Dickens
Mark Dickens
Ollie Dickens
India, Daisy and Flora Dickinson
Rebecca Dillon-Robinson,
   Edward Dillon-Robinson and
   George Dillon-Robinson
Phoebe, Alexander and
   Freya Dingemans
Laura and Harry Dobbs
Julia Doherty
James Dougall
Charlie, Tom and Rich Dowdall
Mr and Mrs Robert Dowdall
John and Sylvia Downe
Mrs F. Drewett
Mrs Pam Duffill

Rebecca Dunstan (née Arnold)
David Duvall
John N.W. Dyball
Hazel Dye

Jim Earle
Joe Earle
R.F. Earle
Alastair Edgell
Angus Edgell
Mrs Rosalyn Edsberg
Alice, Thomas and
　Angus Edwards
Ian Edwards
Dr and Mrs J.D. Edwards
Ruth Edwards
Annabel Elliot
Ben and George Elwes
Christopher Emmott
Joumana Es Said
Caroline and Edward Evans
Martin Evans
Barney Evison

Francesca Faridany Zinsser
Lucy Faridany
Mr Michael Feaver
Mark Fieldhouse
Nicola Finney (née Gurney)
Nicky Finnie
Caryl Fisher
Niall and Ingrid Fitzgerald
Bronte Flecker
Robert Footman
J. Formolli
Barbara and Monty Froud
Tom Furber
Cornelia Furse

Mrs Elizabeth Gabriel
Andrew Gairdner
Wendy Gairdner
Philippa Gibson (née Gurney)
R.H.B. Gilberd
David and Jenni Gilbert
Samantha Gilbert
The Gillespie-Smith Family
Andrew Gilliam
Martin Godber
David Goddard
Francesca Goddard
Nicholas and Barbara Godlee
John P.B. Golding
Crispin Goldsmith

Jamie, Alistair and David Gourlay
Melissa Grafton (née Collum)
Victor and Nell Gratton Parry
Ollie Green
D.J. Guilfoyle
David Gunawardena
Adrian Gurney
Robert Gussman

Robert Halcrow
Clara Hamer
Oliver Hancock
Lucinda Hand (née Collum)
Andrew Harmsworth
Mrs G. Harmsworth Maxwell
Harry Hastings
Hamish Hatrick
Jessie Hatrick
Sophie Hatrick
Emily Hawes and Henry Hawes
Vanessa Hawkings (née Gabriel)
Toby Hayward
Daniel Heath
Nicholas Heath
Christian, Belinda, Alice, Kate,
　Jamie and Georgie Heinrich
Sophie Henderson
Forbes Henley
Savannah Henley
Mrs J. Hepplewhite
John Hignett
Mark and Jamie Hilton
Caroline Hirst
Colin and Giles Holland
Mick Holland
Thomas J. Humphrey
Brook Horowitz
M.B. Houghton
George Howe
John and Caryl Hubbard
Nicholas Humphrey
Trinity Hutton
Andrew Hutton
Patrick Hutton

Margaret and Alec Ibbott
The Irving Family

Adrian Jones
Mrs D. Jones
Kenneth V. Jones
Quentin Jones
Oliver Jory
Kate Jelly

Tom Jelly

Robin Kennard
R. Kilner
Mrs Jane Kilroy
Tom Kilroy
Camilla Kingsland (née
　Campbell)
Georgina Knight
Ian Knill-Jones
Alexander Knowles and
　Victoria Knowles
Jonathan Krish
Becky Kruger
Jessica Kruger
Mike and Janine Kruger
Milly Kruger

Dr Alastair Lack
Alastair, Tom, Andrew and
　Robbie Laing
Mr D. Lawson
Philip and Sally Le Brocq
Robert Leonard
Roland Leonard
Tamora Leonard
R. Lewis
C.C.M. Liddell
Freddie Light
Olivia Light
William Light
Bruce Lightbody
Matthew Likierman
Joanna Lisney
Megan, Ruby and Harry Lloyd
Ann and David Lock
William Lock
Mrs Ann Longley
James Lovegrove and Philippa
　Luddington (née Lovegrove)
Jeff Lowe
Jamie and Toby Lumsden

Colin, Dayle and Emily Mair
Richard Mais
Clare Malins
Alex and Francis Marden
Mrs Cynthia Marney
Julian Marsh
Dr Adrian G. Marshall
Wayne Martin
Elizabeth Maslen
Christopher Matthew
Beverley Matthews

R.V. Maxwell-Gumbleton
Paul J. McColl
Rachel, Ali, Chris and
　James Macgregor
Air Commodore E.J. McGuire
The McIntosh Family
Andrew McKenzie-Smith
Ian MacNeil
F.J. Meikle
Roddy Meikle
Ione Meyer
Martin Middlehurst
Mark and Alison Milhench
Judith Miller
Michael Mills
E.J. Milner-Gulland
Jamie Milner-Gulland
Kate Milner-Gulland
Toby Milner-Gulland
James, Hugh, Eleanor and
　Guy Minch
Andrew Mitchell
John L. Mitchell
Juliet Mitchell
Nick Mitchell
Peter and Threave Mitchell
Matt Mockridge
Charlie Mole
Edward Mole
Rosie Moon
Piers Morgan
Andrew Morpeth
Catherine Morpeth
Sir Douglas and
　Lady Morpeth
Duncan Morpeth
Iain and Angela Morpeth
James Morpeth
Richard Morpeth
Mary Mortimer and
　Donald Denoon
Robin Moss
Elizabeth Muir-Lewis
David P. Mullins
Peter Mullins
Kathy Murphy
Penny Mussell
Oliver and Louisa Myrtle

G.M.T. Nankivell
Duncan and Yolanda Nash
D. J. Newbery
Edmund, Julia and
　Maria Nicholson

Oscar H. Nieboer
The Norfolks

Adam Ogilvie
Michael and James Orchard
J.A. Orssten

Meriel Packman
Claire Packman
Clare Parkhouse
Emma Parkhouse
James Parkhouse
Thomas Parkhouse
The Parnell Family
Sue Paterson
Jeremy Pattie and Harriet Pattie
Martin and Louise Pavey
Judith A.N. Penry-Davey
Nicholas and Susan Perkins
Nick Phillips
R.H.C. Phillips
Christopher Pigott
R. Pike
Bertie A.T. Playle
A. and R. Pollard
Edward and Will Pook
F.E.H. and F.J. Potter
Anthony E. Poulsom
Mark Prescott
Mr B. Price
Louise Pridmore (née Millar)
Robin Pritchard
Fiona Pullan
N.G. Pullan

Janette Scott Rademaekers

Jonathan Ray
R.M. Reardon
Edward Reyes
Alexander Reynolds
  and Emily Reynolds
Mrs J. Richards
Georgie Roberts
James Roberts
Nicola, Paul and
  Sara Robinson
E.H. Robinson
Rosi Robinson
David Ryde

Mrs Isabel Salimbeni
Jackie Sampson/Rosling
Anthony Sargent
Shiraz Satchu
Simeon M.J. Saunders
R.N. Saunders
C. Scaramanga
Abi and Saskia Schade
Curtis Schwartz
Joceline Sharman
William Sharman
Sarah Jane Sherlock
Tom Sherlock
Rein Sillart
Richard Sinclair
Eleanor Sly
Clive Smith-Langridge
Martin Smith
Christopher Snell
Philip Snow
Alexander Soul
Mr and Mrs J. Trevor Spurgen

Michael Stanley
Mrs David Steel
Jonathan Steel
Rob Steel
Gabi Stein (née Cotton)
Rebecca Steinebach
Ruth Steketee-Engledow
Hugh Stevens
Hugo Stewart-Roberts
Madeleine Sumption
Anthony Swing

James and Victoria Tanner
Mark Tanous
Richard Tapper
Gavin Tasker
Andrew Taylor
George Taylor
Stephen Taylor
Michael, Nicola and
  Angus Thatcher
Ann Thirkell
O. Thompson
P. Thompson
Stephanie and Simon Thornton
Tom Tickell
Daniel Ticktum
Elspeth Tissington
William Tissington
Rosamund and Richard Toms
The Tower Family
Susannah Towsey
John Turner
Liz Turner

Rosemary Usborne

The Right Rev'd Michael
  Vickers
Alec Vinter
Annabel Virtue
Peter and Richard Vlasto
Rhoddy Voremberg

Asha Waglé
Alistair Ward and Tom Ward
Anne Marie Webster
Emma Welby
Melanie Welch
William Welton
R.H. Wheeler
Mrs Chrissie White
Stephen White
Peter Wigan
Xa, Bella and Geordie Wilkes
Elizabeth Wilkinson
Freddie Willatt
Tony and Sheelagh Williams,
  parents of Philip, Nick
  and Sean
Mrs A. Williams
Clive Williams
Matthew Williams
Robert Williams
S. Williams
S.J. Williams
Mr Peter Williamson
Tim Williamson
Caroline D. Wilson
Nick Wilson
Gavin Wood
Marcella Wynne

INDEX OF NAMES